WordPress 3 Plugin Development Essenti

Create your own powerful, interactive plugins to extend
and add features to your WordPress site

Brian Bondari

Everett Griffiths

BIRMINGHAM - MUMBAI

WordPress 3 Plugin Development Essentials

First published: March 2011

Production Reference: 1180311

Published by Packt Publishing Ltd.
32 Lincoln Road
Olton
Birmingham, B27 6PA, UK.

ISBN 978-1-849513-52-4

www.packtpub.com

Cover Image by Rakesh Shejwal (shejwal.rakesh@gmail.com)

Credits

About the Authors

Brian Bondari is a musician, composer, and teacher with equal love for both music and technology. His hobbies include reading, hiking, composing music, and playing with his pet rabbit. He also spends an exorbitant amount of time lying on the floor grading papers.

Brian earned his doctorate from the University of Kansas in 2009 and is currently an Assistant Professor of Music Theory and Composition at Trinity University in San Antonio, TX. When he is not writing music or grading papers, he helps run the multi-author technology blog www.TipsFor.us. He is also the author of WordPress 2.9 E-Commerce, also published by Packt.

This book would not have been possible without Everett's mad coding skills and utterly unyielding work ethic. Thanks for the partnership and friendship of many years. I'd also like to thank the team at Packt for helping to organize this project and get it off the ground. Finally, utmost thanks to my wife Katrina for her unending love, support, and patience.

Everett Griffiths is the owner of Fireproof Socks, a development company that specializes in web applications and content management systems including MODx, WordPress, and Expression Engine. Although, he has contributed many educational articles and screencasts to the blog he runs with Brian Bondari, TipsFor.us, this is his first published book. He survives as a coder of fortune in the Los Angeles underground. If you have a problem, if no one else can help, and if you can find him, maybe you can hire... Everett's team.

I'd like to thank Brian for being a steadfast and patient editor of practically every crazy word I've penned or spoken, Nui for the beautiful memories, and my parents for their constant support. I'd also like to thank all the people who didn't believe in me because all their attempts to keep me down only made me stronger.

About the Reviewers

Srikanth AD is a Web Developer and SEO Consultant. He is passionate about developing and optimizing websites for better search engine visibility and user experience. Sharing interesting tools and services pertaining to web development and SEO across technology blogs is one of his active hobbies.

He has written articles for some of the popular blogs such as MakeUseOf, TheNextWeb, QuickOnlineTips, Lost in Technology, 1stWebDesigner, and others.

Portfolio: http://www.adsrikanth.com

Blog: http://www.readaboutseo.com

Sam Rose is a 20 year old Computer Science student living in Wales, UK. He has recently entered his second year of his Computer Science degree at the University of Glamorgan in South Wales.

Sam writes code primarily in Java, PHP and has intermediate knowledge in an array of other languages.

In his spare time, Sam is usually playing pool, watching comedy produced by Chuck Lorre, writing code on his current favorite open source project, ThinkUp, managed by the lovely Gina Trapani, or writing on his blog, http://lbak.co.uk.

This is my first time as a technical reviewer for a book and I would really like to thank Erika from the Packt team for finding and giving me the opportunity to review this book and Michelle, also from the Packt team, for being a wonderfully happy and helpful point of contact throughout the review process.

Paul Thewlis is seasoned web marketing professional. He is currently in charge of the Search Engine Marketing department at a leading full-service digital agency in the UK. Previously, he was the E-Communications Manager for a multinational transport company. He began his web career as a Technical Editor, working on web design books for a well-known publisher. He has extensive experience of many content management systems and blogging platforms. His first book, WordPress For Business Bloggers, was published by Packt. He is an expert in the use of social media within corporate communications, and blogs about that subject, as well as WordPress, SEO, and the Web in general, at `http://blog.paulthewlis.com`.

www.PacktPub.com

Support files, eBooks, discount offers and more

You might want to visit www.PacktPub.com for support files and downloads related to your book.

Did you know that Packt offers eBook versions of every book published, with PDF and ePub files available? You can upgrade to the eBook version at www.PacktPub.com and as a print book customer, you are entitled to a discount on the eBook copy. Get in touch with us at service@packtpub.com for more details.

At www.PacktPub.com, you can also read a collection of free technical articles, sign up for a range of free newsletters and receive exclusive discounts and offers on Packt books and eBooks.

http://PacktLib.PacktPub.com

Do you need instant solutions to your IT questions? PacktLib is Packt's online digital book library. Here, you can access, read and search across Packt's entire library of books.

Why Subscribe?

- Fully searchable across every book published by Packt
- Copy and paste, print and bookmark content
- On demand and accessible via web browser

Free Access for Packt account holders

If you have an account with Packt at www.PacktPub.com, you can use this to access PacktLib today and view nine entirely free books. Simply use your login credentials for immediate access.

Table of Contents

Preface

By picking up this book, there's a good chance that you fall into one of two categories: an existing WordPress user / hobbyist programmer who is interested in building your own plugins for the platform, or a seasoned developer who is new to WordPress and need to complete a project for a client.

In either case, this book is designed to help you along the way. If you can code your own plugins, you can make WordPress do just about anything. By learning how to tap into the additional power and functionality that plugins provide, you can make your site easier to administer, add new features, or even alter the very nature of how WordPress works. Written with the WordPress version 3 in mind, this book will show you how to build a variety of plugins that demonstrate the additional power available to you as a plugin author.

Throughout this book, our goal is to teach you all aspects of modern WordPress development. We will build a variety of WordPress plugins and follow their creation from the idea to the finishing touches. You will discover how to deconstruct an existing plugin, use the WordPress API in typical scenarios, hook into the database, version your code with SVN, and deploy your new plugin to the world.

We have plenty of work to do, so let's get started!

What this book covers

Chapter 1, Preparing for WordPress Development, provides an overview of the development process and discusses a number of tools and practices recommended for a successful WordPress development environment.

Chapter 2, Anatomy of a Plugin, breaks an existing plugin down into its component parts to see what makes it work, and what makes it break.

Chapter 3, Social Bookmarking, walks through the development of an initial plugin, including how to tie into the WordPress API, how to trigger functions, and how to include external JavaScript files.

Chapter 4, Ajax Search, covers the construction of a plugin that augments WordPress' built-in search capability. This chapter provides details on how to utilize Ajax and JQuery, as well as how to use the PHP library classes with static functions in our plugins.

Chapter 5, Content Rotator, explores the wonderful world of WordPress widgets. In this chapter we will show you how to build and manipulate a widget, as well as how to construct a personal preference page for your plugin.

Chapter 6, Standardized Custom Content, begins the process of extending WordPress' usage as a content management system. We will cover how to alter and extend custom fields and how to display custom content in your templates.

Chapter 7, Custom Post Types, continues the discussion on extending WordPress as a CMS. We will also discuss working with shortcodes, and how to customize your plugin by creating custom menus and administration panels in the Dashboard.

Chapter 8, Versioning Your Code with Subversion (SVN), shows you how to maintain and manage your plugin code with a version control system.

Chapter 9, Preparing Your Plugin for Distribution, takes the next logical step in making sure your shiny new plugins are ready for the wider world. We will discuss how to avoid certain pitfalls by writing custom tests to check for failure points.

Chapter 10, Publishing Your Plugin, covers the mechanics of officially making your masterpiece available to the public, including the topics of internationalization, using the WordPress SVN repository, and handling the ubiquitous `readme.txt` file.

Appendix A, Recommended Resources, lists some of our favorite websites, books, and other resources for seeking additional knowledge or getting help with a specific problem.

Appendix B, WordPress API Reference, provides a compendium of functions, actions, and filters referenced in this book.

What you need for this book

To develop plugins for WordPress, all you really need is a text editor, a working installation of WordPress, and your favorite (s)FTP program. Other tools, such as a MySQL editor, can make your life easier, but are optional.

Who this book is for

This book is for WordPress users who want to learn how to create their own plugins and for developers who are new to the WordPress platform. Basic knowledge of PHP and HTML is expected, as well as a functional knowledge of how WordPress works from a user standpoint.

Conventions

In this book, you will find a number of styles of text that distinguish between different kinds of information. Here are some examples of these styles, and an explanation of their meaning.

Code words in text are shown as follows: "We can include other contexts through the use of the `include` directive."

A block of code is set as follows:

```
<h3 class="widget-title">Built In WordPress Search Widget</h3>

<form role="search" method="get" id="searchform" action="http://
localhost:8888/" >
    <div>
        <label class="screen-reader-text" for="s">Search for:</label>
        <input type="text" value="" name="s" id="s" />
        <input type="submit" id="searchsubmit" value="Search" />
    </div>
```

When we wish to draw your attention to a particular part of a code block, the relevant lines or items are set in bold:

```
/*
Theme Name: Twenty Ten v2
Theme URI: http://wordpress.org/
```

Any command-line input or output is written as follows:

```
svn checkout https://my-unique-project-name.googlecode.com/svn/trunk/
--username mygoogleid
```

New terms and **important words** are shown in bold. Words that you see on the screen, in menus or dialog boxes for example, appear in the text like this: " Under the **Hello Dolly** title, click on the **Activate** link.".

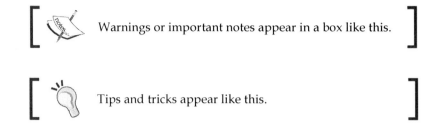

Warnings or important notes appear in a box like this.

Tips and tricks appear like this.

Reader feedback

Feedback from our readers is always welcome. Let us know what you think about this book—what you liked or may have disliked. Reader feedback is important for us to develop titles that you really get the most out of.

To send us general feedback, simply send an e-mail to feedback@packtpub.com, and mention the book title via the subject of your message.

If there is a book that you need and would like to see us publish, please send us a note in the **SUGGEST A TITLE** form on www.packtpub.com or e-mail suggest@packtpub.com.

If there is a topic that you have expertise in and you are interested in either writing or contributing to a book, see our author guide on www.packtpub.com/authors.

Customer support

Now that you are the proud owner of a Packt book, we have a number of things to help you to get the most from your purchase.

Downloading the example code for this book

You can download the example code files for all Packt books you have purchased from your account at http://www.PacktPub.com. If you purchased this book elsewhere, you can visit http://www.PacktPub.com/support and register to have the files e-mailed directly to you.

Errata

Although we have taken every care to ensure the accuracy of our content, mistakes do happen. If you find a mistake in one of our books—maybe a mistake in the text or the code—we would be grateful if you would report this to us. By doing so, you can save other readers from frustration and help us improve subsequent versions of this book. If you find any errata, please report them by visiting http://www.packtpub.com/support, selecting your book, clicking on the **errata submission form** link, and entering the details of your errata. Once your errata are verified, your submission will be accepted and the errata will be uploaded on our website, or added to any list of existing errata, under the Errata section of that title. Any existing errata can be viewed by selecting your title from http://www.packtpub.com/support.

Piracy

Piracy of copyright material on the Internet is an ongoing problem across all media. At Packt, we take the protection of our copyright and licenses very seriously. If you come across any illegal copies of our works, in any form, on the Internet, please provide us with the location address or website name immediately so that we can pursue a remedy.

Please contact us at copyright@packtpub.com with a link to the suspected pirated material.

We appreciate your help in protecting our authors, and our ability to bring you valuable content.

Questions

You can contact us at questions@packtpub.com if you are having a problem with any aspect of the book, and we will do our best to address it.

1
Preparing for WordPress Development

Since you have picked up this book, you are likely to fall into one of two overall categories: developers who are new to WordPress, or WordPress users keen to start or improve their WordPress development skills. No matter which camp you lie in, this book will help you down that path. This book will show you how to customize WordPress using plugins by providing well-structured code and by explaining how the code interacts with the WordPress application. It introduces a variety of development techniques drawn from a range of real-world scenarios that will give you, the reader, a practical understanding of how to write, debug, and deploy WordPress plugins.

Together we will delve through a series of increasingly challenging topics covering a range of scenarios that a developer is likely to encounter when developing and maintaining a WordPress 3 site. While you may read the book from start to finish, each chapter strives to be a self-contained topic for easier reference.

It is expected that the readers of this book have some knowledge of programming concepts and a working understanding of web applications, including HTML and basic CSS. Familiarity with WordPress is also recommended.

WordPress background

WordPress is a popular content management system (CMS), most renowned for its use as a blogging / publishing application. According to usage statistics tracker, BuiltWith (`http://builtWith.com`), WordPress is considered to be the most popular blogging software on the planet—not bad for something that has only been around officially since 2003. It has always sought to allow its users to publish information easily, and although it can be used successfully for sites that are not blog-centric, running a blog has been a guiding star in WordPress' design since its inception.

Extending WordPress

Like many systems, WordPress may not do everything you want right out of the box. Instead, it focuses on a set of core features and allows for customizations in the form of plugins, so if the built-in functionality doesn't meet your needs, your options are to:

- Find an existing third-party plugin
- Write your own plugin
- Look for another CMS entirely

It is well worth your time to search for an existing solution if WordPress doesn't already have the functionality that you require—chances are high that someone out there has already done what you are trying to do. It may not be as much fun or as glamorous as developing your own shiny new code, but it is usually easier and faster to cash in on the work others have done, just be aware that a lot of code in the WordPress repository is written by amateurs and it may contain bugs.

If you do end up extending WordPress with your own plugin, and we hope you do since you are reading this book, make sure that you are doing one of two things: either you are solving a problem that nobody has solved before, or you are coming up with a better mousetrap and re-solving a problem in a new and valuable way.

Understanding WordPress architecture

Spend a few minutes kicking the tires and you will become familiar with WordPress' features:

- Clean blog management
- Flexible permalink structure
- Easy search engine optimization (SEO)
- A simple package management tool
- The ability to update WordPress itself directly from the manager
- Versioning of drafts (so you don't lose data)
- A mature Ajax interface (lets you easily drag-and-drop widgets to customize your experience in the manager)

This is a fine system, but it is a bit like listening to a car salesman—if you really want to see how it performs, you should get your hands greasy and see what's under the hood. For developers, the real aspects of WordPress' customization and extensibility lie in Templating and Plugins.

Templating

WordPress offers a templating system for implementing custom HTML and CSS, but it is not a templating system in the same sense as Smarty (`http://www.smarty.net`) or Perl's Template Toolkit. Instead, like many PHP CMSs (most notably Drupal and Joomla!), WordPress templates are simply PHP files that typically contain a mix of application logic and presentation code, for example, `<div id="footer"><?php wp_footer(); ?></div>`.

Compare that with a Drupal template excerpt: `<div id="footer"><?php print render($page['footer']); ?></div>` or with a MODx excerpt using Smarty placeholders: `<div id="footer">[[*footer]]</div>` and you can get some idea of the spectrum. Typically, the templates used in WordPress do not adhere to the Model-View-Controller (MVC) pattern, so they cause some developers to raise a critical eyebrow.

Be aware that your WordPress templates contain PHP code and that they do execute, so it is naturally possible to "crash" your templates, or to have complex loops and logical statements in them. As a developer, try your absolute best to separate logic from presentation and keep your templates as clean as possible. There are plenty of WordPress theme files out there that contain a dizzying mess of PHP and HTML, which result in an unmaintainable no man's land. Designers won't touch them because they can't decipher the myriad if-statements and sloppy concatenations, and developers won't touch them for the same reason, or perhaps because they contain HTML and CSS that developers don't want to worry about. In the end, just try to avoid the numerous pitfalls that exist in this type of templating system.

Introducing plugins

Like any good CMS, WordPress offers an **application programming interface** (API) for developers to perform common tasks in their plugins. Unlike many CMSs, however, the WordPress API is largely procedural: it exists mostly as a series of globally scoped functions and variables in the main namespace, so you have to be extra careful when naming your functions to avoid naming collisions. There are certain tasks that are object oriented (OO), but there is a decent chance that you could look through a dozen WordPress plugins before encountering a class or an object. In certain programming languages, such an arrangement is unusual if not impossible, but the PHP community in particular often offers procedural equivalents of object-oriented code.

Opening up an existing WordPress plugin is a bit like going into a public restroom: it may be perfectly clean and hygienic, or it may be a rank and apoplectic mess of functions, logic, and HTML. Just be prepared.

What is a plugin?

The term "Plugin" is a bit ambiguous and WordPress' definition differs from other content management systems. In general, a WordPress plugin is any bit of code that extends the core functionality of WordPress. Unlike Expression Engine, Drupal, or MODx, WordPress does not use different terms such as **"module"**, **"snippet"**, or **"add-on"** to distinguish where or how this extension occurs. In WordPress, they are all considered plugins.

WordPress plugins use an event-driven architecture—anyone who has seen a JavaScript function triggered via an HTML "onClick" is familiar with this approach, but in WordPress, the events are typically referred to as hooks. A hook is an event— it is a place where you can attach (or "hook") code. While examining existing plugins, keep an eye out for the `add_action()` and `add_filter()` functions that tie a hook to a function inside the plugin. Depending on the author, `add_action()` and `add_filter()` instances may be scattered throughout the code or consolidated into one place.

The number of hooks available in WordPress has been steadily increasing and with version 3, there are well over 1,000. Unfortunately, they are not well documented. This daunting number represents an unwieldy weak point in the WordPress architecture. How can the developer find the one or two he needs? We have included a list of some of the most common hooks in an appendix at the end of this book.

Many plugins contain convoluted mixtures of logic and HTML within a single function. This scenario is unfortunately common in many PHP CMSs, and it can make it exceedingly difficult to find and fix formatting errors. You may be fighting an uphill battle, but we strongly recommend separating your plugin logic from any formatting code. It will make your plugins easier to maintain and skin.

Another thing to remember when writing plugins is that WordPress 3.1 is the last version of WordPress that is compatible with a dwindling number of PHP 4 users. Be sure your plugin tests the PHP version in use, especially if you use the more advanced language constructs available in PHP 5.

Summarizing architecture

WordPress has put together a solution that works well. This solution is not necessarily better or worse than other platforms, it just has different advantages and disadvantages. When in Rome, it is not necessarily best to do as the Romans do (Rome did fall, after all), but you had better be aware of their modus operandi.

In general, WordPress offers a clean and efficient way to get many sites off the ground. However, its flexibility has allowed some less-experienced developers to create unenviable code patterns that are difficult to maintain and debug, and this is what we are striving to avoid. Above all, we encourage you to strive for clean and concise code while working within this, or any, system.

Tools for web development

The tools you need to develop plugins for WordPress are essentially the same tools you need for developing almost any web application, specifically:

- WordPress
- Text editor
- FTP client
- MySQL client (optional)

WordPress

If you are going to develop plugins for WordPress, you need WordPress itself and an environment that can run it. Download the latest version of WordPress from `http://wordpress.org/download`. It is then just a matter of finding a suitable place to install it.

WordPress 3 runs on a web server (most commonly Apache) that can run at least PHP 4.3 and MySQL 4.1.2—WordPress 3.2 requires PHP 5.2 and MySQL 5.0.15. Since both PHP and MySQL are widespread web technologies and WordPress is such a popular blogging tool, most hosting providers can support running WordPress on their servers. If in doubt, consult your web host's FAQ.

Another option is to run WordPress in a "sandbox" environment on your own computer. This can be more involved since you have to set up your computer as a web server and configure several other inter-related technologies, but thankfully there are bundled packages available that do much of the difficult work for you—we have listed a few options for these types of packages below.

A third option is to run a virtual machine on your local computer using emulation software like Parallels (`http://www.parallels.com`), VMware (`http://www.vmware.com`) or VirtualBox (`http://www.virtualbox.org`). This can be a great way to mimic your intended production environment precisely and still get all the benefits of hosting your site locally, but it does require some solid system administration skills, so this option is mainly recommended for seasoned developers.

If you plan to run a "sandbox" testing ground on your own computer, you have a few options depending on the platform.

Mac

Since Mac OS X ships with Apache and PHP—and MySQL can be compiled to run natively—you can run WordPress directly on your Macintosh. However, this requires a fair amount of non-trivial sysadmin skills, so we strongly recommend that you download an all-in-one pre-configured PHP-MySQL package.

Two solid options are:

- MAMP (`http://www.mamp.info`)
- XAMPP (`http://www.apachefriends.org/en/xampp.html`)

Both are free packages that include all you need to get your Mac ready for WordPress.

Windows

On Microsoft Windows, there are several options. You can try:

- WAMP (`http://www.wampserver.com`)
- EasyPHP (`http://www.easyphp.org`)
- XAMPP (`http://www.apachefriends.org/en/xampp.html`)
- Microsoft Web Platform (`http://www.microsoft.com/web`)

All of the above options are free and will get the job done. For reference, the Microsoft Web Platform uses IIS as the web server instead of Apache. Refer to the relevant website for instructions on how to install and set up any of this software.

Text editor

You don't need anything special when it comes to a text editor, just something that can write plain, unformatted text files. Don't try using a word processor such as Microsoft Word because it will add all kinds of formatting. We strongly recommend, however, that you go a little bit beyond the basic requirement of authoring text files and find an editor that offers the following features:

- **Syntax highlighting**: This could save you hours of frustration by helping you spot variables, missing quotes, or other errata.

- **Locate matching parentheses, brackets, or braces**: Many times syntax errors are caused when you inadvertently omit a curly brace or a parenthesis. Being able to locate the matching unit of these paired symbols will help you track down these types of errors more quickly.

- **Find and replace across multiple files**: A massively timesaving operation.

- **Displays line numbers**: PHP will reference line numbers when it encounters errors.

On a Mac, TextWrangler (`http://www.barebones.com/products/textwrangler`) is a free application that lets you work on multiple files simultaneously, made by the same folks who make the venerable BBEdit (which is a viable option if you need more features and are willing to spend a bit of money). TextMate (`http://macromates.com`) is on par with BBEdit and is a direct competitor. A tremendous editor for Mac OS X is Coda (`http://www.panic.com/coda`). It really is the Swiss Army Knife of web development applications. Coda keeps your files organized, lets you preview HTML and CSS, does syntax highlighting on all kinds of files, offers auto complete on function calls, acts as an FTP, SSH, and a lightweight SVN client, and even has plugins that will help you check your code for errors. If you have a budget for your projects, Coda is a time-saving application.

On Windows, there are several free text editors worth examining, including NotePad++ (`http://notepad-plus-plus.org`), PSPad (`http://www.pspad.com`), and NotePad2 (`http://www.flos-freeware.ch/notepad2.html`). One excellent commercial offering is UltraEdit (`http://www.ultraedit.com`).

Using an IDE

You may consider using a full blown Integrated Development Environment (IDE) such as Eclipse (`http://www.eclipse.org`), Sun's NetBeans (`http://netbeans.org`), Jet Brain's PhpStorm (`http://www.jetbrains.com/phpstorm/`), or the Zend Studio IDE (`http://www.zend.com/products/studio`), all of which run on Mac, Windows, or Linux.

These are powerful programs, but they aren't easy to use so their complexity may be off-putting. Compare a 16 MB footprint for a standalone text editor such as TextEdit to the behemoth 470 MB of the Zend Studio IDE and you get some idea of the resources required to run each program. The more development you do, the more you will gravitate toward IDE applications because they offer unmatched features, but they're not generally recommend for first time developers. NetBeans is free and relatively resource friendly, so it is a good option if you are looking to explore the world of IDEs.

On the lightweight end of the spectrum, you can use one of the feature rich and battle-tested command line editors: vi or eMacs. They offer enormous flexibility and features directly from any *nix command line. Although it is extremely useful for a developer to be capable of editing files from a command line, the keyboard-only interface and steep learning curve of these editors precludes them from mainstream use, so we don't recommend you use them as your primary editing application.

> No matter which editor you choose, make sure it helps you get your work done instead of becoming a chore unto itself. Refer to each vendor's site for instructions on how to install and configure them.

FTP client

In order to transfer files from your local computer to your destination web server and back again, you need an FTP client (or an SSH client) to facilitate the copying. The application need not be fancy, but it should be easy to use because chances are good that you will be using it a lot.

On Mac OS X, the aforementioned text editor Coda includes FTP functionality; CyberDuck (`http://cyberduck.ch`) offers a fine standalone client with the ability to bookmark sites and access Amazon S3 folders. Though not free, Transmit (`http://www.panic.com/transmit`) has a slick interface and it stands out as one of the only FTP clients that offers the OS X "column view" of files and folders.

On Windows, FileZilla (`http://filezilla-project.org`) is a solid offering. There's also the venerable WinSCP (http://winscp.net), as well as Core FTP LE (`http://www.coreftp.com`). All three of these programs are free.

MySQL client

Depending on the level of developing that you do with WordPress, you may not need a MySQL client, but it is extremely handy to have one available, and it can be good to have this window into your database. After all, the database has much of your content and settings, so eventually you will want to see what's going on in there.

On a Mac, if you installed the MAMP package, it comes with phpMyAdmin. This works in a pinch, albeit clumsily because it is a web application. Sequel Pro (`http://www.sequelpro.com`) is one of only a handful of options for desktop SQL clients on Mac OS X.

SQLyog (`http://www.webyog.com`) is the Windows-only benchmark — it's a powerful desktop client with an intuitive interface and sensible shortcuts.

phpMyAdmin is also available for many Windows installations, including XAMPP and EasyPHP, so don't feel obligated to purchase software if it's not in your budget.

Coding best practices

Contrary to the old adage, practice does not always make perfect. Instead, practice makes habit. The more time you spend developing, the more knowledgeable you become, but the benefits or disadvantages of certain development practices may not be obvious to the hobbyist. The wisdom of experienced developers is invaluable as you learn, so here are some general guidelines that should help you make your code easier to design, test, and maintain. You can read through WordPress' coding guidelines (`http://codex.wordpress.org/Writing_a_Plugin`), but this chapter provides more detailed information—we will be putting these into practice over the following chapters.

Basic organization

The simple recommendation here is to keep your code consistently organized. If someone is looking through your code months from now, will he be able to follow the method to your madness? If you are consistent, people will be able to follow your logic more easily, even if they don't agree with it. Consistency should prevail throughout your variable names, function names, documentation, file names, and folder structure: keep it sensible and clean.

One other tip that we have learned through many hours of frustration seems profoundly simple: a "unit" of code should fit on one screen without scrolling. In general, if you can't see it, you can't get it uploaded into your brain for full comprehension. What is a "unit"? Usually it is a function, but sometimes it can be a logical block or a group of related tasks. Functions are easier to test, so they make for better units. The bottom line is to take small bites and if your "units" fit snugly on the screen instead of scrolling across several pages, then your code will be much easier to understand and debug.

Here are the main points to consider when organizing your code:

- Isolate tasks into functions
- Use classes
- Use descriptive variable names
- Use descriptive function names
- Separate logic and display layers
- Go modular, to a point
- Avoid short tags

Isolate tasks into functions

A function, as its name suggests, performs a certain task, but structuring them can be a bit of an art. Any time you find yourself copying and pasting identical code (or even similar code), that should be a glaring red flag that it's time to consolidate it into one place by putting it into a function. Just like having a single stylesheet for your website gives the designer a single place to make global changes, a function should give the developer one place to alter a particular behavior.

A good rule of thumb when writing functions is that they should not accept more than three inputs. Otherwise, they become difficult to use. You can package multiple inputs into a single associative array (a.k.a. a "hash"), or you could restructure your code into multiple functions. Again, find a clean solution.

Use classes

For new developers, the whole notion of objects and classes may seem something of a black art. It may feel needlessly complex, and to be fair, in some scenarios it is. However, the more you develop, the more you will gravitate toward object-oriented code because it allows for better organization, maintainability, and classes are much easier to extend.

Anyone familiar with CSS can appreciate the beauty of overriding a behavior. In the same way that you can override a style declaration from a `*.css` file with a local declaration, you can override a PHP class function by extending the class and redefining the function. We will see some examples of this later in this book.

Use descriptive variable names

PHP does not impose many restrictions on variable names, and there are differing naming strategies that you may employ. Compare this to Java, where using the incorrect case or underscores in your variable names is tantamount to heresy. Common naming strategies include $lower_case_with_underlines and $camelCase, and since PHP does not use distinct glyphs to distinguish arrays from scalar variables (like Perl, which distinguishes a $scalar from a @array), it can be useful to include the data type in the variable name, for example, $records_array.

Whichever method you use, make sure that the names adequately describe the contents of the variable in the context in which they appear. Avoid single letters and avoid long-winded, overly complicated names. In general, find the shortest name that accurately represents the variable's purpose. It may seem esoteric, but in order to understand your code, it must enter your brain through the construct of the English language (or in whatever language you tend to think). If your variable names are unclear, your brain will have to work harder to understand what your code is doing, so take the time to be descriptive and clear.

Use descriptive function names

As with your variable names, your function names should accurately describe what the functions do. It is common in most languages to have functions that get or set attributes, such as `getHeader()` or `setPageWidth()`.

There are a few caveats to mention with PHP function names: first of all they are not case sensitive. For example, `add_action()`, `aDD_aCtIoN()`, or `ADD_ACTION()` are all interpreted identically. For the sake of clarity and ease of searching, always call your functions using the same case as their definitions.

Function names starting with a single underscore (for example, `_my_private_function()`) have historically been used to denote private functions—that is functions intended for use by other functions and not for direct use by the "outside world". With PHP 5, you can control the access to a class's functions as public, private, or protected, but the underscore is still often used as a helpful reminder.

"Magical" functions in PHP use names starting with two underscores (for example, `__construct()`). They are used to perform special tasks inside of a PHP class. Although you can name your functions in this way provided there are no name collisions, it is not recommended because they may be mistaken for magic PHP functions. For example, WordPress uses the `__()` function for localization, but we do not recommend using function names that begin with two underscores or whose names are very non-descriptive.

Lastly, your code will be much easier to navigate if you alphabetize your functions by name. Some text editors, particularly IDEs, will provide a menu to jump to each function. Alphabetizing works especially well if you put the magic functions (with two leading underscores) before the private functions (with a single leading underscore) before the public functions (with no leading underscores). The quicker you can navigate your code, the quicker you will be able to debug and change it.

Separate logic and display layers

It doesn't matter whether you are using procedural or object-oriented code, you should still separate your logic from your presentation. In laymen's terms, that means that you should keep if-statements, loops, or any other logical flows out of your HTML as much as possible.

Endlessly concatenating bits of HTML with variables and having to debug your display layers is a huge waste of time that is accepted as common practice by a staggering number of developers. You will be way ahead of the curve if you keep your HTML display logic as simple and static as possible, and keep your complicated calculations in separate functions and files. We will show you several examples of how to avoid messy concatenations using PHP functions like `sprintf()` as well as a few of our own parsing functions.

Go modular, to a point

Normally, there are strong admonitions to reuse your code whenever possible, but it is necessary to mention the caveats required for making your code portable and modular. When it comes to plugin development, sometimes you can get into trouble if your code pokes its head too far out of its own folder and starts referencing JavaScript libraries, CSS files, or even scripts that it assumes will be present in any WordPress install.

The only tie to the parent application should be through the API. It may go against your instincts to copy a second version of an image or a JavaScript library into your plugin's directory, but it will ensure that your plugin is self-sustaining and not susceptible to changes outside of its own folder.

Avoid short tags

Simply because you can configure PHP to use "<?" and "?>" (a.k.a. "short tags") to demarcate PHP code, that doesn't mean you should. Short tags are fool's gold! Even if your web server supports them, don't expect everyone in the neighborhood to join your club. Apart from making distribution of your plugin risky, short tags can cause XML files to get interpreted as PHP because they too begin with "<?".

We have personally discovered many plugins in the WordPress repository that made the sophomoric mistake of using short tags, forcing us to have to debug them immediately after installing them. It sounds harsh, but using short tags is a sure-fire way to doom your plugin to the rubbish pile.

Planning ahead / starting development

If you have ever worked in a professional development shop, you are probably familiar with the careful preparations, discussions, wireframes, and mock-ups that are made before any code is written. Projects born of haphazard random hacking are always harder to upgrade and maintain, so it is worth your time to plan your actions before writing a single line of code.

The following are a few important aspects to have in mind when starting development of your plugin:

- Interfaces
- Localization
- Documentation for the developer
- Version control
- Environment

- Tests
- Security

Interfaces

As you write code, you should constantly ask yourself, "How should this component be used?" If you are coding a particular function, you should choose what the input and output should be to make it as easy to use as possible. If you are planning a particular plugin, close your eyes and try to imagine every detail of how it should look once it is finished. What configuration options does it need? How many buttons? What will each button do? Choosing how a user will interact with your code can be broadly described as "defining the interface", and it is one of the most important aspects in planning your project because you should strive to "code to the interface". The concept is subtle, but the point is that if you have designed an interface that is easy to use, your plugin will be easy to use, and its code will be easier to maintain.

When you think about interfaces, think about the WordPress API—it is a series of functions that define how you interact with the WordPress application. While the code within each function may change between versions, so as long as the inputs and outputs (that is "the interface") remain the same, all the code using those functions will continue to work.

Localization

Even if you never intend to release your code publicly, it can be helpful to isolate any text that is used for messaging and might at some point be translated. If you are curious, you can skip ahead to the chapter on internationalization.

Documentation for the developer

As you write your plugin, be vigilant about documentation. Most developers do not include enough comments, and some include too many. At a minimum, you should include a synopsis of the plugin itself and list the expected inputs and outputs of each function so that it is clear to anyone looking at the comments what the function does and what data types it requires. If you've followed the advice presented here so far, your code will be broken down into bite-sized "units" that are easier to debug and easier to document. If you find that you are documenting a function that does more than one task, chances are good that you did not break down the functionality into a small enough unit. We have included a section on how to write effective documentation in a later chapter.

Version control

On any software project, it is useful to store versions of your files using one of the common version control applications such as Subversion (SVN), GIT, or Mercurial. The WordPress plugin repositories use SVN, and it is one of the most popular tools, so if you know you will be publishing your plugin, it may save you some time to use SVN right off the bat.

No matter how you do it, make sure that you are storing all revisions of your work so that you can easily roll back. Indeed, in professional projects, one of the first things that gets set up for collaborators is the version-controlled code repository. If you know you are going down this route or if you just want to brush up your chops, you may want to spend around $50 and get a good client for your system. Mac OS X ships with SVN on the command-line (and the Coda editor includes a basic SVN client), but you can also download Versions (`http://www.versionsapp.com`). Windows has the well-liked TortoiseSVN (`http://www.tortoisesvn.net`), while SyncroSVN is available on all platforms (`http://www.syncrosvnclient.com`). GIT also has client software available on all platforms.

We have included a chapter on SVN later in this book, so feel free to refer to it if you need to get your code versioned.

Environment

Just as you should consider the interfaces and possible translations of your code before getting too deep into it, you should also consider the environment on which it will be deployed. Does your code need to work on a specific version of PHP? Does it need to work across a series of load-balanced servers where the default PHP session management won't work? Does the destination environment have all the PHP modules that you have on your development machine?

It is common practice in software development to set up a development server that mimics the production server exactly. Unless you do additional tests, the only environment on which your plugin is guaranteed to work is the one you used while writing it. If you ever write plugins for paying customers, be sure to allow time to test your code in the environment(s) where it will be used.

Tests

Whether informal or not, tests are an integral part of any application. If you have structured your code well, it will be easier to test. Later on, we will talk about writing tests to ensure that your plugin functions properly, but it is also very worthwhile to construct informal proof-of-concept tests as you develop.

Just as an artist will draw a few studies before he paints his masterpiece, it is useful for the developer to isolate tricky bits of code into a separate test or proof. We recommend saving these little proofs in a separate directory and keeping them along with your other project code. They can become valuable notes for you as you progress in your education of PHP development.

Security

Web application security is a massive topic that goes far beyond the scope of this book. Experience is the best teacher, and we encourage you to educate yourself as much as possible when it comes to understanding vulnerabilities. We are devoting only a small amount of time to cover some of the most common exploits. You don't have much control over the underlying technologies that your plugin runs on (that is PHP, MySQL, or WordPress itself), so you should focus your attention on writing your code securely. The following scenarios represent the most commonly exploited areas in a typical web application, but remember: security is a journey, not a destination. No technology or code can ever be guaranteed to be 100% secure, but there are steps you can take to avoid the most common pitfalls.

Printing user-supplied data to a page

This most often comes up when repopulating forms after failed validation and it is often the key ingredient in a cross-site-scripting (XSS) attack. Be extremely careful any time your code handles data supplied by the user. This can be data from the `$_POST`, `$_GET`, `$_REQUEST`, `$_COOKIE`, or even from the `$_SESSION` arrays. If you print any of this data to the page, you must make sure that you have filtered out any malicious content.

Consider this little bit of code:

```php
<?php print $_GET ['x']; ?>
```

That bit of code is deadly. Printing raw request variables is all it takes to convert your site into a distributor of scum and villainy, infect computers with viruses, and get your site blocked by Google.

A better example shows how to force the value of a variable to an integer using type-casting, rendering harmless any hacking attempt:

```php
<?php print (int) $_GET['x']; ?>
```

When handling user-supplied data, you will certainly become intimately familiar with regular expressions and the `preg_match()` and `preg_replace()` functions. Regular expressions represent another topic that is beyond the scope of this book, but keep an eye on our plugins for examples on how they might be used.

Using user-supplied data to construct database queries

This can crop up in search forms, profile pages, surveys, or any other form that interacts with the database. Consider this query:

```
$query = "SELECT * FROM wp_some_table WHERE username='" . $username .
"'";
```

If you did nothing to filter the value of $username, then it is entirely possible that the variable could contain multiple queries instead of just the single username you expected. This could lead to your database being inadvertently read, deleted, or altered. Sending unfiltered user input directly to the database is the prime ingredient in a SQL-injection attack.

The risk can be virtually eliminated if your code uses "prepared statements". Instead of sending arbitrary strings to the database for execution, prepared statements first prepare the basic query and then accept only variables that complete it. Prepared statements are only possible if your web server has a more mature PHP-MySQL driver installed, such as mysqli, and your code is written explicitly to use them; WordPress does not, so be very careful if you ever start constructing your own query strings to send to the database. It is highly recommended that you use WordPress' built-in database accessor functions whenever possible. We have some examples of these in our plugins.

Debugging

If you code, you will need to learn how to debug. PHP can be more difficult to debug than some languages because it lacks a built-in debugger, so you can't step through the code line by line and set break points. PHP also does not require that you declare your variables. The first time it comes across a variable, the variable is automatically typed and scoped. This behavior is both a blessing and a curse; it is guaranteed that you will have times when you will debug a script for hours, only to discover that the root cause was a misspelled variable name.

The following is a list of recommendations for more efficient PHP debugging:

- Clear your browser cache
- Update your `php.ini` file
- Check your syntax
- Configure your `wp-config.php` file
- Check values: `print_r()` and `vardump()`

Clearing your browser cache

This should be old news for anyone who has done web development of any kind, but you must ensure that you are getting the freshest copy each time you view a page. The one caveat here is with Firefox and its "Work Offline" setting. If you are developing locally on your own computer (for example, using MAMP) and you have disconnected from the Internet, Firefox tends to go into "Work Offline" mode, which means that it will not reload any pages. Make sure Firefox never enters the "Work Offline" mode.

Updating your php.ini file

Use the following settings in your `php.ini` file:

```
error_reporting  =  E_ALL
display_errors = On
```

And optionally, use these settings to log errors to a log file:

```
log_errors = On
error_log = "/path/to/php_error.log"
```

For security, make sure the following value is set:

```
register_globals = Off
```

This will make PHP print errors to the screen (and optionally to the logs), including line numbers. Without this type of verbose output, it is virtually impossible to tell if your scripts are having problems, let alone diagnose them. On a shared hosting environment, you may not have much control over the contents of the `php.ini` file, but you can include a line in your scripts to change the error reporting level:

```
error_reporting(E_ALL)
```

Some hosting setups allow you to use your own local `php.ini` file to override system settings found in the main `php.ini` file. Check with your web host for details.

Configuring your wp-config.php file

WordPress has some debugging options of its own. If you are developing on a shared server where you cannot modify the `php.ini` file, it can be just as effective to modify the contents of your `wp-config.php` file so that the `WP_DEBUG` value is set to `true`:

```
define('WP_DEBUG', true);
```

Checking your syntax

From a *nix command line (Linux or Mac OS X), you can easily check whether or not a script has parse errors by using the syntax-check flag:

```
php -l myscript.php
```

If you are using Coda on Mac OS X, you can install the PHP Toolkit (http://www. chipwreck.de) and check for syntax errors directly from Coda. No matter what, check your syntax frequently! Sometimes forgetting a semicolon or a bracket can trigger an error that is nowhere near the actual problem. So, it is best to work on one area of code at a time and check syntax frequently so you will know where to look for the problem.

Checking values

Since PHP does not have a built-in debugger, it is common for developers to temporarily sprinkle their code with print and exit statements to check variable contents at runtime. You should become intimately familiar with the following two functions: print_r and var_dump. The get_defined_vars() function is also useful to help check for misspellings and variables that may be persisting beyond the scope you expected.

It is common to exit your script after performing one of these debugging maneuvers, then comment out the statement once you've verified the values. It can be really easy to forget that you added an exit statement somewhere in your script, so be vigilant when you perform this type of debugging. Don't forget to comment it out when finished.

For example, the following script:

```
<?php
$arr = array('man','bear','pig');
print_r($arr);
?>
```

prints this result, clearly identifying the contents of the array:

```
Array
(
    [0] => man
    [1] => bear
    [2] => pig
)
```

If you are doing any sort of frontend development that involves CSS or JavaScript, then the Firefox Firebug add-on is invaluable (`http://getfirebug.com`).

Exercise

If you're not already a Firebug user, here's a little exercise that you can try in order to get a glimpse of the value that Firebug can do to aid in debugging. First, upload the following HTML file to the root of your site then visit it using Firefox (for example, `http://yoursite.com/firebug.html`):

```
<html>
<head>
    <title>Testing FireBug</title>
    <script type="text/javascript">
            function myFunction(inputValue)
            {
                    console.log('Current value is' + inputValue);
            }
    </script>
</head>
<body>
    <a href="#" onclick="myFunction('man')">Man</a><br/>
    <a href="#" onclick="myFunction('bear')">Bear</a><br/>
    <a href="#" onclick="myFunction('pig')">Pig</a><br/>
</body>
</html>
```

Within FireFox, click on the Firebug icon at the bottom-right corner of your browser to activate it, then enable the console. Do you see how you can track JavaScript variable values in the console?

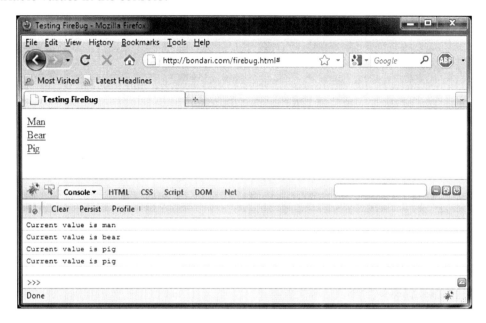

Note that the console.log() function has variants: console.info(), console.warn(), and console.error(). They all accept input in the same format at PHP's printf() function, and they will all help you test your JavaScript. The big thing to remember when using the Firebug console methods is that they are only available when Firebug is active. As soon as you close Firebug, those commands will fail and cause JavaScript processing to stop. The simple workaround is to remove the debugging statements when you are finished debugging, or shepherd them into areas where they can fail safely.

We will show some examples of how to use Firebug and JavaScript in your plugins in some of the later chapters.

Summary

There is a lot to learn about the numerous technologies that work together to allow you to write a plugin. If it did not all sink in, that's okay, because we will be repeatedly exposing you to the ideas and techniques discussed in this chapter as we work through the following chapters. We have included an appendix at the end of the book that lists resources where you can get information about WordPress functions and plugins.

Hopefully, we have painted a decent picture of the landscape of WordPress plugins and their parent technologies. In the next chapter, we will dissect a typical plugin to find out what makes it tick.

2

Anatomy of a Plugin

Before we develop any substantial plugins of our own, let's take a few moments to look at what other people have done, so we get an idea of what the final product might look like. By this point, you should have a fresh version of WordPress installed and running somewhere for you to play with. It is important that your installation of WordPress is one with which you can tinker—in this chapter we will purposely break a few things to help see how they work, so please don't try anything in this chapter on a live production site.

Deconstructing an existing plugin: "Hello Dolly"

WordPress ships with a simple plugin named "Hello Dolly". Its name is a whimsical take on the programmer's obligatory "Hello, World!", and it is trotted out only for pedantic explanations like the one that follows (unless, of course, you really do want random lyrics by Jerry Herman to grace your administration screens).

Activating the plugin

Let's activate this plugin so we can have a look at what it does:

1. Browse to your WordPress Dashboard at `http://yoursite.com/wp-admin/`.
2. Navigate to the **Plugins** section.
3. Under the **Hello Dolly** title, click on the Activate link.

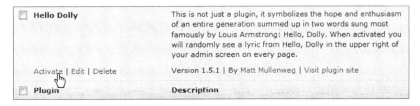

You should now see a random lyric appear in the top-right portion of the Dashboard. Refresh the page a few times to get the full effect.

Examining the hello.php file

Now that we've tried out the "Hello Dolly" plugin, let's have a closer look. In your favorite text editor, open up the /wp-content/plugins/hello.php file. Can you identify the following integral parts?

- The Information Header which describes details about the plugin (author and description). This is contained in a large PHP /* comment */.

- User-defined functions, such as the hello_dolly() function.

- The add_action() and/or add_filter() functions, which hook a WordPress event to a user-defined function.

It looks pretty simple, right? That's all you need for a plugin:

- An information header

- Some user-defined functions

- add_action() and/or add_filter() functions

Now that we've identified the critical component parts, let's examine them in more detail.

Information header

Don't just skim this section thinking it's a waste of breath on the self-explanatory header fields. Unlike a normal PHP file in which the comments are purely optional, in WordPress plugin and theme files, the Information Header is required! It is this block of text that causes a file to show up on WordPress' radar so that you can activate it or deactivate it. If your plugin is missing a valid information header, you cannot use it!

Exercise—breaking the header

To reinforce that the information header is an integral part of a plugin, try the following exercise:

1. In your WordPress Dashboard, ensure that the "Hello Dolly" plugin has been activated.

2. If applicable, use your preferred (s)FTP program to connect to your WordPress installation.

3. Using your text editor, temporarily delete the information header from `wp-content/plugins/hello.php` and save the file (you can save the header elsewhere for now). Save the file.

4. Refresh the Plugins page in your browser.

5. You should get a warning from WordPress stating that the plugin does not have a valid header:

After you've seen the tragic consequences, put the header information back into the `hello.php` file.

This should make it abundantly clear to you that the information header is absolutely vital for every WordPress plugin. If your plugin has multiple files, the header should be inside the primary file—in this book we use `index.php` as our primary file, but many plugins use a file named after the plugin name as their primary file.

Location, name, and format

The header itself is similar in form and function to other content management systems, such as Drupal's `module.info` files or Joomla's XML module configurations—it offers a way to store additional information about a plugin in a standardized format. The values can be extended, but the most common header values are listed below:

- Author: Listed below the plugin name
- Author URI: Together with "Author", this creates a link to the author's site
- Description: Main block of text describing the plugin
- Plugin Name: The displayed name of the plugin
- Plugin URI: Destination of the "Visit plugin site" link
- Version: Use this to track your changes over time

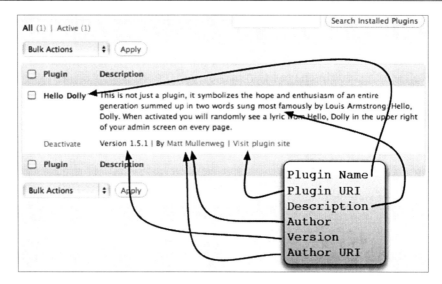

For more information about header blocks, see the WordPress codex at:
http://codex.wordpress.org/File_Header.

In order for a PHP file to show up in WordPress' **Plugins** menu:

- The file must have a .php extension.
- The file must contain the information header somewhere in it (preferably at the beginning).
- The file must be either in the /wp-content/plugins directory, or in a subdirectory of the plugins directory. It cannot be more deeply nested.

Understanding the Includes

When you activate a plugin, the name of the file containing the information header is stored in the WordPress database. Each time a page is requested, WordPress goes through a laundry list of PHP files it needs to load, so activating a plugin ensures that your own files are on that list. To help illustrate this concept, let's break WordPress again.

Exercise – parse errors

Try the following exercise:

1. Ensure that the "Hello Dolly" plugin is active.

2. Open the `/wp-content/plugins/hello.php` file in your text editor.

3. Immediately before the line that contains function hello_dolly_get_lyric, type in some gibberish text, such as "asdfasdf" and save the file.

4. Reload the plugins page in your browser.

5. This should generate a parse error, something like:

```
Parse error: syntax error, unexpected T_FUNCTION in /path/to/
wordpress/html/wp-content/plugins/hello.php on line 16
```

Yikes! Your site is now broken. Why did this happen? We introduced errors into the plugin's main file (`hello.php`), so including it caused PHP and WordPress to choke. If you did not see any errors and instead saw only a blank white page, you need to refer back to the previous chapter and the section on debugging to ensure that you have configured PHP to report errors. This is vital!

Delete the gibberish line from the `hello.php` file and save to return the plugin back to normal.

The parse error only occurs if there is an error in an active plugin. Deactivated plugins are not included by WordPress and therefore their code is not parsed. You can try the same exercise after deactivating the plugin and you'll notice that WordPress does not raise any errors.

Bonus for the curious

In case you're wondering exactly where and how WordPress stores the information about activated plugins, have a look in the database. Using your MySQL client, you can browse the `wp_options` table or execute the following query:

```
SELECT option_value FROM wp_options WHERE option_name='active_
plugins';
```

The active plugins are stored as a serialized PHP hash, referencing the file containing the header. The following is an example of what the serialized hash might contain if you had activated a plugin named "Bad Example". You can use PHP's unserialize() function to parse the contents of this string into a PHP variable as in the following script:

```
<?php
    $active_plugin_str = 'a:1:{i:0;s:27:"bad-example/bad-example.
php";}';
    print_r( unserialize($active_plugin_str) );
?>
```

And here's its output:

```
Array
(
    [0] => bad-example/bad-example.php
)
```

User-defined functions

Each plugin will store the majority of its code inside functions that you define. While it is technically possible to have a plugin that has nothing but a header, or to have a plugin that does not use user-defined functions, it is highly unlikely you would ever write such a plugin outside of a purely academic exercise.

Ready to proceed? Let's make a doomed plugin.

Exercise—an evil functionless plugin

You may not be used to writing your own functions in your code, especially for trivial tasks. However, when you are writing WordPress plugins, it is virtually impossible to get away with having all your code naked in the main code block. Let's take a closer look at how WordPress works and you will see why you need to shepherd your code into functions.

Normal users will use the **Add New** button in the Dashboard to search the WordPress repository for published plugins, but we as developers will be creating our own plugins from scratch. To do this, all we need is our trusty text editor (and our FTP client to upload it to the web server, if you're running WordPress remotely).

This exercise will illustrate how *not* to code a plugin:

1. Create a new PHP file inside the /wp-content/plugins directory. In this example, we've named ours evil-example.php.

2. Copy the <?php opening tag and the header information from the "Hello Dolly" hello.php file and take a moment to customize the header.

3. Add a single print statement to your plugin and save it. The following is what our full example looks like:

```php
<?php
/*
Plugin Name: Bad Example
Plugin URI: http://wordpress.org/#
Description: Showing what NOT to do.
Author: Everett's Twin from an Evil Parallel Universe
Version: 0.666
Author URI: http://goo.gl/us9i
*/

// Worst plugin ever
print " -------- I think I'm getting a clue!";

/* End of File */
```

Downloading the example code

You can download the example code files for all Packt books you have purchased from your account at http://www.PacktPub.com. If you purchased this book elsewhere, you can visit http://www.PacktPub.com/support and register to have the files e-mailed directly to you.

In case you didn't notice, we have omitted the closing ?> tag. We'll explain why, later in this chapter.

4. Once you've saved your new plugin, head back to your browser and refresh the **Plugin** admin page. Your new plugin should appear on the list, as follows:

5. As soon as you activate the plugin, a few horrible things may happen.

6. You may see a PHP warning, such as **Cannot modify header information...**.

7. WordPress itself may show you a warning, as follows:

The plugin generated 37 characters of unexpected output during activation. If you notice "headers already sent" messages, problems with syndication feeds or other issues, try deactivating or removing this plugin.

You will see the text you printed at the top of every page on your site, including your home page! This obnoxious text appears before the opening HTML and DOCTYPE tags.

What just happened

This is a pretty simple script, so why did everything explode? If you already know the answer, keep quiet for the folks who are still figuring this out. The answer will help keep you out of trouble when writing PHP code.

Before we go any further, if you did not see the PHP errors, then you really need revisit the previous chapter on setting up your environment and debugging. This will be your last reminder.

Now, to answer the question of all those header errors—what's going on? The whole point of using a hook is to have your function executed at a certain time. When you include a file, its code is parsed and any code not inside classes or function-blocks gets executed (whereas the classes and functions are merely loaded). The problem here revolves around PHP's `header()` function, which WordPress is using to declare the content type of its output—for example, the scripts generating the main pages use the text/HTML content type, whereas the scripts generating the RSS feeds use an RSS/XML content type.

All you really need to understand here is that the `header()` function must be called before any output is sent. From PHP's documentation:

> *"Remember that* `header()` *must be called before any actual output is sent, either by normal HTML tags, blank lines in a file, or from PHP."*

It also warns that header errors are common when using `include()` or `require()` functions. A brief analogy is seen when you mail a letter—you must address the envelope before you drop it into the mailbox.

Consider the following two scripts:

Example 1

```
<?php
header('Content-type: text/plain');
print "Headers come first.";
/* End of File */
```

Example 2

```
<?php
print "This will raise a warning.";
header('Content-type: text/plain');
/* End of File */
```

The first example works normally—if you uploaded this to the root of your website and named it `test.php`, then loaded it in your browser (for example, `http://yoursite.com/test.php`), you would see the printed text. However, the second example generates the now familiar PHP warning: **Cannot modify header information**. It's as if you are trying to change the address on your letter after you posted it.

Back in our "Bad Example" plugin, this is exactly what was happening. The print statement was executed when the file was included, and this jumped the gun on the `header()` function, even though the code was otherwise syntactically correct. Our "Bad Example" is, in fact, a good example of what not to do. This should help drive home the point that you must define your own functions in order to write WordPress functions—you cannot simply put naked code into your plugin file.

Omitting the closing "?>" PHP tag

So why do we omit the closing tag in our plugins? PHP will automatically terminate a file with a closing ?> tag if needed, but we're not just being lazy here. The reason is predicated on our discussion about headers—if your plugins have any trailing whitespace after the closing ?>, it gets interpreted in the same way as if you had printed something, and that can cause the same header warnings. Look closely at the following example. Notice the extra lines after the closing PHP tag?

```php
<?php
/*
Plugin Name: Evil Whitspace
Plugin URI: http://wordpress.org/#
Description: Undoing the Madness
Author: Senor Having a Little Trouble
Version: 0.7
Author URI: http://homestarrunner.com/
*/

// The whitespace after the closing tag
// will cause header errors!!!
?>


```

It is exceedingly difficult to spot extra newlines or spaces when debugging a script, so we omit the closing PHP tags whenever possible simply because they may trigger header errors. It is helpful to include a comment at the end of the file, such as /*End of File*/ or simply /*EOF*/ just as a reminder that yes, the omission is intentional and not the result of a corrupted file.

A better example: Adding functions

Now that we know what we can't simply print data directly from our plugin's main block, let's fix our example to make it a bit more like the "Hello Dolly" plugin:

```php
<?php
/*
Plugin Name: Better Example
Plugin URI: http://wordpress.org/#
Description: Undoing the Madness
Author: Everett's sometimes obnoxious Twin
Version: 0.7
Author URI: http://theonion.com/
*/

function safe_print() {
    print " -------- I think I'm getting a clue!";
}

/* End of File */
```

What's different about this example? This version of our plugin isolates the print statement inside a function block so that it does not execute immediately once the file is loaded. If you change the code in your sample plugin and save it, the warnings caused by the previous version of this plugin should disappear once you refresh the page. This gets us out of trouble, but it doesn't get our statement printing and visible just yet. To do that, we must add a hook to trigger execution of our function.

Referencing hooks via add_action() and add_filter()

The final vital component in a WordPress plugin is the hook, which defines when the plugin is executed. This is arguably the most confusing component of a plugin, so we will be thorough in our explanations. Just as in pop-music, the term "hook" is sometimes ambiguous—different people use the term to refer to different things. Technically, the term "hook" should refer to a WordPress event, such as get_header or the_content, but sometimes it is used generally to refer to the add_action() or add_filter() functions which reference the hook. Pay attention to the context, and it should be clear which meaning was intended. The most important thing to understand here is that you determine when your functions execute by attaching them to a WordPress event by using the add_action() or add_filter() functions. **Remember: hooks are events**.

The syntax for both functions is exactly the same. We'll discuss the reasoning for this shortly, but for now, just compare the two:

```
add_filter( string $hook, mixed $your_function_name [, int $priority =
10 [, int $accepted_args = 1]])
```

versus

```
add_action( string $hook, mixed $your_function_name [, int $priority =
10 [, int $accepted_args = 1]])
```

In practice, the most common usage includes only the name of the WordPress event and the name of your function, such as:

```
add_action('admin_footer', 'hello_dolly');
```

In "Hello Dolly", admin_footer is the action or event, and hello_dolly is the name of the function which we want WordPress to run when the admin_footer event occurs. Note that we have intentionally digressed from WordPress' official terminology for the sake of clarity.

Actions versus Filters

This is another confusing area in the land of WordPress plugins. What exactly is the difference between an action and a filter? Well, even if you've read through the forums and official documentation, the answers there likely left you more confused, so let's get this clarified once and for all.

Actions and filters are simply two different types of events. Remember that WordPress refers to events as "hooks". The difference between them is predicated on how WordPress handles the hook in question. Some hooks are designated as action hooks, others as filter hooks. When you link one of your functions to a filter hook, your function must accept an input and return an output because it is intended to modify or "filter" output. When you link a function to an action hook, your function is not passed input parameters, and any value returned is simply ignored. It is all a matter of how WordPress handles a given hook. On his site, Adam Brown maintains lists of all available WordPress hooks, and you can verify whether a given hook is a filter or an action hook (`http://adambrown.info/p/wp_hooks/`).

The truth of the matter is that the architecture here is showing its age, and there are some caveats that can be confusing. Actions and filters are simply types of events, and the `add_action()` and `add_filter()` functions are actually one and the same — one function merely references the other. If you are curious, have a look for yourself inside the `/wp-includes/plugin.php` file. In other words, you can replace any instance of `add_action()` with `add_filter()` and vice versa, and it will have no effect on the functionality of your plugin. They both simply tie a WordPress event to a function you have defined. Even though the `add_action()` and `add_filter()` functions are fundamentally the same, we do not recommend that you swap them! There is a recommended usage here that should be followed for mnemonic purposes.

Just once, however, let's demonstrate that the `add_action()` and `add_filter()` functions are equivalent by modifying the "Hello Dolly" plugin once again. This will help us understand that both functions tie to an event, and the behavior of the event is determined by the event in question, not by the function used to reference it.

Exercise—actions and filters

Using your favorite text editor, let's modify the "Hello Dolly" plugin once more.

Try replacing both instances of `add_action()` with `add_filter()` and save the file. The following is what the important lines now look like:

```
add_filter('admin_footer', 'hello_dolly');
// ...
add_filter('admin_head', 'dolly_css');
```

Remember: We haven't changed anything else about this plugin, only these two lines.

Try refreshing the WordPress Dashboard—the plugin still functions in exactly the same way. The takeaways from this exercise should be that actions and filters are simply classifications of events, and the behavior of a particular event is inherent in the event itself, not in the function we use to reference it. In other words, `admin_footer` and `admin_head` are action-events, not filter-events, and they remain action-events no matter how we hook into them.

Return the functions to their original state once you're done:

```
add_action('admin_footer', 'hello_dolly');
// ...
add_action('admin_head', 'dolly_css');
```

Now that we've demonstrated that the event is the important thing here, not the function, let's try using a different event so we can see how it behaves differently.

Exercise—filters

Let's suppose we want to repurpose the "Hello Dolly" plugin so it prints random lyrics into posts on the frontend of our site instead of just inside the WordPress manager. We will call this new plugin "Hello Knock Off". The change in behavior will revolve around the event that we hook into. Instead of tying into the `admin_footer` event, we are going to hook into the `the_content` event. `the_content` is a filter event, so we have to use it slightly differently than we did the `admin_footer` action event. Comparing the "Hello Knock Off" plugin to the original "Hello Dolly" will be a simple example that demonstrates the differences between an action and a filter. Let's get started.

First, let's make a copy of the "Hello Dolly" plugin—just copy the `hello.php` file and name the copy `knockoff.php`. You should save it in the same directory: `/wp-content/plugins`. Be sure you deactivate the original "Hello Dolly" plugin to avoid confusion.

Next, modify the information header so we can spot this plugin inside the WordPress manager. The following is what our example looks like:

```
<?php
/*
Plugin Name: Hello Knock Off
Plugin URI: http://wordpress.org/#
Description: Our first filter event
Author: Some Puerto Rican Guy
Version: 0.1
```

```
Author URI: http://goo.gl/kMEc
*/

/*EOF*/
```

Activate the plugin from inside the WordPress manager—it should show up in the Plugin administration area under the name "Hello Knock Off". Before we change the functionality, verify that the copy of the plugin works just like the original. You should see the same random messages at the top of each page in your WordPress Dashboard just like you did with the original plugin.

Next, let's change the event that is referenced here. Instead of using the `admin_footer` hook, let's use the `the_content` hook. Change the following line:

```
add_action('admin_footer', 'hello_dolly');
```

So it reads:

```
add_filter('the_content', 'hello_dolly');
```

Even though we have demonstrated that both functions are effectively the same, do not confuse yourself or others by mixing these up! `the_content` is a filter event, so we should always reference it using the `add_filter()` function.

Save your work, then try visiting your home page. You'll notice that all of your posts have been replaced with random Hello Dolly lyrics, all simply because we are hooking the code into a different event.

> ### Hello world!
> Posted on October 30, 2010 by everett
>
> Dolly'll never go away
>
> Posted in Uncategorized | 1 Comment | Edit

Let's make some adjustments here so that instead of replacing the post content, we append the quote to it. That is what a filter normally does: it modifies some text, not replaces it entirely.

Edit the `hello_dolly()` function in your `knockoff.php` so that it accepts an input, and instead of echoing a string, it returns it:

```
function hello_dolly($input) {
    $chosen = hello_dolly_get_lyric();
    return $input . "<p id='dolly'>$chosen</p>";
}
```

The `$input` here represents the content for each post—it is passed into the filter function, acted on, and then returned. Do you see how we have appended the chosen lyric to the `$input`? The result is that now we are appending a random lyric to each blog post instead of overwriting it.

Hello world!

Posted on October 30, 2010 by everett

Welcome to WordPress. This is your first post. Edit or delete it, then start blogging!

Dolly'll never go away again

Posted in Uncategorized | 1 Comment | Edit

To reiterate what just happened, the bulk of changes were caused by simply changing the event that was referenced from `admin_footer` to `the_content`. We also had to change some of the syntax in the user-defined function to correctly use a filter event instead of an action event. This should help reinforce the fact that some events are filters, and some events are actions, and now you have seen the differences in syntax between these two types of events. A function called by an action event does not accept or return input, whereas a function called by a filter does.

You may have noticed that some parts of this knock-off plugin are not being used. So let's simplify our knock-off plugin by deleting the following two functions: `dolly_css()` and the function that hooks into it: `add_action('admin_head', 'dolly_css');`

Deleting those functions simply helps clean up superfluous code. The original "Hello Dolly" plugin required those extra functions in order to correctly style and position the output, but in our "Hello Knock Off" plugin, we don't need the extra styling because we are simply appending the quotes to post content.

Reading more

Hopefully these exercises have clarified how WordPress handles actions and hooks. It is worth your time and effort to skim through the online documentation that lists the most common actions and filters, just so you have some awareness of what actions and filters are available. WordPress has thousands of hooks, but there are still some key places that you cannot easily hook into. We recommend bookmarking the following two pages for reference:

http://codex.wordpress.org/Plugin_API/Action_Reference

http://codex.wordpress.org/Plugin_API/Filter_Reference

The hooks referenced on those pages are only a fraction of those available, but we recommend that you stick to the short list as much as possible. For a full list of all WordPress hooks, see:

`http://adambrown.info/p/wp_hooks/`

We have included a short list of actions and filters used in this book in Appendix B. You'll find that you can achieve a lot of what you need by using a small number of actions and filters.

Summary

After completing this chapter, you should know how to create a simplistic WordPress plugin and you should know where you have to put the file in order for it to show up in the WordPress Dashboard. You should have learned a couple debugging techniques that will apply to your work as a plugin developer. We've learned the differences between filters and actions and seen how WordPress sends data to your functions in each case. You should now have a working understanding of the most common plugin patterns and you should now be ready to write a couple of your own.

Up next, we're going to create our first full and functional plugin: Social Bookmarking.

3
Social Bookmarking

Now that we've covered the component parts of a WordPress plugin, it's time to write something more substantial. In this chapter, we will create a plugin that allows visitors to bookmark each of our posts using the social bookmarking service `http://www.digg.com`. We are going to learn a bit more about the WordPress API and by the time we're done, we will have in our toolbox a simple coding pattern that is applicable to many other plugins we may want to write, such as one that creates a Facebook "Like" button.

In this chapter, you will learn or review the following points:

- How to plan your plugin architecture and write code in a methodical and testable way
- How to use several WordPress API functions, such as how to retrieve the title and permalink URL of each post
- How to use WordPress hooks to execute your plugin code
- How to check the WordPress version
- How to include external JavaScript files

We're going to build this slowly and test it as we go so you can see how each component works. Let's get started!

The overall plan

In our opening chapters, we talked about the importance of planning ahead, so here is a picture of what our plugin should do. It should add a **Submit to digg** button to each post:

Proof of concept

Before we get WordPress involved at all, let's make sure that Digg's button works on a simple static page. If we can't make it work outside of WordPress, it's unlikely that we can make it work inside of WordPress. Take a look at the guide at `http://about.digg.com/downloads/button/smart` and get familiar with the sample code and the options available. We're going to try to make a simple static HTML page that implements a "Medium Smart Digg Button". According to Digg's documentation, all we need to do is add a bit of JavaScript to the document head and then use a special anchor tag on our page. Taking Digg's lead, the following is the HTML we've saved in a file named `proof_of_concept.html`:

```
<html>
<head>
    <title>Proof of Concept</title>
    <script type="text/javascript">
        (function() {
        var s = document.createElement('SCRIPT'), s1 = document.
getElementsByTagName('SCRIPT')[0];
        s.type = 'text/javascript';
        s.async = true;
        s.src = 'http://widgets.digg.com/buttons.js';
        s1.parentNode.insertBefore(s, s1);
        })();
    </script>
```

```
</head>
<body>
    <p>My post content goes here...</p>
    <a class="DiggThisButton DiggMedium"></a>
</body>
</html>
```

Visiting this page in a browser should look something like the following screenshot:

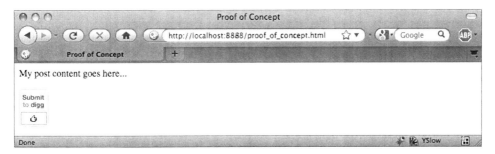

Make sure you see something like the preceding screenshot before you go on. This gives you an opportunity to troubleshoot the basic functionality before WordPress or PHP are involved.

Avoiding conflicting function names

Remember from *Chapter 1* that WordPress' architecture normally relies on globally scoped functions in the main namespace, so name collisions are a big concern. In layman's terms, each function must have a unique name to avoid PHP errors. For example, the following PHP script would die with a fatal error:

```php
<?php
function main() {
    // Do something
}
function main() {
    // Oops... "Fatal error: Cannot redeclare main()"
}
?>
```

Even if the functions are declared in different files, the names must be unique. As we write plugins, we must be careful to avoid using function names that are already in use by WordPress or by other plugins.

In this chapter, we will ensure unique function names by adding a prefix to each name, for example, `my_plugin_main()` or `my_plugin_some_function`. Usually this prefix is inspired by your plugin's name. We're naming our plugin Digg This, so we've used "diggthis" as a prefix to each function's name.

In later chapters, we will show you how to avoid conflicting function names by using PHP classes, objects, and static functions. Object-oriented coding represents a cleaner solution to the problem of namespace pollution, but it is a bit harder to follow, so we have dedicated this chapter to show you how we solved this problem using simple function names. We'll tackle the more advanced solutions later.

The master plugin outline

After looking over the examples on `Digg.com` and trying out our own proof of concept, we know what we're aiming for, so let's think through the structure of the PHP code that is required. When you write your own plugins, it's a great habit to sketch an outline of the main components before you start any serious coding because it will force you to identify problems and establish a structure. Keep in mind there are many different ways in which a plugin could be written, so don't be discouraged if your outline differs from ours.

We know our plugin needs an information header and either the `add_action()` or the `add_filter()` functions. We also want to test the WordPress version in use and we're going to outline some of the helper functions we expect we'll need to achieve all of this. To help organize our thoughts, we are going to sketch an outline for our plugin by creating some PHP comments in the file that will become our plugin. Our plugin will slowly become functional as we replace those comments with working functions. Let's get started!

Create a folder for your plugin inside `/wp-content/plugins`. We're naming our plugin Digg This, so the folder will be named `digg-this`—we have simply replaced spaces with dashes to come up with a valid folder name. Next, create an `index.php` file inside your plugin's folder. This `index.php` will contain your plugin's information header, and we will refer to it as your plugin's "main" file.

Many WordPress developers use a file named after the plugin as their plugin's "main" file, for example, `digg-this.php`, but we find it more intuitive to use `index.php` instead. As a web developer, you should already be accustomed to looking for this common file any time you scan through a directory. It may seem overly nitpicky when we are writing plugins that only have a couple files, but once your plugin grows to include multiple files, it can become increasingly difficult for you or others to find your plugin's "main" file. Here is the code we've saved inside of `/wp-content/plugins/digg-this/index.php`:

```php
<?php
/* Information Header Goes here */

// include() or require() any necessary files here...

// Settings and/or Configuration Details go here...

// Tie into WordPress Hooks and any functions that should run on load.

// "Private" internal functions named with a leading underscore
function _diggthis_get_post_description() { }
function _diggthis_get_post_media_type() { }
function _diggthis_get_post_title() { }
function _diggthis_get_post_topic() { }
function _diggthis_get_post_url() { }

// The "Public" functions
function diggthis_add_js_to_doc_head() { }
function diggthis_check_wordpress_version() { }
function diggthis_get_button() { }

/* EOF */
```

That's the skeletal framework of our plugin, and it's a simple outline you can copy for similar plugins. This code should execute without errors, even though it doesn't do anything yet because our functions are empty. Regardless, you should be able to get a decent idea about how the plugin will work just by looking at this outline— we've used descriptive function names that give an idea of what each function will do. As discussed in the previous section, we have prepended "diggthis" to each function's name to help avoid naming collisions.

You can see that we've created three "public" functions to correspond with the three main things we want this plugin to do. We want it to add some JavaScript to the document head, we want it to generate a valid Digg button, and we also want it to test the version of WordPress in use. The public functions represent the main tasks for our plugin, and they are the functions that will be tied to a WordPress event.

Our "private" functions are meant to assist the public functions. Technically, they aren't private functions per se, but we are isolating them as functions that will be called by one of the "public" functions instead of being called directly. Notice that the names of these functions too begin with an underscore. It is common practice to use a leading underscore to identify functions that should be considered "private", for "internal use only". The private functions we have outlined will help the `diggthis_get_button()` function by getting the component parts needed to create the button: title, description, and URL. Just to be clear, the private functions we have outlined are a product of the Digg API. If Digg offered a way to transmit a post's author, for example, we would have included a corresponding `_diggthis_get_post_author()` function to isolate the task of getting the author's name into its own function.

Lastly, notice that we have alphabetized our functions by name for better organization.

> In this chapter, we are not using object oriented code, so we are not enforcing any permissions on our functions. We are referring to some functions as "public" and others as "private" merely as a way to help distinguish between primary functions and helper functions. In later chapters, we will use PHP classes and we will implement true public and private functions.

Now that we've outlined our script with comments and empty functions, let's start filling in the gaps. Here are all the areas in our plugin outline that we need to address:

- The plugin information header
- Adding JavaScript to the head
- Adding a link to the post content
- Adding a button template
- Getting the post URL
- Getting the post title
- Getting the description
- Getting the media type
- Getting the topic

As we work through this chapter, we will show small bits of code that are meant to replace individual sections within the master plugin outline. This is intended to allow you to focus on one section of the code at a time.

The plugin information header

We know from the previous chapter that each plugin requires an information header before it shows up in WordPress' plugin administration panel. You can copy and modify the plugin header from the Hello Dolly plugin. Take a moment to customize it and save the result. The following is the plugin header we're using in our /content/wp-content/plugins/digg-this/index.php file:

```
/*
Plugin Name: Digg This
Plugin URI: http://www.tipsfor.us/
Description: This plugin will add a "Digg This" button link to each
post on your WordPress site.
Author: Everett Griffiths
Version: 0.1
Author URI: http://www.tipsfor.us/
*/
```

In your browser—information header

Remember that this header information is what causes the plugin to show up on WordPress' radar, so as soon as you've saved the file, you should be able to see it in the WordPress plugin administration screen. Before you go any further, check to ensure that your plugin is now showing up in the plugin administration page.

If your future plugin has more than one PHP file, the plugin information header should be placed only in your main file, the one which will `include()` or `require()` the other plugin PHP files.

Before you continue, try activating your plugin to ensure that you do not have any syntax errors. It should work, even though it doesn't do anything yet. It is critical to start testing your script early and often. This helps you catch any errors more quickly!

Adding a link to the post content

Let's begin by focusing on modifying the post content so we can append a clickable link. It can be a challenge to know whether you need to use an action or a filter, but experience will teach you. If we examine our options in the WordPress Codex about filter references (`http://goo.gl/whqA`) and action references (`http://goo.gl/qAps`), eventually we can narrow our choices down to the `the_content` filter. This, by the way, is exactly the same filter we demonstrated in the previous chapter. As this is a filter and not an action, we will use the `add_filter()` function to reference it, and the custom function that we reference must accept an input and return an output. We've already earmarked the `diggthis_get_button()` as the one that will generate the button link, so we'll reference it by name in the `add_filter()` function.

The following is how we've edited our `/content/wp-content/plugins/digg-this/index.php` file:

```
add_filter('the_content', 'diggthis_get_button');
// [ . . . ]
/**
* Adds a "Digg This" link to the post content.
*
* @param    string   $content   the existing post content
* @return   string   appends a DiggThis link to the incoming $content.
*/
function diggthis_get_button($content) {
    return $content . '<a class="DiggThisButton DiggMedium"></a>';
}
```

Documenting our functions

You may have noticed that we used a special syntax for documenting the `diggthis_get_button()` function. We are using a PHP equivalent to the often-emulated Javadoc syntax, which is a standard syntax used for documenting functions so that your comments can be automatically converted to HTML pages. The principle is similar to Wikipedia formatting or BBCode, both of which use special symbols to specify various HTML elements. The PHPDoc syntax isn't strictly necessary, but since it is a common feature of a lot of open source PHP code, we will be using it throughout this book.

Ironically, the documentation on how to use the PHPDoc syntax is confusing and hard to follow. The official quick start is here (`http://goo.gl/5CyZg`), but we find the third-party tutorial at `http://goo.gl/oTARc` to be much more to the point and easier to follow.

No matter which syntax you use, make sure you document your functions clearly by including a brief overview of what the function does, specifying the input parameters, and specifying the value returned. Adding proper documentation to your code is a "time" investment that will save you (and others) lots of time in the long run, so please don't neglect it!

In your browser—linking to the post content

Save your file, then try refreshing your homepage. At first, everything might look the same, but try viewing the source HTML and verify that the Digg anchor tag is appearing after your post content.

Congratulations! It doesn't look like much yet and it doesn't quite work, but a little bit of JavaScript will bring it to life.

Adding JavaScript to the head

From our proof of concept, we learned that the Digg button needs to have some special JavaScript in the HTML document head. Although we could simply paste the necessary JavaScript into our template files, that defeats the purpose of dynamically adding it via a plugin. Besides, we want a solution that doesn't break when we switch templates.

As we've already done this a couple of times, you might be ready to scan through the available actions and filters in the WordPress Codex to find a viable event you can hook into. If you did that, you might come to the conclusion that using the `wp_head` action would be your ticket to making this work. It's true that the `wp_head` action would allow you to print the necessary HTML into the head of your pages, but that's actually not the recommended way of accomplishing this.

When working with plugins in any CMS, it is a common need to add both JavaScript and CSS to augment your plugin – the scripts expect to have certain JavaScript and CSS available to them in order to function correctly. WordPress, like other CMS's, has dedicated a few API functions designed explicitly to help solve this problem: `wp_register_script()` and `wp_enqueue_script()`. Together, these functions allow you to include an external JavaScript file exactly once. When used correctly, they prevent you from including the same file multiple times. That's important with JavaScript because many plugins might require the same JavaScript library, but including the same file multiple times can cause conflicts in the same way as redeclaring PHP functions. It's also inefficient to include the same file multiple times, so WordPress' functions here are an effective solution.

Our fist task then is to get the necessary JavaScript into a separate file. If you have working JavaScript inside a `<script>` tag, you can put its contents into an external file and reference it using the `src` attribute. Create a new file named `digg.js` and paste the contents of the `<script>` tag into it. Here is what we have added to our newly created `digg-this/digg.js` file:

```
(function() {
var s = document.createElement('SCRIPT'), s1 = document.
getElementsByTagName('SCRIPT')[0];
s.type = 'text/javascript';
s.async = true;
s.src = 'http://widgets.digg.com/buttons.js';
s1.parentNode.insertBefore(s, s1);
})();
```

To include this on our pages, we would typically add something like this to our document head:

```
<script type="text/javascript" src="http://yoursite.com/plugins/digg-
this/digg.js"></script>
```

In order to have WordPress do this automatically for us, we are going to make use of the aforementioned `wp_register_script()` and `wp_enqueue_script()` as well as the `plugins_url()` function, which helps us generate the correct URL to our new JavaScript file:

```
function diggthis_add_js_to_doc_head() {
    $src = plugins_url('digg.js', __FILE__);
    wp_register_script( 'diggthis', $src );
    wp_enqueue_script( 'diggthis' );
}
```

The function `plugins_url()` generates a URL to the `digg.js` file inside of our plugin's folder when we pass it the `__FILE__` constant, which PHP interprets as the path and name of the current file. Now we have a function that will cause the necessary JavaScript file to be loaded, but we need to tie this to a WordPress event so that this function executes. The event to which we want to tie this is the `init` action that fires when WordPress is initialized.

```
// Tie into WordPress Hooks and any functions that should run on load.
add_action('init','diggthis_add_js_to_doc_head');
```

When we've finished this, our `index.php` file looks like the following:

```php
<?php
/*----------------------------------------------------------------
-----------
Plugin Name: Digg This
Plugin URI: http://www.tipsfor.us/
Description: This plugin will add a "Digg This" button link to each
post on your WordPress site.
Author: Everett Griffiths
Version: 0.1
Author URI: http://www.tipsfor.us/
----------------------------------------------------------------
---------*/

// include() or require() any necessary files here...

// Settings and/or Configuration Details go here...

// Tie into WordPress Hooks and any functions that should run on load.
add_filter('the_content', 'diggthis_get_button');
add_action('init', 'diggthis_add_js_to_doc_head');

// "Private" internal functions named with a leading underscore
function _diggthis_get_post_description() { }
function _diggthis_get_post_media_type() { }
function _diggthis_get_post_title() { }
function _diggthis_get_post_topic() { }
function _diggthis_get_post_url() { }

// The "Public" functions
/**
* Add the local digg.js to the <head> of WordPress pages
*
* @return   none   adds HTML to the document <head>
*/

function diggthis_add_js_to_doc_head() {
    $src = plugins_url('digg.js', __FILE__);
```

```
        wp_register_script( 'diggthis', $src );
        wp_enqueue_script( 'diggthis' );
    }
    function diggthis_check_wordpress_version() { }
    /**
     * Adds a "Digg This" link to the post content.
     *
     * @param     string    $content   the existing post content
     * @return    string    appends a DiggThis link to the incoming $content.
     */
    function diggthis_get_button($content) {
        return $content . '<a class="DiggThisButton DiggMedium"></a>';
    }

    /* EOF */
```

If you haven't already, activate this plugin and then visit the homepage of your site. You should now see a functioning Digg button. Try viewing the source HTML and verify that the Digg JavaScript is being added to the head. You should see something like the following show up in your document head when you view the source HTML:

```
<script type='text/javascript' src='http://yoursite.com/wp-content/
plugins/digg-this/digg.js?ver=3.0.4'></script>
```

Tricky, eh? We are now dynamically modifying our pages and we have achieved basic functionality! If you are developing locally on your own desktop computer, you may get some errors when you try to submit a link to Digg: **Unable to access this content**. This is normal—Digg is trying to connect to your site, but if you are developing locally, your site is not publicly available, so it throws this error.

If you get any other errors, the PHP information printed to the screen should help you track down their source.

Making our link dynamic

We have the basic functionality in place, but our link doesn't yet send any data to Digg.com. Remember from Digg's documentation that we can supply each link with a URL, a title, a description, a media type, and a topic. That's why we set up those other functions.

In order to pass all that additional information, we need to modify the format of our link, so we have to refer back to Digg's documentation. Arguably, we could have done this right off the bat in our proof-of-concept page, but it was good to first test the basic functionality. Let's revisit our proof_of_concept.html page and try to use a "fully qualified" link that passes along the extra attributes.

While tinkering with Digg's format on our `proof_of_concept.html`, we realized a couple of things that may throw you off. First, submitting a page is a two-part process, and only after Digg has evaluated your submission can you see whether or not the attributes you passed actually came through. In short, it takes a bit of mouse work to test if it is working properly.

Secondly, Digg uses "&" to separate name/value pairs in their URL instead of the traditional "&". This might seem perplexing, but it has to do with URL encoding, and "&" is actually correct.

We had to piece together various parts of the Digg documentation to get what we wanted, but when we finished, our `proof_of_concept.html` file contained a link that looked like this:

```
<a class="DiggThisButton DiggMedium" href="http://digg.com/
submit?url=http%3A//tipsfor.us&amp;title=Tips%20For%20Us" rev="news,
tech_news">
<span style="display:none">This site will make you smarter.</span>
</a>
```

In your browser—dynamic links

Before going further, take a moment to verify that the static proof-of-concept still works and that all attributes are passed correctly. You can log into `Digg.com` using your Facebook or Twitter account. If everything was passed correctly, you should see a page on `Digg.com` that has all the information you specified in your proof-of-concept link.

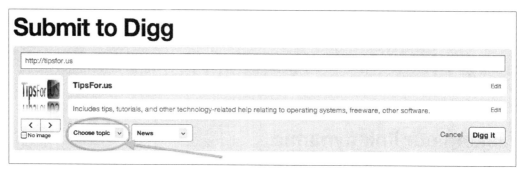

Unfortunately, at the time of writing, we had problems getting all attributes to pass correctly. In particular, the description and the topic that we defined in our proof of concept never showed up on `Digg.com`; they had to be re-entered manually. Rather than trying to tell you that web service integrations like this are always peaches and cream, this can be a good reality check: API's do not always work as advertised. It's fairly common that the documentation is incomplete or the examples don't work. If this frustrates you, then it should be a strong motivation for you to make sure that your functions work and are documented properly.

Adding a button template

Now that we've tested it, let's update our `diggthis_get_button()` function so that we can pass information dynamically using the full link format. We will now take the opportunity to reference the other functions, even though they still are empty. As always, it's important to keep your code as organized as possible, so we're going to use the PHP `sprintf()` function to format our link string and replace instances of "%s" with values returned by our functions. If you're not familiar with `sprintf()`, take a moment to look over its manual page: `http://php.net/manual/en/function.sprintf.php`. It's a really useful function for cleanly formatting strings.

We are also going to make use of a PHP constant. PHP constants are declared using the `define()` function. Constants are declared in the global namespace, so like functions, you have to be careful that their names are unique. Unlike variables, they cannot be overwritten once defined, so they are perfect for configuration details that should not be changed.

We're going to create a PHP constant in the section of our plugin that we have earmarked for configuration details:

```
// Settings and/or Configuration Details go here...
define ('DIGGTHIS_BUTTON_TEMPLATE',
    '<a class="DiggThisButton DiggMedium"
        href="http://digg.com/submit?url=%s&amp;title=%s"
        rev="%s, %s">
        <span style="display:none">
            %s
        </span>
    </a>');
```

This constant contains instances of "%s", which will be replaced by PHP's `sprintf()` function. Here's our updated `diggthis_get_button()` function, now using the `sprintf()` function. Notice that we have used PHP's `urlencode()` function to encode the values for `$url` and `$title`:

```
/**
 * Adds a "Digg This" link to the post content.
 *
 * @param      string   $content   the existing post content
 * @return     string   appends a DiggThis link to the incoming $content.
 */
function diggthis_get_button($content) {
    $url         = urlencode( _diggthis_get_post_url() );
    $title       = urlencode( _diggthis_get_post_title() );
    $description  = _diggthis_get_post_description();
```

```
$media_type  = _diggthis_get_post_media_type();
$topic       = _diggthis_get_post_topic();

return $content . sprintf(
    DIGGTHIS_BUTTON_TEMPLATE,
    $url,
    $title,
    $media_type,
    $topic,
    $description);
}
```

There are more concise ways of writing this function that would have required fewer variables, but here we are striving for clarity. **Never** optimize your functions prematurely—your first priorities should always be functionality and readability. A more conventional way to construct the link would have been via concatenation, as shown below:

```
return '<a class="DiggThisButton DiggMedium"
    href="http://digg.com/submit?url=' . $url . '&title=' . $title.
'"
    rev="' . $media_type . ', ' . $topic . '"
    <span style="display:none">
       ' . $description. '
    </span>
    </a>';
```

Concatenation works, but can you see how much more difficult it is to read? Particularly, keeping track of the quotes and periods is prone to error, so we prefer the sprintf() function. Its first argument is the string or template that contains placeholders (that is %s). The following list of parameters correspond to values that will replace the placeholders; the first instance of %s will be replaced by the value of $url, and the second %s by the value of $title and so on. It can be an elegant way to keep your code clean.

Getting the post URL

Let's start fleshing out the helper functions that retrieve the link's URL, title, and other attributes. Can you see the logic of our approach here? We've framed the script in a way that lets us develop gradually and test as we go, function by function.

We're going to start introducing some elements from the WordPress API to help us get the information we need about each post. Our primary source of information here is the WordPress function reference: http://codex.wordpress.org/ Function_Reference.

Can you find a function that retrieves a post's URL? We did it using the `get_permalink()` function. By default, it will return the URL of the current post, which is what we want.

```
/**
 * Gets the URL of the current post.
 *
 * @return    string    the URL of the current post.
 */
function _diggthis_get_post_url() {
return get_permalink();
}
```

It's worth mentioning that there are multiple ways we could have gone about this. We have opted to use the built-in WordPress functions whenever possible because we feel they offer a cleaner interface to the application. It is entirely possible, however, to rely on WordPress variables instead. Look at the following variation on the same function:

```
function _diggthis_get_post_url() {
    global $post;
    return get_permalink($post->ID);
}
```

Notice our use of the `global` keyword. This has nothing to do with the notorious PHP security vulnerability that arises when *register globals* are enabled. Rather, it is a command which instructs PHP to inherit the globally scoped variable of that name, rather than creating a new locally scoped variable. In other words, WordPress already has a global `$post` variable floating around, and we want to use it. The `$post` variable is actually an object, and it has all kinds of information about the current post. If you are curious, try temporarily printing its contents using `print_r()` and observing the result when you refresh the page:

```
function _diggthis_get_post_url() {
    global $post;
print_r($post); exit; // <-- temporarily add this line if you're
curious!
    return get_permalink($post->ID);
}
```

Once you've seen what's contained in the `$post` object, be sure to delete or comment out the `print_r` and the exit lines.

Accessing post data directly from the `$post` object has some advantages, but in general we feel it's clearer to rely on WordPress' accessor methods to retrieve post attributes.

We could have forgone our custom function altogether, since the only thing it did was to reference a single WordPress function. We did construct a sensible outline, though, and we have isolated a single function dedicated to a single purpose, and that clarity is useful.

In your browser—getting the post URL

Once you have implemented the `_diggthis_get_post_url()` function you should be able to save your work and then refresh your home page in your browser. By examining the source of the HTML, you should be able to see some values coming through. In the HTML of our page, we can see that we are now getting a value for the URL:

```
<a class="DiggThisButton DiggMedium"          href="http://digg.com/subm
it?url=http%3A%2F%2Flocalhost%3A8888%2F%3Fp%3D1&amp;title=" rev=", ">
<span style="display:none"></span></a>
```

We still have a lot of empty attributes, though, so let's keep going!

Getting the post title

We're going to do something very similar for the `_diggthis_get_post_title()` function. First, we'll find a viable WordPress API function that can return the post's title, and then we'll add it to our function earmarked for the purpose:

```
/**
 * Gets the title of the current post.
 *
 * @return    string   the title of the current post.
 */
function _diggthis_get_post_title () {
$id = get_the_ID();
return get_the_title($id);
}
```

As before, save the result and check the result in your browser.

Getting the description

Getting the post description is slightly more complicated because Digg requires that the excerpt be no longer than 350 characters. There are some built-in WordPress functions that return excerpts, but nothing does exactly what we want. So, we're going to roll up our sleeves and write our own function that grabs the first 350 characters of the content.

We have to think a bit more ahead, though. Digg wants only text, but our content may contain HTML tags or WordPress shortcodes (more about those in a later chapter). So we need to make sure we strip all of those out of the excerpt before we count our 350 characters.

Lastly, we want to make sure that we don't chop a word in half when we return the excerpt. As we are perfectionists, we are going to ensure that only whole words are sent to Digg for their description.

The following is the function we came up with. Note that we used WordPress's `strip_shortcodes()` function and PHP's `strip_tags()` function:

```php
/**
 * Gets a short description/excerpt of the post from the content.
 *
 * @return    string    stripped of html tags and shortcodes.
 */
function _diggthis_get_post_description() {
    $excerpt        = get_the_content();
    $excerpt        = strip_shortcodes($excerpt);
    $excerpt        = strip_tags($excerpt);
    $excerpt        = substr($excerpt, 0, 350);
    $words_array    = explode(' ', $excerpt);
    $word_cnt       = count($words_array);
    return implode(' ', array_slice($words_array, 0, $word_cnt - 1));
}
```

Wow. We did some crazy stuff in there. Let's walk you through what we did. Firstly, we retrieved the post content using WordPress' `get_the_content()` function. Next, we removed WordPress shortcodes from the content using WordPress' `strip_shortcodes()` function. Shortcodes are macro codes that can appear in your post content, so they can throw off the total number of characters in a text-only excerpt. We also need to remove any HTML tags from the excerpt, so for that we used PHP's `strip_tags()` function. After those functions have operated on the content, we should have only raw text, of which we need only 350 characters. The next few functions help us prevent chopping a word in half—if we had simply grabbed 350 characters from the raw content, chances are that we'd end up with half a word at the end of our excerpt, and that's just as bad as half a worm in your apple. The way we prevent chopping a word in half means that we grab the first 350 characters using PHP's `substr()` function, then we effectively count the words using PHP's `explode()` function, which converts the string to an array of words. Since the last word in that array might be half a word, we omit the last word from the excerpt using the `count()` function and the `array_slice()` function. Finally, we glue the array of words back together using the `implode()` function. Our solution here might be somewhat complicated, but it is thorough enough to cover our bases.

Getting the media type

The media type is not something we are going to support in this first version, so we are going to return a static value from our function:

```
/**
 * Get the media type for the current post
 *
 * @return   string   a valid media type: news, image, or video.
 */
function _diggthis_get_post_media_type() {
return 'news';
}
```

"Shenanigans!" you might be saying. "That's not legit!" Calm down. It is actually quite common for programmers to earmark certain functionality as "Future" or "To-Do". We should be happy that we've isolated this particular functionality into its own function, and if we so choose, we can at a later date make this plugin dynamically determine the media type. However, for now, we're going to leave it alone.

It would be a great exercise for the reader to figure out a way to determine whether a post's media type was "image" or "video". We can give you a hint: search for "post types".

Getting the post topic

The post topic is something that we could return statically as well, but there is the possibility that our post has been grouped into a category that might match up favorably with a Digg topic. From Digg's documentation, we can see a list of viable topics: `arts_culture`, `autos`, `baseball`, and so on. If our site is predominantly about baseball, then we could set this to a static value and forget about it, but let's do this instead: if one of a post's categories matches up with one of Digg's topics, we'll use that as the topic, but if not, we'll fall back on a default topic.

To accomplish this plan, we're going to use another PHP constant in our script in the area we've reserved for settings and configuration details:

```
// Must be one of the allowed Digg topics: http://about.digg.com/
button
define ('DIGGTHIS_DEFAULT_TOPIC','tech_news');
```

For our site, we've decided to use `tech_news` as our default. Like before, we're going to look through the available WordPress functions to use in our `_diggthis_get_post_topic()` function. We can get all of a post's categories using WordPress' `get_categories()` function. Then we need to see if any of them match up with the viable Digg topics. The following is how we did it:

```
/**
 * Checks current post categories to see if any WP Category is a viable
 *   Digg topic; if yes, return the first match. Otherwise, the
 *   DIGGTHIS_DEFAULT_TOPIC will be returned.
 *
 * @return   string   a viable Digg topic.
 */
function _diggthis_get_post_topic() {

    $digg_topics_array = array(
        'arts_culture','autos','baseball','basketball','business_
finance',
        'celebrity','comedy','comics_animation','design','educational',
        'environment','extreme_sports','food_
drink','football','gadgets',
        'gaming_news','general_sciences','golf','hardware','health',
        'hockey','linux_unix','microsoft','mods','motorsport',
    'movies','music','nintendo','odd_stuff','olympics','other_sports',
 'pc_games','people','pets_animals','playable_web_games','playstation',
        'political_opinion','politics','programming','security','socc
er',
        'software','space','tech_news','television','tennis','travel_
places',
        'world_news','xbox',);

    $category_array = get_categories();

    foreach ( $category_array as $cat ) {
        // WP replaces spaces w '-', whereas Digg uses '_'
        $category_name = preg_replace('/ \-/','_',$cat->category_
nicename);
        if ( in_array ( $category_name, $digg_topics_array ) ) {
            return $category_name;
        }
    }

    // if no match, then fall back to the default
    return DIGGTHIS_DEFAULT_TOPIC;
}
```

We have used WordPress' `get_categories()` function to retrieve all the categories that the current post has been placed in. We can iterate through these categories and use the PHP `in_array()` function to determine if a category matches any of Digg's topics. We have to manipulate WordPress' categories a bit so they match up with the Digg topics: we replace spaces and dashes with underscores. We have opted to use PHP's powerful `preg_replace()` function for this purpose, but we could have used the `str_replace()` function as well:

```
$replace_me = array(' ', '_');
$category_name = str_replace($replace_me, '_', $cat->category_
nicename);
```

Although `str_replace()` and similar functions are simpler to understand, the `preg_replace()` function offers a flexible solution using Perl's powerful regular expressions. Regular expressions represent a huge topic in and of themselves, so we can't get too far into their syntax. However, if you ever use other program languages, it's more likely that you will end up using the Perl syntax, so we favor its use.

In your browser—title, description, and topic

Once you complete this function, your Digg button should be fully functional! Try refreshing your home page and clicking your Digg button. Verify whether the title, description, and the topic come through to the Digg page when you click on the button. If you are developing locally on your computer, remember that Digg will complain that the URL is not properly formatted, so you can temporarily modify your `_diggthis_get_post_url()` function to return the URL of a publicly available page:

```
function _diggthis_get_post_url() {
    return "http://www.tipsfor.us/";    // <-- temporary for testing
    // return get_permalink();
}
```

Be sure to change the function back to normal after testing.

Checking WordPress versions

It is common for scripts to perform some "pre-flight" tests at runtime to ensure that they can execute correctly. Common examples of these types of tests include checking the version of PHP or of WordPress. To avoid any potential catastrophes that could occur if our plugin is activated on incompatible WordPress versions, we will perform a simple WordPress version check, and you can use this format as a guideline for how you might perform similar pre-flight tests. Let's add another PHP constant to define the minimum version of WordPress required. We want this plugin to require WordPress version 3 or greater:

```
define('DIGGTHIS_MIN_WORDPRESS_VERSION', '3.0');
```

Again, we place this near the top of our plugin in the area we allotted for configuration and settings.

In order to check the current version of WordPress, we can use the global WordPress variable $wp_version. We can then use the PHP function version_compare() to compare the current version with the minimum required. The following is how we updated the diggthis_check_wordpress_version() function:

```
/**
 * Checks that the current version of WordPress is current enough.
 *
 * @return    none    exit on fail.
 */
function diggthis_check_wordpress_version() {
    global $wp_version;

    $exit_msg='"Digg This" requires WordPress '
        .DIGGTHIS_MIN_WORDPRESS_VERSION
        .' or newer.
        <a href="http://codex.wordpress.org/Upgrading_WordPress">Please
update!</a>';

    if (version_compare($wp_version,DIGGTHIS_MIN_WORDPRESS_
VERSION,'<'))
    {
        exit ($exit_msg);
    }
}
```

This will ensure that only users who are running WordPress 3.0 or later will be able to use the plugin. Technically, everything we've done would work on many older versions of WordPress, but since we authored this plugin on WordPress 3, it's best not to assume that it will work on older versions.

To execute this function, we will tie into the same init method as we did before. Simply add this below our existing add_action() and add_filter() functions:

```
add_action('init', 'diggthis_check_wordpress_version');
```

To ensure that this works, try temporarily changing the minimum version constant:

```
define('DIGGTHIS_MIN_WORDPRESS_VERSION', '4.0');
```

Save your file and refresh your browser. You should see the `$exit_msg` displayed:

"Digg This" requires WordPress 4.0 or newer. Please update!

Once you've verified that the error message works, you can change the constant back.

Summary

We've gone through a lot of topics in this chapter, and we've taken you step by step through a sensible development flow. Here's what we've covered:

- Structuring a plugin: How to prepare an outline of key components and implement them slowly, allowing you to test as you go

- Accessing post information: Different ways of obtaining data from the post such as title, permalink and content

- Checking WordPress version: How to check that our plugin is compatible with the user's version of WordPress

- Using WordPress hooks: How to use actions and filters to get to trigger functions in our plugin

- Include external JavaScript files in your plugins using WordPress' `wp_register_script()` and `wp_enqueue_script()` functions

Now that we've learned a bit more about WordPress hooks, the API, and how to handle some of the external files, we are ready to look at some more complex code patterns. We will do this in the next chapter as we improve upon the built-in WordPress search feature.

4
Ajax Search

In this chapter we will continue our exploration of the WordPress universe by using Ajax to create a cleaner user experience for the WordPress site search form. Don't worry if you've never used Ajax before. We'll explain what it is, how to use it in your plugins, and also how to debug it.

In this chapter, you will:

- Learn a bit about Ajax
- Augment the default search functionality using jQuery and Ajax
- Learn how to include Ajax functionality in your plugins
- Create a plugin that displays search results automatically without you having to submit the form
- Learn techniques for debugging Ajax scripts
- Learn how to tie jQuery into your plugins
- Learn how to test your PHP version
- Use more API features
- Create a plugin that uses classes and external files
- Learn some templating techniques for creating skins that are easy to maintain

What is Ajax?

Ajax stands for "**Asynchronous JavaScript and XML**". Once merely a party trick of Web 1.0 sites, Ajax has now firmly established itself as the *wunderkind* component of interactive Web 2.0 and Web 3.0 sites. Despite its impressive *resumé*, don't forget that on a functional level, everything that is done with Ajax can also be done *without* Ajax — its only function is to enhance user experience. Any site built with Ajax can be fully operational without Ajax, albeit with more mouse clicks.

The following is a simple but relevant example: go to `http://www.pandora.com` or `http://www.google.com` and try searching for something. You'll notice that search results appear *without* you having to submit the form.

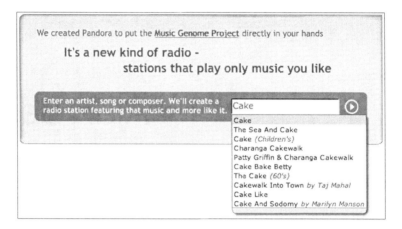

You didn't have to click anything. This is the magic of asynchronous JavaScript. You received your search results and the page did not have to reload. We have all been on websites where we had to click a button to submit a form, but the user experience is smoother when Ajax is used.

To help demonstrate how this all happens, have a look at the following diagrams that compare a "normal" search form to an Ajax search form. In a normal search form, the user requests the first page containing the search form, and then a second page is requested when the user submits the form. Two page requests are made, both by the user.

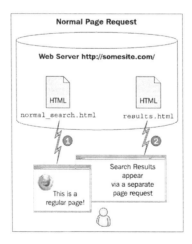

The Ajax search form also makes two page requests, but instead of the user making both requests, the user requests only the first page, then the page makes the second request. The Ajax page acts like a browser.

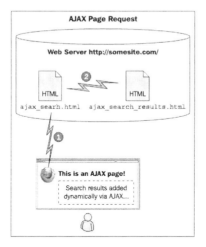

Can you see how the Ajax scenario might be harder to debug? Instead of any error messages being delivered to you, they are delivered to the page that made the request, and unless you are looking for them, you might never realize that a problem occurred.

The slick features and smooth interface that Ajax sites provide come at a price. Special JavaScript functions have to be loaded and there are hidden dependencies on other pages. In short, Ajax-enabled pages are larger and thus slower to load, and their added complexity makes them more difficult to test and troubleshoot. As you design and develop plugins and pages, be sure to evaluate whether the clean Ajax interface is an absolute necessity or merely a "nice to have".

WordPress includes jQuery, a popular JavaScript library that makes it easy to perform Ajax tasks. Most importantly, jQuery solves many of the cross browser issues that plague many JavaScript functions. If you have never used jQuery before, then this chapter will introduce you to some of what it can do. If you are already familiar with jQuery, this chapter will show you how well it integrates with WordPress.

"Why use Ajax?" you might ask yourself. To answer that question, it's worthwhile to review the mechanics of how a web page works. When a browser requests a page, the web server constructs it using server-side technology such as PHP and then sends the assembled page to your browser. After the page request has been fulfilled, it is out of PHP's hands. JavaScript, however, can run client-side on the user's browser. It is for this reason that it is extremely valuable. It can do things long after PHP has packed up and gone home.

The overall plan

In order to demonstrate how to integrate Ajax into your WordPress plugins, we've chosen a textbook example: automatically showing search results. Later in this book, we'll use Ajax to do more complicated things, but first we're going to cover the basics by breathing life into the standard search widget.

If you don't have the search widget enabled on your site, enable it now so you can see what we're talking about. In the WordPress manager, click on the **Appearance | Widgets** link and then drag the **Search** widget into the **Primary Widget Area** so that it becomes active. On a tangential note, WordPress uses Ajax to save your widget selections without you having to click anything.

Take a look at your home page to verify that you see the search widget. Try searching for a few terms to get a feel for how this process works.

Pretty basic, eh? You've seen this type of thing before, but let's take a moment to talk about what is really going on here. On a technical level, here is what happens when you perform a simple search:

1. You type a search term, for example, "sparky".

2. You submit the form—in this case it submits to same page via the "GET" method. After submitting, you can see the query term in your URL, for example, `http://yoursite.com/?s=sparky`.

3. The data is sanitized and a database query is constructed.

4. The database executes the query and returns zero or many rows matching the criteria.

5. The results are formatted and displayed on the results page.

We don't want to change the behavior of the normal results page—we just want to have some "live" results that appear without the user having to submit the form. So in order to do that, we need to do a few extra things.

A common Ajax implementation for this type of situation uses the following components:

- The original page (just as we have with our standard search form)

- Another page that executes a search and provides "naked" search results that are meant to be dynamically inserted into the original page

- An Ajax script on the original page that fetches the data from the other page and inserts it dynamically into the original page

Remember that the other page's sole purpose is to provide a payload meant for the original page; it is never visited by the normal user. The original page uses a CSS selector to designate where this payload will be placed, for example, `<div id="ajax_search_results_go_here"></div>`.

The proof of concept mock up

Just like we did in the previous chapter, we're going to mock this up using static HTML before we try to do it dynamically. This forces us to test the solution in its simplest implementation (remember: test early and often). Our goal with this mock up is to test the necessary JavaScript—we'll deal with the PHP components later.

First, let's copy the HTML from our home page into a new file:

1. Go to your site's home page, then view the source HTML (you can right-click the page or look under the browser's **View** menu).

2. Do a **Select all** from your browser's **Edit** menu, copy the text, then paste it into a new file named `mockup.html`.

3. Save the `mockup.html` file to the root of your site—this will ensure that paths to assets remain the same.

4. Visit this page in your browser (`http://yoursite.com/mockup.html`) and verify that it displays correctly.

Now we need to choose where to display the search results. We are choosing to show our dynamic search results right below the search box, just as they do on Facebook and on Pandora. By searching for the `<form>` tag, we can find where we need to insert our HTML, and we're going to make sure we use a unique ID attribute in the `<div>` tag.

Here is the excerpt of our static HTML mock-up. We have added the `ajax_search_results_go_here` div following the closing `</form>` tag:

```html
<h3 class="widget-title">Built In WordPress Search Widget</h3>

<form role="search" method="get" id="searchform" action="http://
localhost:8888/" >
    <div>
        <label class="screen-reader-text" for="s">Search for:</label>
        <input type="text" value="" name="s" id="s" />
        <input type="submit" id="searchsubmit" value="Search" />
    </div>
</form>
<div id="ajax_search_results_go_here">
    <div id="ajax_search_results">
        <ul>
            <li><a href="#">First result</a></li>
            <li><a href="#">Second result</a></li>
            <li><a href="#">Third result</a></li>
            <li><a href="#">More...</a></li>
        </ul>
    </div>
</div>
```

Let's go ahead and add a wee bit of styling to the page so we can more easily see the results. Put the following into your page's head:

```css
<style type="text/css">
    #ajax_search_results {
        background: gray;
        border:1px solid black;
        padding:5px;
        width:115px;
    }
</style>
```

Notice that we're using two nested `div` tags (this helps isolate our styling) and that we are putting some styling information in-line for now; this is not *best practices*, but it is only temporary! Later, we will put the styling information into a dedicated CSS file. Don't waste too much time styling your search results yet—let's get the functionality in place first.

The following is what it looks like in a browser:

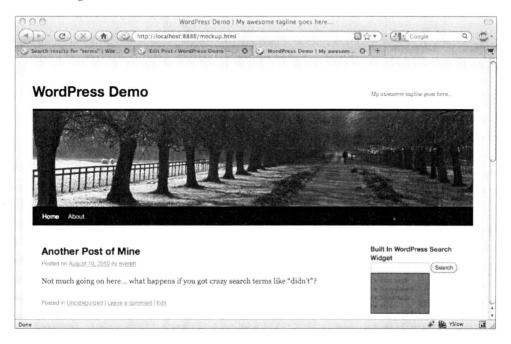

Next, let's mock up the second page. It will generate mock search results meant to be used on the first page, so for now we can just copy and paste our unordered list to this page. Paste your sample search results into a new file named `ajax_search_results.php`:

```
<div id="ajax_search_results">
    <ul>
        <li><a href="#">First result</a></li>
        <li><a href="#">Second result</a></li>
        <li><a href="#">Third result</a></li>
        <li><a href="#">More...</a></li>
    </ul>
</div>
```

Remember, that's the **only** thing in `ajax_search_results.php`: there are no `<html>`, `<head>`, or `<body>` tags.

By now you should have two self-contained pages: `mockup.html` and `ajax_search_results.php`. Our next task is going to be setting up the JavaScript that will dynamically manipulate access and modify the content of these pages. Make sure you can navigate to each of these pages in your browser before continuing.

Hooking up jQuery

Some PHP developers don't like dealing with JavaScript because it can be more difficult to debug. If you are in this camp, we can sympathize with you—we're going to take things slowly so that we can verify exactly what is happening in our mockup. Here's a task list of everything we're going to be doing with jQuery:

1. Test that jQuery is loading.
2. Writing HTML dynamically into a target div.
3. Create the target div automatically (and continue to write HTML to it).
4. Create a listener that is triggered when someone types a search term.
5. Get HTML from `ajax_search_results.php` after passing it the search term.

Test that jQuery has loaded

The first thing we are going to do is ensure that the jQuery library is loading. In your `mockup.html` file, add a line that includes `jquery.js`, something like the following:

```
<script type="text/javascript" src="http://yoursite.com/wp-includes/
js/jquery/jquery.js"></script>
```

WordPress ships with jQuery and it is enabled by certain themes and plugins, so it may already appear in your `mockup.html`.

Let's brush up our JavaScript debugging chops right off the bat and verify that jQuery has indeed loaded correctly. We're going to use the FireBug console for a lot of things in this chapter, so make sure you've got the FireBug plugin installed in Firefox, as we mentioned in the first chapter. It is *imperative* you have this plugin installed—it is nearly impossible to debug JavaScript without it.

Add the following script tag to the end of your `mockup.html` head (make sure this comes after the `jquery.js` include):

```
<script type="text/javascript">
    jQuery.noConflict();
    console.log( jQuery().jquery );
</script>
```

Now refresh the `mockup.html` page in Firefox and open up the FireBug console. This is done by clicking the little lightning bug icon at the bottom of your Firefox window and then selecting the **Console** tab. You should see the current jQuery version printed to the console:

If you do not see the valid version number and instead see an error saying that *jQuery is not defined*, then you know that the jQuery library was not loaded correctly — double check the path to `wp-includes` to ensure you are including the right file. Maybe you put the carriage before the horse. Remember that the `jquery.js` file must be loaded *before* our test script which makes use of it.

What happened?

The *noConflict* method is used to avoid conflicts in JavaScript libraries that can arise when too much shorthand is used — different JavaScript libraries use the "$" variable in different ways. jQuery uses the "$" variable as an alias for the jQuery object, so we could have used the following function to retrieve the jQuery version:

```
$().jquery;
```

However, we have opted instead to use the verbose form in our examples, and we went one step further in conflict resolution by running the `jQuery.noConflict()` function, which destroys the "$" variable entirely. Strictly speaking, for these examples the `noConflict` method is probably unnecessary but we introduce it here to remind the reader that conflicts between libraries may occur.

Once you have verified that jQuery is loading you can remove the `console.log()` statement.

Using the FireBug console directly

To further your understanding of FireBug, let's point out one thing quickly, anything that you enter into a `<script>` tag can be typed directly into the FireBug console. Try pasting the `console.log(jQuery().jquery )`; statement into the right-side of the FireBug console, and then clicking on **Run**. The result is the same as it would have been if you had put the statement into a `<script>` tag and reloaded the page.

This is a useful way to check variable values without having to edit the page.

Writing HTML dynamically to a target div

Now that we have jQuery loaded, let's take advantage of the cool features it brings to the table. We're going to use it to dynamically insert text into our page. Before we try bringing in content from a separate page, let's keep it in the house and try writing text from our script to a `div` tag in the same file.

To prepare, delete the sample search results from `mockup.html` — we just want an empty `div` tag, like this:

```
<div id="ajax_search_results_go_here"></div>
```

Let's start things off with a common mistake. You can set the contents of a particular `div` using jQuery's `.html` method, so you would think the following would be a valid way to write text to our page (where `#ajax_search_results_go_here` is a valid CSS selector identifying our empty `<div>` tag). Try adding this script to the document head in `mockup.html`:

```
<script type="text/javascript">
    // This won't work!!!
    jQuery('#ajax_search_results_go_here').html('<b>Tripmaster
Monkey!</b>');
</script>
```

If you refresh the page, you won't see any new text inserted inside the `<div id="ajax_search_results_go_here"></div>`, but why? It has to do with timing. Remember that the page loads head first, top down. So when your browser reads this script in the document head, the rest of the page has not yet loaded. As far as the browser is concerned, it doesn't even exist yet!

If you're curious to test this, try putting that script at the end of the page right before the closing `</body>` tag. Then it will work, because the HTML will have loaded by that point.

So in order to make this work in the head of the document, we have to tell it to wait until the page has loaded. jQuery does this through the use of the `.ready()` function. Let's modify our script:

```
<script type="text/javascript">
    jQuery(document).ready(main);

    // Runs once the DOM is ready
    function main()
    {
```

```
        jQuery('#ajax_search_results_go_here').html('<b>Tripmaster
Monkey!</b>');
    }
</script>
```

Here we've created a JavaScript function and we've referenced it by name as an argument to the `.ready()` function. Now when you refresh your `mockup.html` page, you should see the **Tripmaster Monkey!** text just below the search box:

Multi-line strings

Let's point out a few things before moving on (hey, we warned you that JavaScript can be more difficult to debug). If you received an error message in the FireBug console about an "unterminated string literal", it's because your HTML text contained a carriage return, and JavaScript is more sensitive to multi-line strings than PHP. Your HTML text must appear all on one line, or you must separate it in a way that JavaScript respects. Consider the following options for separating multi-line strings:

```
<script type="text/javascript">
        var multiline_str1 = 'Well,'
            + 'well,'
            + 'well...';
        var multiline_str2 = 'Something \
            something \
            something \
            Dark Side';
        var invalid_multiline = 'They
            killed
            Kenny!'; // <-- Invalid!
</string>
```

The first two examples are valid, but the third will cause JavaScript to error out. If you are not using FireBug, you might never see the error message! Consider this your last warning to install and use FireBug.

Viewing the generated page

Let's point out something else here that's really important. When you start manipulating pages using JavaScript, it becomes more difficult to see what's going on. As a web developer, you are probably accustomed to viewing the source HTML of a page (for example, **View | Page Source**). If you've got the "Tripmaster Monkey" text from our previous example being added dynamically to your target `div`, go ahead and try viewing the page source. According to "View Source", the target div is still empty. What happened? Remember that the source HTML is created when the page is loaded, and everything we're doing with jQuery occurs *after* the page has loaded.

It's a bit maddening because the HTML that you look at may no longer bear any resemblance to the HTML that first arrived from the web server. For example, when a web page gets hacked, JavaScript is often used to *completely* alter the page. Viewing the page source only tells you what the HTML looked like when it left the server, sort of like the police description of a missing person.

An extremely useful tool for dealing with this problem comes in the form of another Firefox add-on that we mentioned back in the first chapter: the Web Developer toolbar (available at `https://addons.mozilla.org/en-US/firefox/addon/60`). It has an option to **View Generated Source** which shows you the actual condition of the page after any JavaScript manipulations.

When we use the Web Developer Toolbar and **View Source | View Generated Source**, we can see our text both in the head and where we inserted it in the target div. We highly recommend using this plugin to check your work as you manipulate pages using JavaScript.

Anonymous functions

Another thing that can be difficult for PHP developers is JavaScript's use of anonymous functions. This language construct is not available to PHP until version 5.3.0, so the code pattern may be unfamiliar to you. The gist is that you can put an unnamed function where you would put a function callback. Consider our earlier script:

```
<script type="text/javascript">
    jQuery(document).ready(main);

    // Runs once the DOM is ready
    function main()
    {
        jQuery('#ajax_search_results_go_here').html('<b>Tripmaster
Monkey!</b>');
    }
</script>
```

And now consider this variation that uses an anonymous function in place of the named function callback ("main" in our example):

```
<script type="text/javascript">
    jQuery(document).ready( function(){
            jQuery('#ajax_search_results_go_here').html("<b>Tripmaster
Monkey!</b>");
        });
</script>
```

Generally, we feel anonymous functions are a bit harder to read, but it is important to point out how they are used because they are used frequently in JavaScript examples on the Web.

Now that we've brushed up our JavaScript chops, let's get back to the tasks at hand.

Adding a div on the fly

We are walking you through this process step by step so you can test your work as you go and hopefully keep any frustrations to a minimum. In our `mockup.html` page, we manually added the `<div id="ajax_search_results_go_here"></div>` to hold our search results, but this was really a crutch. In WordPress, we may not have the luxury of manipulating the search form's HTML—this widget is built into the core, so it is especially hard to get to. Besides, we prefer to create plugins that are template agnostic, and we don't want to edit templates unless we absolutely have to.

Our solution to this is to use jQuery to add the div on the fly. We can use the `.append()` method to write the div to the list item identified by `<li id="search-2">` (this is the list item that houses the search form).

1. First, delete the `<div id="ajax_search_results_go_here"></div>` from `mockup.html`.

2. Next, modify the JavaScript in your document head to use the `.append()` method:

```
<script type="text/javascript">

    jQuery(document).ready(main);

    function main()
    {
        // Create a div where we can dynamically send results
        jQuery('#search-2').append('<div id="ajax_search_results_go_
here"></div>');

        // Write some text to the target div
        jQuery('#ajax_search_results_go_here').html('<b>Tripmaster
Monkey!</b>');
    }
</script>
```

3. Save your work and refresh the `mockup.html` page in Firefox.

If everything worked, you should see the exact same results. Use the Web Developer toolbar's **View Source | View Generated Source** to verify that the `div` tag and the sample content are being placed correctly inside the `"search-2"` `<li>`. Remember, you can't write HTML to the `ajax_search_results_go_here` element unless that element exists.

Create a listener

Next, we need to add a listener to the form. When someone begins typing a search term, we need to capture the input before they submit the form. We are going to listen for the `keyup` event inside the search query box: `<input id="s" type="text" />`.

jQuery can use any valid CSS selector to identify a page component, but we've been sticking to id tags for simplicity. Let's modify our JavaScript once again:

```
<script type="text/javascript">

    jQuery(document).ready(main);

    function main()
    {
        // Create a div where we can dynamically send results
        jQuery('#search-2').append('<div id="ajax_search_results_go_
here"></div>');
```

```
        // Listen for changes in our search field (<input id="s" >)
        jQuery('#s').keyup(get_search_results);
    }

    function get_search_results()
    {
        // Write some text to the target div
        jQuery('#ajax_search_results_go_here').html('<b>Tripmaster
Monkey!</b>');
    }

</script>
```

We added another function to the mix: `get_search_results`. For now, the expected behavior is that the "Tripmaster Monkey" text should only appear after a `keyup` event has occurred in the search box. Save your work and refresh the page. Try typing something in the search box to verify that "Tripmaster Monkey" appears after you've typed something in the search box.

Again, we've opted for the use of a callback function (`get_search_results`) instead of an anonymous function; this creates a bit of a waterfall effect: the `.ready()` method calls the "main" function, and the `.keyup()` method calls the `get_search_results`. Too much waterfall is confusing: feel free to structure your code differently if you feel it would make it clearer.

Fetching data from another page

Up until now, we've been writing sample text to our target `div` locally, from within the same page. The final component in our mockup is to grab the text from an external file, `ajax_search_results.php`, and insert it into the `mockup.html` page. jQuery makes it easy to grab data asynchronously from an external page. All we need to do is to make use of jQuery's `.get()` method.

We are going to take this opportunity to refine the `get_search_results` function so it requests the `ajax_search_results.php` page only if more than two characters have been typed into the search box. This is simply a practical matter: we won't get very meaningful search results with character combinations shorter than three letters. We are also now passing data to the `ajax_search_results.php` page via the second argument to the `.get()` method. We are passing the search query inside of the `$_GET['s']` array.

We are also going to add some documentation to our functions to make them easier to understand and easier to read. Since these are JavaScript functions, we will forgo the PHPDoc syntax for commenting them. Update the JavaScript in `mockup.html` so it matches the following:

```
<script type="text/javascript">
   jQuery(document).ready(main);
   function main()
   {
      // Create a div where we can dynamically send results
      jQuery('#search-2').append('<div id="ajax_search_results_go_
here"></div>');
      // Listen for changes in our search field (<input id="s" >)
      jQuery('#s').keyup(get_search_results);
   }
   /*------------------------------------------------------------
SYNOPSIS:
   Query our external search page
INPUT:
   none; reads values from the id='s' text input (the search query)
OUTPUT:
   triggers the write_results_to_page() function, writes to console
for logging.
   ------------------------------------------------------------*/
   function get_search_results()
   {
      var search_query = jQuery('#s').val();
       if(search_query != "" && search_query.length > 2 ) {
         jQuery.get("ajax_search_results.php", { s:search_query },
write_results_to_page);
       }
       else
       {
          console.log('Search term empty or too short.');
       }
   }
   /*------------------------------------------------------------
SYNOPSIS:
   Write the incoming data to the page.
INPUT:
   data = the html to write to the page
OUTPUT:
   Writes HTML data to the 'ajax_search_results_go_here' id.
   ------------------------------------------------------------*/
   function write_results_to_page(data)
   {
      jQuery('#ajax_search_results_go_here').html(data);
   }
</script>
```

We added some console logging, so you should see some messages coming across as you type a search term. If all went well, the HTML from the `ajax_search_results.php` page should be inserted into the `mockup.html` page as soon as you type three or more characters into your search field.

If you are having problems, double check your spellings and make sure that you have used the correct identifier in your JavaScript functions. The FireBug console should help you isolate errors. Make sure you have the mockup working before you go on. Our goal here was to complete a proof-of-concept mockup using the necessary Ajax functions, and we've done that entirely without PHP. Make sure it's working *without* PHP before continuing. The next step will be porting this over into a plugin where we will be dealing with the added complexity of PHP and WordPress.

Creating our plugin

Now that we have a working mockup, we can finally create our plugin. As before, we will start with a simple outline and then flesh it out. This time, however, we're going to introduce a new structure for our plugin and its related files, including several directories and PHP classes. Learning good organization and some object-oriented structures is an important step in your education as a developer.

We are choosing the name "Live Search" for our plugin, so our first step is to create a directory named `live-search` inside the `wp-content/plugins/` directory.

Inside that directory, we recommend the following items:

- An `index.php` file which houses the Information Header for the plugin
- A directory for style sheets, named `css`
- A directory for images, named `images`
- A directory for included PHP files, named `includes`
- A directory for JavaScript files, named `js`
- A directory for tests, named `tests`

You may not need all these directories for this plugin, but it is a useful structure.

Before we start creating files and our outline, let's take a moment to think through the overall tasks our plugin must perform:

- Test the version of PHP
- Include a CSS stylesheet in the document head
- Include some JavaScript in the document head
- Handle Ajax requests and return search results

We covered all of this in our mockup, but this time we are not going to have a simple one-to-one correlation with public functions and WordPress events. The Ajax search handler has to act as its own standalone page, and there are some caveats involved with using JavaScript that needs to inherit values from PHP. This is about the simplest Ajax scenario we could come up with, but you'll find that its implementation isn't quite as linear as our previous plugin. Let's get started.

Creating index.php and activating the plugin

We want to activate our skeleton plugin as early as possible so that we can test if there are any errors. So let's create the index.php file inside the live-search directory. We know that at a minimum, we need to have an Information Header inside the file, so let's add that now. If you have forgotten the format, just copy it from the "Hello Dolly" plugin like we did in the previous chapter.

We're also going to sketch out a couple of items in this file because we know we need to add more to it to make it a viable plugin. The following is what our index.php looks like:

```php
<?php
/*-------------------------------------------------------------------
Plugin Name: Live Search
Plugin URI: http://www.tipsfor.us/
Description: Sample plugin for integrating jQuery with your WordPress
plugins
Author: Everett Griffiths
Version: 0.1
Author URI: http://www.tipsfor.us/
-----------------------------------------------------------------*/
// include() or require() any necessary files here...

// Tie into WordPress Hooks and any functions that should run on load.

/* EOF */
```

You should notice right away that it's a bit simpler than the outline we introduced in *Chapter 3*. That's because we are going to move the public and private functions associated with this plugin into a PHP class file that will live inside the `includes/` directory.

Once you've created the `index.php` file, log in to the WordPress administration area and activate the plugin. Try visiting your homepage and verify that no errors are showing. We might sound like a broken record, but it's so much easier to test your code now when it's simple!

Creating our first PHP class

PHP classes come in two flavors: objects and libraries. We're going to introduce you to the latter. What we want here is simply a collection of functions under one roof. This helps us stay organized by keeping related functions together and it helps us avoid conflicting function names. PHP classes are a more mature solution to the namespace problem.

It is standard practice in PHP programming to capitalize the first letter of your class name. Most often, there is only one class per file and the filename uses the same naming convention as the class. The first letter is capitalized.

Inside our plugin's `includes/` directory, let's create a file named `LiveSearch.php`. We're going to outline a couple of functions in it—it's hard to know exactly what we're going to need beforehand, but we're going to take a stab at the public functions. If we need to add more, we can always do that later. Here is what our outline inside of `includes/LiveSearch.php` looks like:

```php
<?php
/**
 * class LiveSearch
 *
 * Adds basic Ajax functionality to the built-in WordPress search
 * widget: it displays results matching your query without the user
having to
 * submit the form.
 */
class LiveSearch
{
    const plugin_name = 'Live Search';
    const min_php_version = '5.2';

    /**
     * Adds the necessary JavaScript and/or CSS to the pages to enable
the Ajax search.
```

```
    */
    public static function head() {

    }

    /**
    * The main function for this plugin, similar to __construct()
    */
    public static function initialize() {

    }
}
/* EOF */
```

Notice that we are declaring our functions using the `static` keyword. This is what makes our class a library of related functions instead of an object that must be instantiated — we do not need to instantiate our class using the `new` keyword.

Since we are now using PHP classes, we get to use visibility keywords for our functions and variables in our class, so when we say that a function is "public" or "private", now we really mean it. From the PHP manual:

> *A property or method can be defined by prefixing the declaration with the keywords public, protected or private.*

Before we only earmarked functions as *public* and *private*, but now we actually can control access to them. This is a more advanced feature that is only available in later versions of PHP, but remember that WordPress 3.1 and later versions will require PHP version 5.2 at a minimum. Public functions can be called from anywhere, simply by prefacing their name with the name of the class, for example, `LiveSearch::initialize();`. Private functions, you will see, can only be called from inside the class where they were declared.

We have also added a couple of class constants to our class. These are similar to PHP constants that were defined using the `define()` function, but class constants are defined using the `const` keyword. In order to retrieve their value, you must include the class name, for example:

```
<?php print LiveSearch::min_php_version; ?>
```

Now that we've created our first class, let's hook it up to `index.php` and make sure it works.

Updating index.php

In order to use the functions in our new class, we simply have to include it. Modify your `index.php` file to include the `includes/LiveSearch.php` file:

```
// include() or require() any necessary files here...
include_once('includes/LiveSearch.php');
```

Save it, then refresh your homepage and check for errors.

Next, let's add a couple of actions to the `index.php` file so we can make use of the two functions we outlined. We are going to tie into the `init` and `wp_head` actions, so the following is what our `index.php` looks like:

```
// Tie into WordPress Hooks and any functions that should run on load.
add_action('init', 'LiveSearch::initialize');
add_action('wp_head', 'LiveSearch::head');
```

Notice how we have called the static functions by including the name of the class. Do you see how much cleaner those names are? We could have also used the following syntax:

```
add_action('init', array('LiveSearch', 'initialize'));
```

This latter version is the required method for calling functions in an object; we got by with the `LiveSearch::initialize` version because we were dealing with `static` functions. If you're curious about the specifics of the syntax, refer to the PHP documentation for the `call_user_func()` function: `http://php.net/manual/en/function.call-user-func.php`.

Save the `index.php` file and refresh your homepage again. If you have any errors, clean them up now while your classes are virtually empty. The most common causes of errors at this point are missing braces "}" or semicolons ";"—sometimes the line number that PHP references in its error message is several lines after the missing brace or semicolon, so keep your eyes peeled.

Testing your version of PHP

We are going to create another PHP class where we can store testing functions. Create a file named `Test.php` inside the `tests` directory. The following is what we have written for `tests/Test.php`:

```
<?php
/**
* class Test
*
* Basic library for run-time tests.
*/
if ( !class_exists('Test') ):
class Test
{
```

```
    /**
     * min_php_version
     *
     * Test that your PHP version is at least that of the $min_php_
version.
     * @param $min_php_version    string    representing the minimum
required version of PHP, e.g. '5.3.2'
     * @param $plugin_name    string    Name of the plugin for messaging
purposes.
     * @return none        Exit with messaging if PHP version is too old.
     */
    static function min_php_version($min_php_version, $plugin_name) {
        $exit_msg = "The '$plugin_name' plugin requires PHP $min_php_
version
            or newer. Contact your system administrator about updating
your version of PHP";
        if (version_compare( phpversion(),$min_php_version,'<'))
        {
            exit ($exit_msg);
        }
    }
}
endif;
/*EOF*/
```

This is a useful library we are building. We can add additional functions to it as needed. Notice that we've wrapped the entire class with an `if` statement in an attempt to avoid naming collisions, this time with conflicting class names.

The astute reader may realize that this class definition omits the visibility statements (that is `public`). It does this to be compatible with PHP 4—it wouldn't be a very useful version test if it couldn't actually execute on older versions. Although technically, PHP 4 would have probably crashed when including the `LiveSearch.php` file due it its use of visibility statements.

Let's include `Test.php` in our `index.php` file. Now, the `include` section of `index.php` should read as follows:

```
// include() or require() any necessary files here...
include_once('includes/LiveSearch.php');
include_once('tests/Test.php');
```

Save your work, then try refreshing your home page to check for errors.

Next, we need to actually run this test. Instead of hooking the tests directly to a WordPress event, we are going to execute them from within the `LiveSearch::initialize()` function. Update the `includes/LiveSearch.php` file so the `initialize` function looks like the following:

```
/**
 * initialize
 *
 * The main function for this plugin, similar to __construct()
 */
public static function initialize() {
    Test::min_php_version(self::min_php_version, self::plugin_name);
}
```

Notice how we referenced the class constants using the `self` keyword. Technically `LiveSearch::min_php_version` would also work just fine, but using `self` is the recommended way to refer to class constants from within the class.

In order to properly verify that this test is working, we need to goose the system a bit. Let's pretend that our script requires PHP version 7. Simply edit the class constant at the top of the `LiveSearch` class:

```
const min_php_version = '7';
```

Now save the file and refresh your homepage. You should be greeted with the message from the `Test::min_php_version()` function:

> *The 'Live Search' plugin requires PHP 7 or newer. Contact your system administrator about updating your version of PHP.*

Once you have verified that this test is working properly, please edit `includes/LiveSearch.php` and restore the public variable to the value of PHP that you're using for development:

```
public static $min_php_version = '5.2';
```

Testing for searchable pages

Next, we need to focus on adding the necessary JavaScript and CSS to our pages to enable the Ajax search results. Since this plugin is only intended to be used on pages that are searchable, let's add a private function to our `includes/LiveSearch.php` file that tests whether or not a page is searchable. For now, we are going to consider everything that is not in the WordPress admin area as "searchable". We are going to rely on WordPress' `is_admin()` function for this purpose. Add the following function to `includes/LiveSearch.php`:

```
/**
 * _is_searchable_page
 *
 * Any page that's not in the WP admin area is considered
searchable.
 * @return boolean   Simple true/false as to whether the current
page is searchable.
 */
private static function _is_searchable_page() {
    if (is_admin()) {
        return false;
    } else {
        return true;
    }
}
```

It's worth pointing out that the use of the `private` keyword means that this function can only be called from within the `LiveSearch.php` class. If you tried to reference it in your `index.php` and tie it to a WordPress action, you'd get a permission error. Even though we are now controlling the access to this function, we still name it with a leading underscore as a reminder that it is for "internal use only".

We will use this function momentarily to control if and when we add our custom CSS to a page, but first, let's prepare our CSS file.

Adding your own CSS files

We did some basic styling in our `mockup.html` file. Let's copy everything from our `<style>` tag and paste it into a new file: `css/live-search.css`:

```
#ajax_search_results {
    background: gray;
    border:1px solid black;
    padding:5px;
    width:115px;
}
```

Now we just need to dynamically add this stylesheet to pages that utilize our plugin. We're going to do this by making use of two WordPress API functions, which are very similar to the functions we used to reference external JavaScript files in the previous chapter:

*   `wp_register_style()`
*   `wp_enqueue_style()`

They are designed to be used together and their purpose is to let you reference shared assets while avoiding multiple includes of the same files. If you are creating interrelated plugins, these functions can help you easily share assets between them. We are going to make use of the previous function to ensure that this CSS file is only included for searchable pages. Make the following changes to the `initialize()` function in your `includes/LiveSearch.php` file—remember, we've already declared this function; you just need to add a few lines to it:

```
/**
 * initialize
 *
 * The main function for this plugin, similar to __construct()
 */
public static function initialize() {
    Test::min_php_version(self::min_php_version, self::plugin_name);

    if(self::_is_searchable_page()) {
        $src = plugins_url('css/live-search.css',dirname(__FILE__) );
        wp_register_style('live-search', $src);
        wp_enqueue_style('live-search');
    }
}
```

We are again relying on WordPress' `plugins_url()` function to help us get the plugin's URL, but this time, we need to modify the second argument. Our `LiveSearch.php` file is inside the `includes/` directory, so we need to make use of PHP's `dirname()` function to help retrieve the path of the directory above where this appears.

Save your work and then refresh your homepage. Look for the following in your source HTML:

```
<link rel='stylesheet' id='live-search-css'  href='http://
localhost:8888/wp-content/plugins/live-search/css/live-search.
css?ver=3.0' type='text/css' media='all' />
```

You can even test by refreshing your administration page to verify that the `_is_searchable_page()` function is working—your CSS file should not appear in any of the WordPress admin pages because those are not considered searchable.

Adding your search handler

If you recall from the `mockup.html` page, search requests were submitted via JavaScript to a dedicated search handler, `ajax_search_results.php`. This page lived at the root of the site, but that's a poor location for any of a plugin's ancillary files—we should try to keep all of our toys inside the toy box. We want our search handler to reside inside our plugin's dedicated directory.

Let's create a new search handler inside our plugin directory. Create a new file, `wp-content/plugins/live-search/ajax_search_results.php`, with some simple text in it:

```
<div id="ajax_search_results">
    <ul>
        <li>Sample search result</li>
    </ul>
</div>
```

Try navigating this page in a browser, just to make sure it comes through without errors, for example, `www.your-site.com/wp-content/plugins/live-search/ajax_search_results.php`.

We will come back to this page and make it dynamic momentarily, but first let's see if we can get some JavaScript on our pages that dynamically include the contents of our search handler.

Adding your own JavaScript

Once you have verified that the search handler file is error free, we need to set up the JavaScript file that requests that page. In the `mockup.html` file, we simply wrote the JavaScript inside of a `<script>` tag. In the previous chapter, we used the `wp_register_script()` and `wp_enqueue_script()` functions to include an external JavaScript file, and normally we would use them as we did previously. It's a matter of some debate, but in this situation, we are going to advise you not to add JavaScript that way. The difficulty here revolves around the fact that the JavaScript file needs to inherit some values from PHP, and the integration between JavaScript and PHP is sometimes tenuous. In particular, the JavaScript that we need to make the Ajax requests requires the URL of our plugin. That's easy enough for us to calculate when we include a file via PHP, but it's much more difficult if we were to reference an external file via a script tag and a `src` attribute.

It's not an ideal solution, but we're going to emulate the mockup here very closely because we intend to literally print the `<script>` tag and its contents into the document head. We wince a bit as we tell you to do this, but we winced even more at the alternative. First, let's copy the JavaScript from our mockup into a dedicated PHP file (yes, a PHP file). We are calling this file `dynamic_javascript.php` and we are storing it inside the `includes` directory because it is technically a PHP file that executes and is not a static JavaScript file. Add a little bit of PHP to the front of our JavaScript file. Here's what the `js/live-search.js.php` file looks like — again, most of this is simply pasted from `mockup.html`:

```php
<?php
/*-----------------------------------------------------------------
A "mostly" static page. We do however, have to supply one of the
functions with
a valid URL to where the search handler page lives.
-----------------------------------------------------------------*/
header('Content-type: text/javascript');
include_once('../includes/LiveSearch.php');
$plugin_url = LiveSearch::get_plugin_url();
$search_handler = $plugin_url . 'ajax_search_results.php';

//-----------------------------------------------------------------
?>
jQuery(document).ready(main);

function main()
{
    // Create a div where we can dynamically send results
    jQuery('#search-2').append('<div id="ajax_search_results_go_
here"></div>');

    // Listen for changes in our search field (<input id="s" >)
    jQuery('#s').keyup(get_search_results);
}

/*-----------------------------------------------------------------
SYNOPSIS:
    Query our external search page
INPUT:
    none; reads values from the id='s' text input (the search query)
OUTPUT:
    triggers the write_results_to_page() function, writes to console
for logging.
-----------------------------------------------------------------*/
function get_search_results()
{
    var search_query = jQuery('#s').val();
```

```
        if(search_query != "" && search_query.length > 2 ) {
            jQuery.get("<?php print $search_handler; ?>", { s:search_query
}, write_results_to_page);
        }
        else
        {
            console.log('Search term empty or too short.');
        }
    }
    /*-------------------------------------------------------------------
SYNOPSIS:
    Write the incoming data to the page.
INPUT:
    data = the html to write to the page
    status = an HTTP code to designate 200 OK or 404 Not Found
    xhr = object
OUTPUT:
    Writes HTML data to the 'ajax_search_results_go_here' id.
    ----------------------------------------------------------------*/
    function write_results_to_page(data,status, xhr)
    {
        if (status == "error") {
            var msg = "Sorry but there was an error: ";
            console.error(msg + xhr.status + " " + xhr.statusText);
        }
        else
        {
            jQuery('#ajax_search_results_go_here').html(data);
        }
    }
}
```

Make sense? We've just added a wee bit of PHP to the otherwise static file—the alternative would be to simply hardcode the path to the search handler and forgo all this drama. A hard-coded URL would work in a pinch, but it would fail in cases where the user changed his content directory in the `wp-config.php` file (which has been possible since WordPress 2.6), or in cases where WordPress was installed to a subdirectory, for example, `http://yoursite.com/myblog/`. For those reasons, we need to dynamically read the path to this search handler.

We now need to ensure that this JavaScript is added to the document head. Modify the `head()` function inside the `includes/LiveSearch.php` file:

```
/**
* head
*
* Prints some JavaScript into the document head. We are printing
directly
* to the document head because we need our JavaScript to contain a
dynamic
* value that identifies the search handler script.
*
* @return none    This does, however, create some HTML output
*/
public static function head() {
    if(self::_is_searchable_page()) {
        $search_handler_url = plugins_url('ajax_search_results.
php',dirname( __FILE__ ) );
        include('dynamic_javascript.php');
    }
}
```

We are almost done, but we also need to ensure that jQuery has been loaded so our custom JavaScript works correctly. Update your `includes/LiveSearch.php` script so that the `initialize()` function looks like the following:

```
/**
* initialize
*
* The main function for this plugin, similar to __construct()
*/
public static function initialize() {

    Test::min_php_version(self::min_php_version, self::plugin_name);

    if(self::_is_searchable_page()) {
        wp_enqueue_script('jquery'); // make sure jQuery is loaded!
Otherwise our JS will fail!
        $src = plugins_url('css/live-search.css',dirname( __FILE__ )
);

        wp_register_style('live-search', $src);
        wp_enqueue_style('live-search');
    }
}
```

The only thing added was a reference to WordPress' `wp_enqueue_script` function; that will ensure that jQuery is loaded before we print our JavaScript to the document head.

Save the file and refresh your homepage in a browser. View the source code and verify that jQuery and our custom JavaScript are being included. Make sure you test this in Firefox with the FireBug plugin enabled. That will alert you to JavaScript errors.

Finally, try typing in a search term. If all goes correctly, the static text that you have sitting on the `ajax_search_results.php` page should be inserted into the area below your search form. If you encounter any errors, track down the problematic areas using Firebug.

Was this an ideal solution? No. However, by including the `dynamic_javascript.php` file, we were more easily able to ensure that the JavaScript had the correct value passed to it from PHP. Some readers may prefer to try this the other way around by using the `wp_enqueue_script()` function to include the JavaScript, but as we mentioned, it's more difficult to pass a PHP value to an external JavaScript file. If you want to try that method, read the next section for some ideas first. You will see that you can gain access to WordPress' functions and constants when you include the `wp-config.php` file. That, along with the use of PHP's header function could be your ticket to dynamically generating an external JavaScript file for inclusion via the `wp_enqueue_script()` function, but we're getting ahead of ourselves.

The only task remaining for us is to actually do the dynamic searches in the `ajax_search_results.php` page. Let's finish this thing.

Handling Ajax search requests

We've created a page that is meant to handle Ajax search results: `ajax_search_results.php`. Technically, this type of page can be called a "controller", and it's not intended to be accessed by the normal user. It's intended to be accessed by the Ajax requests made by our JavaScript functions.

How does this work? We built our JavaScript so that it sends the search term to this page in the `$_GET` array. So we just need to pass that value to a valid database query to get our matching search results.

What we're actually going to do is to tie into WordPress' backdoor—we will include the `wp-config.php` file and thereby gain access to the built-in WordPress functions and classes, including the database API methods. We're going to completely rewrite the static text on the `ajax_search_results.php` page with some heavy hitting PHP.

Let's modify our `ajax_search_results.php` file so that we connect with the WordPress application. We're going to verify that this connection has taken place by printing out the defined classes. If the connection is successful, PHP's `get_declared_classes()` function will spew out hundreds of classes that WordPress has defined. Make your `ajax_search_results.php` file look like this, paying careful attention to the `realpath()` function—that's the critical one that identifies how many levels up the `wp-config.php` file is:

```php
<?php
/**
* This file is an independent controller, used to query the WordPress
database
* and provide search results for Ajax requests.
*
* @return string  Either return nothing (i.e. no results) or return
some formatted results.
*/
if (!defined('WP_PLUGIN_URL')) {
    require_once( realpath('../../../').'/wp-config.php' );
}

print_r( get_declared_classes() );

/* EOF */
```

Now try hitting that file in a browser, for example, www.yoursite.com/wp-content/plugins/live-search/ajax_search_results.php.

If successful, you should see an array beginning with something like the following:

```
Array
(
    [0] => stdClass
    [1] => Exception
    [2] => ErrorException
    [...]
```

Congratulations! If you see the WordPress classes, then we can commence using them. In particular, we're going to use the WP_Query class and its query method. Update your ajax_search_results.php so it looks like the following:

```php
<?php
/**
* This file is an independent controller, used to query the WordPress
database
* and provide search results for Ajax requests.
*
* @return string  Either return nothing (i.e. no results) or return
some formatted results.
*/
if (!defined('WP_PLUGIN_URL')) {
    // WP functions become available once you include the config file
    require_once( realpath('../../../').'/wp-config.php' );
}

// No point in executing a query if there's no query string
```

```
if ( empty($_GET['s']) )
{
    exit;
}
$max_posts = 3;

$WP_Query_object = new WP_Query();
$WP_Query_object->query(array('s' => $_GET['s'], 'showposts' => $max_
posts));

foreach($WP_Query_object->posts as $result)
{
    print_r($result);
}
/* EOF */
```

Again, we need to hit this in a browser, but this time, we need to include a query string. Use a URL with the s parameter set to a search term that is likely to return some results, such as:

www.yoursite.com/wp-content/plugins/live-search/ajax_search_results. php?s=term.

If all goes well, the print_r() statement should print up to three matching posts. The object structure looks something like the following:

```
stdClass Object
(
    [ID] => 7
    [post_author] => 1
    [post_date] => 2010-08-10 03:36:47
    [post_date_gmt] => 2010-08-10 03:36:47
    [post_content] => Not much going on here...
    [...]
```

If you've gotten this far, you have successfully tied into WordPress' database API to safely pass a query term to the database—you are relying on WordPress to sanitize your input and prevent SQL injection attacks. It is highly recommended that you rely on WordPress' API functions to access the database because chances are high that their data sanitization will be more thorough than yours, and besides, it's easier to use the functions they have already provided.

Once you've got the posts being returned, the only task that remains is to format them.

Formatting your search results

We are going to introduce a little bit of templating here. Although we could simply concatenate variables from our search results, it's more readable and maintainable to use some kind of templates for formatting. We are going to create one additional sub-directory in our plugin's directory: `tpls/`, short for "templates". In it will we store our template files that will be used to format our search results. We're going to use three different templates, designated with a `.tpl` extension:

1. A template to use when there are no search results: `no_results.tpl`.
2. A template to format each individual search result: `single_result.tpl`.
3. A template which will contain the individual results: `results_container.tpl`.

This is not traditional PHP per se, but it does represent some valuable principles garnered from other MVC applications and it can be a great way to create customizable layouts. We will provide sample text for each template before we show you how to parse them. The name of the game here is placeholders. We will denote placeholders by flanking a word with "[+" and "+]". Let's take a look at some examples so you can see what we mean.

The `tpls/single_result.tpl` will make use of a couple placeholders:

```
<li>
    <a href="[+permalink+]">[+post_title+]</a>
</li>
```

The `tpls/results_container.tpl` will wrap the collective individual results. It will only use a single "[+content+]" placeholder to denote where the individual results will appear:

```
<div id="ajax_search_results">
    <ul>
        [+content+]
    </ul>
</div>
```

Lastly, `tpls/no_results.tpl` contains no placeholders, just a message to display if no results were found:

```
<div id="ajax_search_results">
    <p>No results found.</p>
</div>
```

Can you see how each result is formatted as a list item, and then the collection of results is formatted into an unordered list?

Previously, we showed you the `sprintf()` function, which makes use of `%s` as a type of placeholder. `sprintf()` can even swap the order of the arguments by using placeholders such as `%1$s` and `%2$s` — look at the manual page under "argument swapping" for more information. However, this is hard to read. It is not clear what value might be substituted into `%s`, whereas a placeholder such as "[+permalink+]" gives you a good idea of what will replace the placeholder.

Now that we have our templates set up, how do we parse them? We are going to create a simple function that relies on PHP's `str_replace()`. To get the template files as raw strings (without executing any PHP in them), we load them using PHP's `file_get_contents()` function.

When we put it all together, our `ajax_search_results.php` file ends up looking like the following:

```php
<?php
/**
 * This file is an independent controller, used to query the WordPress
database
 * and provide search results for Ajax requests.
 *
 * @return string   Either return nothing (i.e. no results) or return
some formatted results.
 */
if (!defined('WP_PLUGIN_URL')) {
    // WP functions become available once you include the config file
    require_once( realpath('../../../').'/wp-config.php' );
}

// No point in executing a query if there's no query string
if ( empty($_GET['s']) )
{
    exit;
}

$max_posts = 3; // Number of results to show

$WP_Query_object = new WP_Query();
$WP_Query_object->query(array('s' => $_GET['s'], 'showposts' => $max_
posts));

// If there are no results...
if (! count($WP_Query_object->posts) ){
    print file_get_contents( 'tpls/no_results.tpl');
    exit;
}

// Otherwise, format the results
```

```
$container = array('content'=>''); // define the container's only
placeholder
$single_tpl = file_get_contents( 'tpls/single_result.tpl');
foreach($WP_Query_object->posts as $result)
{
    $result->permalink = get_permalink($result->ID);
    $container['content'] .= parse($single_tpl, $result);
}
// Wrap the results
$results_container_tpl = file_get_contents( 'tpls/results_container.
tpl');
print parse($results_container_tpl, $container);

/**
* parse
*
* A simple parsing function for basic templating.
*
* @param $tpl    string    A formatting string containing
[+placeholders+]
* @param $hash    array   An associative array containing keys and
values e.g. array('key' => 'value');
* @return    string      Placeholders corresponding to the keys of the
hash will be replaced with the values the resulting string will be
returned.
*/
function parse($tpl, $hash) {
    foreach ($hash as $key => $value) {
        $tpl = str_replace('[+'.$key.'+]', $value, $tpl);
    }
    return $tpl;
}
/* EOF */
```

While testing this, it's useful to refresh a page that navigates to it directly, just remember to include a valid search term: `http://yoursite.com/wp-content/plugins/live-search/ajax_search_results.php?s=something`.

You may have noticed that we manipulated the search results as objects in PHP, using arrow notation:

```
$result->new_value = 'something';
```

This was as opposed to an associative array:

```
$result['new_value'] = = 'something else';
```

Our `parse()` function can reliably iterate over the properties of an object in the same way as the elements of an associative array.

Although building our own template parsing functions like this is slower and it may be more confusing for you the first time you set it up, it is much easier to maintain and change over a longer term. Any inebriated frontend designer can make alterations to the template files contained in the `tpls/` directory without fear of breaking some delicate PHP concatenation. The worst thing that could happen when using our templating system is that a placeholder is unrecognized and comes out the other end unparsed.

Save your work and give this one final test. Refresh your home page and try searching for a word. You should get the Ajax search results to appear directly below your search form.

Summary

We've come a long way. We have learned about how Ajax works and we've learned how to tie into jQuery and how to debug some JavaScript. We have also learned how to use PHP library classes with static functions in our plugins and how to tie into the WordPress application from the backdoor. In order to pull this off, we have created a total of nine files:

- `ajax_search_results.php`
- `css/live-search.css`
- `includes/dynamic_javascript.php`
- `includes/LiveSearch.php`
- `index.php`
- `tests/Test.php`
- `tpls/no_results.tpl`
- `tpls/results_container.tpl`
- `tpls/single_result.tpl`

We have constructed a working Ajax search, but as you may have noticed, it was fairly complex to set up, and even after all that work, it is still fairly primitive. The goal here was to teach you how to construct a plugin that relied on Ajax; if you want a full-featured Ajax search for your site, try downloading an existing plugin. One example is Dave's WordPress Live Search (`http://wordpress.org/extend/plugins/daves-wordpress-live-search`). We think our code is cleaner, but Dave's plugin has a lot of customizable options and it handles edge cases that are beyond the scope of this chapter.

Next, we will dive into the world of WordPress widgets. The next chapter will expand our understanding of PHP classes by introducing us to some real object-oriented code, and everything we learned about Ajax will come in handy. Get ready for some widgets!

5
Content Rotator

In this chapter, we will learn about a special type of WordPress plugin: the widget. The architecture of widgets has undergone a radical change starting with the release of WordPress 2.8, so now we must talk about Object Oriented programming. We will learn a bit about its power as we extend the `WP_Widget` class to create our widget. We will also learn how to create a preference page in the manager so we can store our plugin's configuration details.

The plan

What exactly do we want this plugin to do? Our widget will display a random bit of text from the database. This type of plugin is frequently used for advertisement rotations or in situations where you want to spruce up a page by rotating content on a periodic basis. Each instance of our plugin will also have a "shelf life" that will determine how frequently its content should be randomized.

Let's take a moment to come up with some specifications for this plugin. We want it to do the following:

- Store multiple chunks of content, such as bits of Google Adsense code
- Be able to randomly return one of the chunks
- Set a time limit that defines the "shelf life" of each chunk, after which the "random" chunk will be updated

As with our other chapters, there are existing plugins you can download that do this already, but our focus here is showing you how to write the code.

Widget overview

Even if you are already familiar with widgets, take a moment to look at how they work in the WordPress manager under **Appearance | Widgets**. You know that they display content on the frontend of your site, usually in a sidebar, and they also have text and control forms that are displayed only when you view them inside the manager. If you put on your thinking cap, this should suggest to you at least two actions: an action that displays the content on the frontend, and an action that displays the form used to update the widget settings inside the manager. There are actually a total of four actions that determine the behavior of a standard widget, and you can think of these functions as a unit because they all live together in a single widget object. In layman's terms, there are four things that any widget can do. In programmatic terms, the `WP_Widget` object class has four functions that you may implement:

- The constructor: The constructor is the only function that you **must** implement. When you "construct" your widget, you give it a name, a description, and you define what options it has. Its name is often `__construct()`, but PHP still accepts the PHP 4 method of naming your constructor function using the name of the class.

- `widget()`: It displays content to users on the frontend.

- `form()`: It displays content to manager users on the backend, usually to allow them to update the widget settings.

- `update()`: It prepares the updated widget settings for database storage. Override this function if you require special form validation.

In order to make your widget actually work, you will need to tell WordPress about it by registering it using the WordPress `register_widget()` function. If you want to get a bit more information about the process, have a look at WordPress' documentation here: `http://codex.wordpress.org/Widgets_API`.

Let's outline this in code so you can see how it works.

Preparation

As always, we're going to go through the same setup steps to get our plugin outlined so we can get it activated and tested as soon as possible.

1. Create a folder inside the `wp-content/plugins/` directory. We are naming this plugin "Content Rotator", so create a new folder inside `wp-content/plugins/` named `content-rotator`.

2. Create the `index.php` file.

3. Add the Information Head to the `index.php` file. If you forgot the format, just copy and modify it from the *Hello Dolly* plugin like we did in previous chapters.

   We're giving you bigger sections of code than before because hopefully by now you're more comfortable adding and testing them. Here is what our `index.php` looks like:

   ```php
   <?php
   /*----------------------------------------------------------------
   --------------
   Plugin Name: Content Rotator
   Plugin URI: http://www.tipsfor.us/
   Description: Sample plugin for rotating chunks of custom content.
   Author: Everett Griffiths
   Version: 0.1
   Author URI: http://www.tipsfor.us/
   ----------------------------------------------------------------
   ------------*/
   // include() or require() any necessary files here...
   include_once('includes/ContentRotatorWidget.php');

   // Tie into WordPress Hooks and any functions that should run on
   load.
   add_action('widgets_init', 'ContentRotatorWidget::register_this_
   widget');

   /* EOF */
   ```

4. Add the folders for `includes` and `tpls` to help keep our files organized.

5. Add a new class file to the `includes` directory. The file should be named `ContentRotatorWidget.php` so it matches the `include` statement in the `index.php` file. This is a subclass which extends the parent `WP_Widget` class. We will name this class `ContentRotatorWidget`, and it should be declared using the `extends` keyword.

   ```php
   <?php
   /**
   * ContentRotatorWidget extends WP_Widget
   *
   * This implements a WordPress widget designed to randomize chunks
   of content.
   */
   class ContentRotatorWidget extends WP_Widget
   {
       public $name = 'Content Rotator';
   ```

```
public $description = 'Rotates chunks of content on a
periodic basis';
/* List all controllable options here along with a
default value.
The values can be distinct for each instance of the
widget. */
public $control_options = array();

//!!! Magic Functions
// The constructor.
function __construct()
{
    $widget_options = array(
        'classname'     => __CLASS__,
        'description'    => $this->widget_desc,
    );

    parent::__construct( __CLASS__, $this->name,$widget_
            options,$this->control_options);
}

//!!! Static Functions
static function register_this_widget()
{
    register_widget(__CLASS__);
}

}
/* EOF */
```

This is the simplest possible widget—we constructed it using only the __ construct() function. We haven't implemented any other functions, but we are supplying enough information here for it to work. Specifically, we are supplying a name and a description, and that's enough to get started. Let's take a moment to explain everything that just happened, especially since the official documentation here is a bit lacking.

When we declared the ContentRotatorWidget class, we used the extends keyword. That's what makes this PHP class a widget, and that's what makes object-oriented code so useful.

The __construct() function is called when an object is first created using the new command, so you might expect to see something like the following in our index. php file:

```
<?php
    $my_widget = new ContentRotatorWidget();
?>
```

However, WordPress has obscured that from us—we just have to tell WordPress the classname of the widget we want to register via the `register_widget()` function, and it takes care of rest by creating a new instance of this `ContentRotatorWidget`. There **is** a new instance being created, we just don't see it directly. Some of the official documentation still uses PHP 4 style examples of the constructor function—that is to say that the function whose name shares the name of the class. We feel that naming the constructor function `__construct` is clearer.

You may have wondered why we didn't simply put the following into our `index.php` file:

```
register_widget('ContentRotatorWidget'); // may throw errors if called
too soon!
```

If you do that, WordPress will try to register the widget before it's ready, and you'll get a fatal error:

"Call to a member function register() on a non-object".

That's why we delay the execution of that function by hooking it to the `widgets_init` action.

We are also tying into the construct of the parent class via the `parent::__construct()` function call. We'll explain the hierarchy in more detail later, but "parent" is a special keyword that can be used by a child class in order to call functions in the parent class. In this case, we want to tie into the `WP_Widget __construct()` function in order to properly instantiate our widget.

Note our use of the PHP `__CLASS__` constant—its value is the class name, so in this case, we could replace it with `ContentRotatorWidget`, but we wanted to provide you with more reusable code. You're welcome.

Lastly, have a look at the class variables we have declared at the top of the class: `$name`, `$description`, and `$control_options`. We have put them at the top of the class for easy access, then we have referenced them in the `__construct()` function using the `$this` variable. Note the syntax here for using class variables. We are declaring these variables as class variables for purposes of scope: we want their values to be available throughout the class.

Please save your work before continuing.

Activating your plugin

Before we can actually use our widget and see what it looks like, we first have to activate our plugin in the manager. Your widget will never show up in the widget administration area if the plugin is not active! Just to be clear, you will have to activate two things: your plugin, and then your widget.

The code is simple enough at this point for you to be able to quickly track down any errors.

Activating the widget

Now that the plugin code is active, we should see our widget show up in the widget administration area: **Appearance | Widgets**.

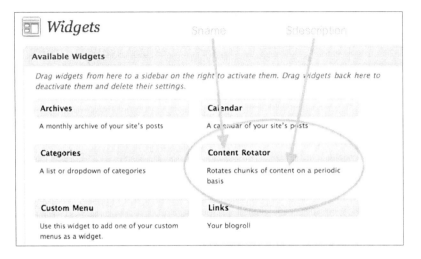

Take a moment to notice the correlation between the widget's name and description and how we used the corresponding variables in our constructor function. Drag your widget into the primary widget area to make it active.

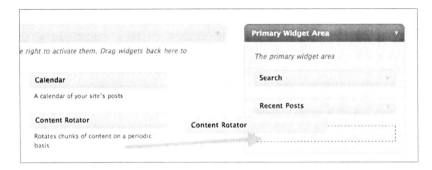

Once it has been activated, refresh your homepage. Your active widget should print some text in the sidebar.

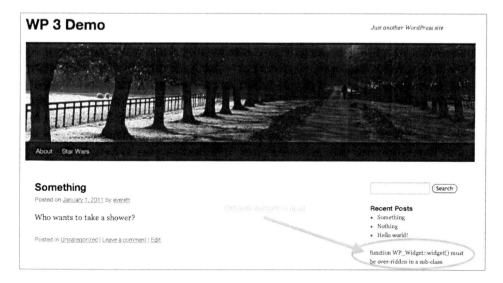

Congratulations! You have created your first WordPress widget! It is printing a default message: **function WP_Widget::widget() must be over-ridden in a sub-class**, which is not very exciting, but technically speaking you have a functional widget. We still need to enable our widget to store some custom options, but first we should ensure that everything is working correctly.

Having problems?

No widget? If you have activated your plugin, but you do not see your widget showing up in the widget administration area, make sure you have tied into a valid WordPress action! If you misspell the action, it will not get called! The action we are using in our `index.php` is `widgets_init` — don't forget the "s"!

White screen? Even if you have PHP error-reporting enabled, sometimes you suddenly end up with a completely white screen in both the frontend and in the manager. If there is a legitimate syntax error, that displays just fine, but if your PHP code is syntactically correct, you end up with nothing but a blank page. What's going on?

A heavy-handed solution for when plugins go bad is to temporarily remove your plugin's folder from `/wp-content/plugins`, then refresh the manager. WordPress is smart enough to deactivate any plugin that it cannot find, so it can recover from this type of surgery.

If you are experiencing the "White Screen of Death", it usually means that something is tragically wrong with your code, and it can take a while to track it down because each time you deactivate the plugin by removing the folder, you have to reactivate it by moving the folder back and reactivating the plugin in the WordPress manager.

This unenviable situation can occur if you accidentally chose a function name that was already in use (for example, `register()` — don't use that as a function name). You have to be *especially* careful of this when you are extending a class because you may inadvertently override a vital function when you meant to create a new one. If you think you may have done this, drop and do 20 push-ups and then have a look at the original parent `WP_Widget` class and its functions in `wp-includes/widgets.php`. Remember that whenever you extend a class, it behooves you to look at the parent class' functions and their inputs and outputs. If this sounds like Greek to you, then the next section is for you.

Parents and children: extending classes

If this is your first foray into the world of Object-Oriented programming or if you just need a refresher, let's take a moment to explain what is going on here. First of all, even though it is common parlance in the programming world, the "parent/child" terminology does not necessarily provide an accurate description of what's happening in our PHP classes. We find it helpful instead to think in terms of *overriding* and *redefining* — when you extend a class, you can redefine the parent's functions and thereby override their behavior.

Let's look at a more familiar example: CSS. If you have done much web development, you have used Cascading Style Sheets to stylize your content. If you follow the rules of good semantic web development, you put your style definitions into a separate `.css` file which you reference in the head of your HTML documents:

```
<link href="/css/default.css" rel="stylesheet" type="text/css" />
```

If you want all paragraphs on your site to be black and regularly sized, you would add something like the following to the default `.css` file:

```
p {
    font-size: medium;
    color: black;
}
```

However, there will always be exceptions. Let's say you have a `legalese.html` page with legal terms, so you want the paragraph text to be impossibly small and hard to read. What's the solution? You *override* the default style by redefining the style declaration in the head of your page:

```
<link href="/css/default.css" rel="stylesheet" type="text/css" />
<style type="text/css">
    p {
        font-size: x-small; /* <-- overrides the declaration in default.
css */
    }
</style>
```

Now all the paragraphs on legalese.html will be extra small. Good job—nobody will bother to read text so small! Now is your chance to disclose your plans to take over the world!

What if you have one paragraph on legalese.html that needs yet another style? Well, you can override the style *again* by redefining it inside that particular paragraph, for example:

```
<p style="font-size: large; font-weight: bold;">I AGREE TO THE
TERMS.</p>
```

Do you see how in each case we overrode the previous definition of the font-size attribute? Of course, we could have used different classes and definitions for each type of text, but we wanted to demonstrate the concept of inheritance and our ability to override inherited attributes. When the browser renders a particular paragraph, it will use the last style declaration it encountered. If the last declaration was in the CSS file, it uses that; if the last declaration was in the document head, it uses that; if a declaration was used inline alongside the content, it uses that. The browser literally remembers the last thing you told it about how to style any given content.

Imagine taking your mother out to dinner, and she can't make up her mind, so she keeps changing her order. The last thing she tells the waiter is what she'll be served.

What does this have to do with PHP and WordPress widgets? Similar to CSS style definitions, PHP functions describe behavior. Similar to CSS inheritance, the class hierarchy defined by extending classes tells our scripts which behavior should be implemented. In our example, the WP_Widget has a widget() function, which is what is currently displaying the default message reminding us that it must be "over-ridden in a sub-class". In other words, our ContentRotatorWidget class must define its own widget() function and thereby override it. The widget() function in the parent WP_Widget class is used until you define your own version of the widget() function and override it in the child class. Make sense?

In terms of the the parent/child terminology, imagine visiting a friend's house, knocking on their door, and having their kid answer it. You ask the child, "Hey, what content should be displayed here for this widget?" If the child knows the answer, your pages will get that text in their sidebars. If the child doesn't know the answer, he might say, "I don't know, let me go ask my dad", and then the parent `WP_Widget` class (the dad) would provide the "answer" to your "question". This chain can keep going—if the dad doesn't know, he asks the grandfather, and so on. Sorry, but in this hierarchical chain of authority, there is no PHP equivalent of "wife" or "girlfriend".

Hopefully this makes the concept of classes and inheritance clearer for you.

Objects vs. libraries: when to use static functions

You may have noticed that in our `ContentRotatorWidget` class some functions are static and some are not. What's going on?

In our example, we are using a static function to register the widget's class name. Even if we had thousand instances of this widget, the class name remains the same for all of them, so it is a good candidate for a static function. As the name suggests, a static function should be used to implement behavior that does not change.

The rest of the widget properties, however, are dynamic and will change from instance to instance. Objects distinguish themselves from libraries because you can have multiple *instances* of an object. You may not have noticed this, but in the widget administration area, you can in fact drag several instances of your widget into the "Primary Widget Area" drop zone.

Even though they are all instances of the ContentRotatorWidget, each instance has its own properties. If our class were "Books", then one instance might have a title of "No Country for Old Men" and another instance might have a title of "I Hope They Serve Beer in Hell". For each instance the title changes.

Objects use the $this variable to refer to the current instance of the object, that is THIS instance. So if you need to call a function inside the class, you call it via $this->function_name(), or if you need to access a "class variable", you use $this->variable_name. We'll see more examples of this as we go along.

Add custom text

Our simple widget is technically functional, but it doesn't do anything yet. After you have activated your widget and viewed your homepage, you will see some default text that we pointed out earlier: **function WP_Widget::widget() must be over-ridden in a sub-class.**

This is the output of the WP_Widget class' widget() function. If we think about our parent/child analogy, here we are getting a message from the parent telling the kid that he needs to take care of this function himself. How do we override the WP_Widget::widget() function? We simply add a widget() function to our ContentRotatorWidget class. Add the following function to the ContentRotatorWidget.php file, somewhere below the __construct() function (remember we like to keep our functions alphabetized):

```
/**
 * Displays content to the front-end.
 *
 * @param array   $args     Display arguments
 * @param array   $instance   The settings for the particular instance
 of the widget
 * @return none  No direct output. This should instead print output
 directly.
 */function widget($args, $instance)
{
    print "Hi, I'm a sneezing unicorn.";

}
```

Note that this function takes two arguments, and the official documentation currently does a poor job of explaining them. You can have a look at the original class and read the documentation for the function we are overriding inside of `wp-includes/widgets.php`, but it's not entirely clear what those arguments do. Just remember that when you override a function, it must take the same inputs and return the same output as the original. We'll use these arguments later so you can get some idea of how they're used.

Save your work and then refresh your homepage. You should see your text printed in place of the default message. Congratulations! You have successfully overridden your first function! Your `ContentRotatorWidget` stuck it to his old man and is now handling this function on his own.

Adding widget options

The other place where we need to customize our widget's content is in the manager—we need to provide a custom form for editing our widget's options. Let's start by adding a single option for the title. In order to do this, we need to implement another function in our widget and add some options:

1. Create a `form()` function that prints out some HTML. Later, this function will print out some HTML form elements, but for now, let's just make sure this works. Add the following function to your `ContentRotatorWidget.php` file:

```
/**
* Displays the widget form in the manager, used for editing its
settings
*
* @param   array    $instance   The settings for the particular
instance of the widget
* @return none   No value is returned directly, but form elements
are printed.
*/
function form( $instance )
{
    print "Form elements go here";
}
```

2. Save your file and refresh your manager page. You should see your handiwork when you open your widget for editing:

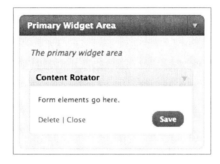

You may be thinking that all we need to do is print some form elements here, but the process here is deceptively complex because we need to handle multiple instances (and multiple HTML forms) of your widget. Each form element must have a unique name and ID. What to do? We let WordPress handle it via the `WP_Widget` class' `get_field_id()` and `get_field_name()` functions. We are going to build a simple template that allows you to adjust your form elements, and we will feed it the `$control_options` that we defined at the top of our `ContentRotatorWidget` class. Let's add a control option now.

3. Update your `ContentRotatorWidget` class and edit the `$control_options` array so we have a control option for "title". Later, we can expand this array to include as many options as our widget requires.

```
/* List all controllable options here along with a default value.
The values can be distinct for each instance of the widget. */
public $control_options = array(
    'title'    => 'Content Rotator',
);
```

4. It's finally getting to the point where we need some helper functions that do things that are not directly related to this widget. We need to put the functions somewhere, but they don't necessarily belong in the `ContentRotatorWidget` class. So let's create a new class named `ContentRotator`, and save it inside the `content-rotator/includes/` directory as `ContentRotator.php`. The following is what our `ContentRotator.php` looks like:

```php
<?php
/**
 * ContentRotator
 *
 * Helper functions that assist the ContentRotatorWidget class
 */
class ContentRotator {
```

```
}
/*EOF*/
```

It's empty for now. We will be adding a handful of functions to it later, but first let's test it.

5. Update the `content-rotator/index.php` file so it includes your new class. Add the following line to your `index.php` file:

```
include_once('includes/ContentRotator.php');
```

Save your work and refresh your homepage to check for any errors. You should now have a helper class hooked up and ready for use.

6. The first helper function we are going add to `ContentRotator.php` is one we've used before: a simple parsing function. This lets us use simple templates and `[+placeholders+]` in order to avoid the confusing mess of PHP concatenation.

Add this static function to the `ContentRotator` class:

```
/**
 * parse
 *
 * A simple parsing function for basic templating.
 *
 * @param $tpl     string    A formatting string containing
[+placeholders+]
 * @param $hash    array    An associative array containing keys
and values e.g. array('key' => 'value');
 * @return    string        Placeholders corresponding to the keys
of the hash will be replaced with the values the resulting string
will be returned.
 */
static function parse($tpl, $hash) {
    foreach ($hash as $key => $value) {
        $tpl = str_replace('[+'.$key.'+]', $value, $tpl);
    }
    return $tpl;
}
```

Save your work, refresh your homepage, and verify that no errors occurred.

7. Add a `tpls/` folder to your plugin's folder if you haven't already, and add a `widget_controls.tpl` file that contains the following text:

```
<!--
This .tpl file is used when editing a widget's options in the WP
manager.
```

```
It should only contain form *elements*; WordPress will supply the
opening and closing <form> tags.

For each key in the ContentRotatorWidget::$control_options array,
you will have
the following placeholders available:

   [+your_key.id+]       - used inside id attributes, e.g.
id="[+your_key.id+]"
   [+your_key.name+]     - used inside name attributes, e.g.
name="[+your_key.name+]"
   [+your_key.value+]    - contains the current value of the option

WordPress appends text to the names and id's to allow for multiple
instances
of the widget, so don't try hard-coding values here.
-->

<label for="[+title.id+]">Title</label><br/>
   <input id="[+title.id+]" name="[+title.name+]" value="[+title.
value+]" /><br/>
```

Notice that we've included a comment with some basic instructions for how to use this file. This is an important concept when it comes to good documentation: **put the documentation where people need it**.

We're preparing a system that can handle more complex widgets. The placeholders are pretty easy to read, and there's no danger of crashing PHP with a bad concatenation because it's only a text file—it does not execute. Any frontend designer would be comfortable editing this template, and that's a big deal. Consistently throughout this book, we want to separate the logic from the presentation layer as much as possible because it makes for better code and better HTML.

We still need to hook this template up to the wagon, so let's update our form() function next so it outputs some form elements instead of just static text.

8. After the footwork of adding a helper class, we're ready to beef up the
   `form()` function in the `ContentRotatorWidget` class. Update the function so
   it looks like the following:

```
/**
* Displays the widget form in the manager, used for editing its
settings
*
* @param   array    $instance   The settings for the particular
instance of the widget
* @return none   No value is returned directly, but form elements
are printed. */
public function form( $instance )
{
    $placeholders = array();

    foreach ( $this->control_options as $key => $val )
    {
        $placeholders[ $key .'.id' ]    = $this->get_field_id( $key
);
        $placeholders[ $key .'.name' ]    = $this->get_field_name(
$key );
        // This helps us avoid "Undefined index" notices.
        if ( isset($instance[ $key ] ) )
        {
            $placeholders[ $key .'.value' ]   = esc_attr( $instance[
$key ] );
        }
        // Use the default (for new instances)
        else
        {
            $placeholders[ $key .'.value' ]   = $this->control_
options[ $key ];
        }
    }

    $tpl = file_get_contents( dirname(dirname(__FILE__)) .'/tpls/
widget_controls.tpl');

    print ContentRotator::parse($tpl, $placeholders);
}
```

Save your work and refresh your admin page. We have just put together a handful of moving parts, so it may take a little debugging before they all work together. We are making use of the helper class' `ContentRotator::parse()` function, and we are also using PHP's `__FILE__` constant, which returns the name of the current file (`ContentRotatorWidget.php`). We use this in order to get a full path to the `widget_controls.tpl` file.

We are utilizing the parent class' `get_field_id()` and `get_field_name()` functions. We call them using the `$this` variable. Since our child class does not contain these functions, PHP looks for these functions in the parent class. This is how we let WordPress handle the naming and identification of form fields. This ensures that we don't get into trouble when we have several instances of our widget active.

Once it all works, head to the widget administration page in your browser, and try adding a title to your activated widget. The default title, by the way, comes from the value you set back in the `$control_options` array at the top of `ContentRotatorWidget.php`. You may need to deactivate the widget and then drag a new instance into the primary widget area before everything refreshes. Remember to refresh your admin page frequently when developing widgets! Enter a new title for the widget instance and try saving it.

If you got this all working, then take a deep breath and congratulate yourself. You have built a reusable component for your widgets, and it follows some good architectural design. That's no small feat! The next step is to tackle this widget's namesake—we need to generate some random content and put it into rotation.

Generating random content

It's time to flesh out the `widget()` function. This is the function that prints out the content that is visible on the frontend, and we want it to print out some *random* content. We are going to approach this in phases so that we can test it.

1. Firstly, add a helper function to ContentRotator.php that generates some random content. For now, we're going to generate a random number. Later, we will pull up some random content from the database, but always keep things simple the first time around so you can test them. Add the following static function to ContentRotator.php:

```
/**
Fetch and return a piece of random content
*/
static function get_random_content()
{
    return rand(1, 1000000);
}
```

This relies on PHP's rand() function, and it returns a random number between one and 1,000,000. It will suffice for our current testing.

Before we go much further, let's "templatize" our widget output. This is another case where the solutions offered on most websites and in most books would have you concatenating a messy bunch of PHP and HTML, but we want to avoid that.

2. Create a new template file named widget.tpl inside your content-rotator/tpls/ directory:

```
[+before_widget+]
    [+before_title+]
        [+title+]
    [+after_title+]

    [+content+]

[+after_widget+]
```

What's all that about? Well, remember how the widget() function takes two arguments? Those arguments are directly related to the widget's output, and we are going to use those arguments to create [+placeholders+] so we can easily control the output and formatting of our widget. If you had added a print_r($args) statement to your widget() function, you can inspect the arguments that WordPress is sending this function:

```
// Output of print_r($args) from inside the widget() function;
Array
(
    [name] => Primary Widget Area
    [id] => primary-widget-area
    [description] => The primary widget area
    [before_widget] => <li id="contentrotatorwidget-6"
```

```
class="widget-container ContentRotatorWidget">
    [after_widget] => </li>
    [before_title] => <h3 class="widget-title">
    [after_title] => </h3>
    [widget_id] => contentrotatorwidget-6
    [widget_name] => Content Rotator
)
```

Changing what these arguments are is beyond the scope of this chapter, but we are going to allow you a way to use these values as you customize your widget display. Unfortunately, we can't provide documentation in a comment because it may throw things off. For example, if our widget were used to returning bits of Google Adsense JavaScript, they would still execute even if they were inside an HTML comment. However, we have an obligation to explain the format and purpose of this .tpl file to our users, so we are going to create a readme.txt file with further information.

3. Create a content-rotator/tpls/readme.txt file with the following instructions in it:

The file called widget_controls.tpl contains the form elements necessary to edit a widget's settings. See widget_controls.tpl for more instructions on using that file.

The widget.tpl template is used to format the output of the widget as it is seen by the outside world, for example, on your homepage.

There are 4 primary built-in placeholders which are dictated by the template in use:

[+before_widget+]

[+after_widget+]

[+before_title+]

[+after_title+]

There are also placeholders corresponding to the ContentRotatorWidget::$control_options array keys. The values of these are bound to an instance of the widget, so two instances of the same widget may have completely different values. These placeholders include:

[+seconds_shelf_life+]

[+title+]

Lastly, the most important placeholder:

[+content+] -- contains the random text as defined in the plugin's administration page

There are additional placeholders created from the widget() function's $args array, for example:

```
Array
(

    [name] => Primary Widget Area
    [id] => primary-widget-area
    [description] => The primary widget area
    [before_widget] => <li id="contentrotatorwidget-6"
class="widget-container ContentRotatorWidget">
    [after_widget] => </li>
    [before_title] => <h3 class="widget-title">
    [after_title] => </h3>
    [widget_id] => contentrotatorwidget-6
    [widget_name] => Content Rotator
)
```

Each key in this array corresponds to a placeholder. For example [+name+] and [+id+] are placeholders you can use in your widget. tpl file.

The documentation for the available placeholders occurs in this readme.txt file so that it does not display publicly.

We won't bother repeating ourselves and we'll assume you read the `readme.txt` file—we have listed a few placeholders that we haven't implemented yet. If our templating method is too unorthodox for you, have a look at the official documentation for more conventional examples: `http://codex.wordpress.org/Widgets_API`.

4. Next, let's call the `get_random_content()` helper function in the `ContentRotatorWidget.php` `widget()` function so our widget can get some random content. Currently, our random content consists of a random number, but the important thing here is to get it so it displays on the frontend. Update the `widget()` function so it looks like the following:

```
/**
 * Displays content to the front-end, using the tpls/widget.tpl
template.
 *
 * @param array   $args    Display arguments
 * @param array    $instance   The settings for the particular
instance of the widget
 * @return none  No direct output. This should instead print
output directly.
 */
public function widget($args, $instance)
{
    $placeholders = array_merge($args, $instance);
```

```
    $placeholders['content'] = ContentRotator::get_random_
content();
    $tpl = file_get_contents( dirname(dirname(__FILE__)) .'/
tpls/widget.tpl');
    print ContentRotator::parse($tpl, $placeholders);
}
```

Save your work and refresh your homepage. You should now see a new random number each time you refresh your homepage. Furthermore, the format of the output should be entirely controlled by the `widget.tpl` file. To test this, you can edit it to include some additional HTML formatting, but we will leave that up to you.

Expiration dates: adding options to our widget

One of the key specifications for this plugin is the ability to set how often content is refreshed. Maybe you want to include a "quote of the day" on your site, or maybe you want to update a chunk of content every hour. Each instance of our widget needs an expiration date.

How do we do that? The solution is a bit tricky, so pay attention. First, we need to add another control option to our widget that allows the managers to set how often the content expires in each widget instance. We are referring to this as the "shelf life", in keeping with some common grocery terms.

Update the `ContentRotatorWidget.php` file so the `$control_options` array has an additional option:

```
public $control_options = array(
    'title'               => 'Content Rotator',
    'seconds_shelf_life'  => 86400,   // 86400 seconds in a day
);
```

We have given it a default value of 86400; we are opting to use seconds as our refresh interval, where 86,400 seconds is equal to 24 hours.

Next, we need to include some form elements so managers can submit new values for this option. The hard work we did previously pays off now. Simply add the form element to the `tpls/widget_controls.tpl` file so it contains elements for both control options:

```
<label for="[+title.id+]">Title</label><br/>
    <input id="[+title.id+]" name="[+title.name+]" value="[+title.
value+]" /><br/>
```

```
<label for="[+seconds_shelf_life.id+]">Shelf Life (in seconds)</
label><br/>
<input id="[+seconds_shelf_life.id+]" name="[+seconds_shelf_life.
name+]" value="+seconds_shelf_life.value+]" />
```

Save your work and refresh your manager page. You may need to deactivate your widgets and reactivate them before you see the new options available for editing.

Now we can tell each widget instance how long its content should persist, but we have not yet solved the trickier problem of enforcing this behavior. We handle that in the next section.

Expiration dates: enforcing the shelf life

Expiration dates are fairly simple. For example, if a container of milk is stamped with a date, we can read that date and compare it with today's date in order to know if that milk is past its prime. How does this apply to our rotating content? We have already solved the problem of determining how long a chunk of content should last before it gets refreshed, but what is our content's "manufacture date"? When exactly is our content considered new?

We are choosing to determine the "manufacturing date" as the time when a user first views our content. The expiration date will be determined by adding the `seconds_shelf_life` value to this date. Since PHP and UNIX typically work in seconds, the arithmetic is simple: If the time right now is later than the manufacturing date plus the shelf life, then it is time to refresh the content. Alternatively, in pseudo code:

```
if ( $now > ($manufacturing_date + $shelf_life) ) {
// Refresh the content
}
```

Make sense? Sometimes these little logical quandaries are the most difficult part of a script. Now we have to integrate this logic into our code, and to do that, we are finally going to make use of the second argument to the `widget()` function: `$instance`. That's where information is stored about the specific instance of our widget. Since each instance has the potential to have different attributes (for example, "shelf life"), our calculations must be made according to each instance. In our grocery store analogy, we need to be able to say *this* bottle of milk is still good, but *this* bottle of milk needs to be replaced.

Update the `ContentRotatorWidget.php widget()` function so it looks like the following:

```php
public function widget($args, $instance)
{
    if ( !isset($instance['manufacture_date'])
        || time() >= ($instance['manufacture_date']
        + $instance['seconds_shelf_life'] ) )
    {
        $instance['content'] = ContentRotator::get_random_
content($instance);
        $instance['manufacture_date'] = time();
        $all_instances = $this->get_settings();
        $all_instances[ $this->number ] = $instance;
        $this->save_settings($all_instances);
    }

    $placeholders = array_merge($args, $instance);

    $tpl = file_get_contents( dirname(dirname(__FILE__)) .'/tpls/
widget.tpl');

    print ContentRotator::parse($tpl, $placeholders);
}
```

A lot is going on there, so let's devote some time to breaking it down.

Explaining the $instance

You can see our "expiration date" logic in the `if-statement`, which relies on PHP's `time()` function to determine the current time (in seconds). The trickiest part of this code is when we actually have to refresh the content. To pull this off, we are tying into `WP_Widget`'s `get_settings()` and `save_settings()` methods (remember, a "method" is simply a function inside of a class). Those functions get and save settings for ALL instances of a widget, not just the current instance, which complicates things.

If you were to `print_r($this->get_settings())` inside the widget function, you would see an array of arrays. Each widget gets its own array; we just need to know which number our widget is. To distinguish our widget's unique place inside that array of arrays, we are making use of a class variable from the parent class: `$this->number`. We make the necessary changes to our `$instance`, and then we slip our `$instance` back into `$all_instances` by overwriting the unique spot in the `$all_instances` array:

```
$all_instances[ $this->number ] = $instance;
```

So what data is stored in a particular `$instance`? Performing a `print_r($instance)` would yield something like the following:

```
Array
(
    [content] => 924297
    [manufacture_date] => 1295813716
    [title] => Content Rotator
    [seconds_shelf_life] => 3
)
```

You can see that this is information about our `ContentRotatorWidget` and not WordPress widgets in general. How did all that information get in there? We have to apologize for this, because it probably qualifies as "clever", and in computer code, "clever" is usually a euphemism for "complicated and poorly documented". Normally a widget's options would only be created and changed via the backend manager by the form you displayed via the `form()` function, but we only created options for `title` and `seconds_shelf_life`, so how did the `content` and `manufacture_date` get in there? These two lines populate the other values of `$instance`:

```
$instance['content'] = ContentRotator::get_random_content();
$instance['manufacture_date'] = time();
```

The "clever" thing about this is that they are populated when a user on the frontend views a page, not when you save the widget in the manager. Since this is a bit uncommon, we don't have a nice WordPress API function to use, so we have to use the parent class' `save_settings()` function, which does in fact save data to the database. How do we know to use that function? We read through the parent class and its functions in `wp-includes/widgets.php`.

Save your work, and then try activating two instances of the `Content Rotator` widget: one should have a shelf-life of *five* seconds and the other should have a shelf life of *zero* seconds. Refresh your homepage a few times to get the full effect. You should see one instance of the widget spit out a random number with each page request, and the other instance should only refresh every five seconds.

This was the hardest part of our widget. The only thing we have left to do is to replace our random number generator with something that pulls real content from the database. To do that, we must modify the `ContentRotator::get_random_content()` function so it picks some content at random. Some readers may feel they can take it from here, but we're going to carry on and show you how to create a custom manager page inside of the WordPress manager so you can add and remove chunks of content.

Adding a custom manager page

It's not written anywhere as a hard core rule, but in general, we try to put a plugin's configuration page under the **Plugins** menu. There is nothing that prevents you from creating our own custom menus, but often developing a custom menu item for your plugin is nothing but pure vanity; it's a plugin, not the second coming! So we are going to add a custom menu item to the **Plugins** menu.

Let's first create a sample page that will show up when we click on our custom menu item. Later on, we'll customize this, but for now, let's keep it simple. Create a new file inside the `content-rotator/includes/` directory named `admin_page.php` and put some sample text into it:

```
<div class="wrap">
    <?php screen_icon(); ?>
    <h2>Content Rotator Administration</h2>
    <p>We're remodeling...</p>
</div>
```

Notice that we're wrapping everything with a `div` tag that uses the `wrap` class. Use this class for best results. We are also using a theme function, `screen_icon()`. This is not required; it's just common practice.

You may have noticed that we are not using a `.tpl` file for this. We try to avoid sloppy mixes of PHP and HTML whenever possible, but it is a blurry line when it comes to building forms, so here we are using a "standard" PHP file.

Now that we have a target page, we have to make a function that displays that page. Inside of `ContentRotator.php`, add a static function as shown in the following code snippet:

```
/**
 * Controller that generates admin page
 */
static function generate_admin_page()
{
    include('admin_page.php');
}
```

We also need a function that will create our custom menu item. Add the following static function to `ContentRotator.php`:

```
/**
 * Adds a menu item inside the WordPress admin
 */
static function add_menu_item()
{
    add_submenu_page(
        'plugins.php',                        // Menu page to attach to
        'Content Rotator Configuration',      // page title
        'Content Rotator',                    // menu title
        'manage_options',                     // permissions
        'content-rotation',                   // page-name (used in the URL)
        'ContentRotator::generate_admin_page' // clicking callback
function
    );
}
```

We pause for a moment to remind you to distance yourself from this WordPress function. Having six inputs is too confusing, so we've added some comments to help you out. The rule of thumb is that having any more than three inputs probably means that you should rewrite your function or repackage your inputs. Please, don't write functions like this.

Finally, we need to hook our `add_menu_item()` function to a WordPress event. Add the following function call to your `content-rotator/index.php` file:

```
add_action('admin_menu', 'ContentRotator::add_menu_item');
```

Save your work and then refresh your manager page. Try clicking on the **Plugins** menu—you should see a custom menu item for **Content Rotator**. Click on it and verify that you can see your custom `admin_page.php`.

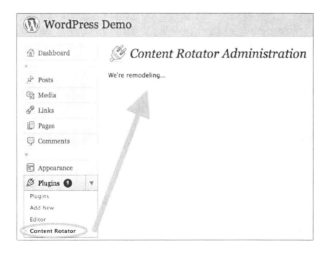

Adding options to the custom manager page

Let's face it: a static manager page isn't very useful for anything other than testing. We want to use this page to add our custom content, so what we really need on it is a form. There are many ways to store content and randomize it, and what we are going to show you isn't necessarily the best way, but it will demonstrate how you can store options in the database using a custom manager page. A more thorough solution would not be as valuable as a teaching tool.

We are going to build a form with two fields: one that allows the user to enter a block of content, and another that accepts the character (or characters) that separates that content into units. For example, this could be our content block:

```
man, bear, pig
```

Then, our separator would be a simple comma (","). If your content is more complex, you may need a more complex separator.

We need to store two settings in the database, so let's make the following changes. First, update your `admin_page.php` file so it contains two form elements:

```
<div class="wrap">
      <?php screen_icon(); ?>
      <h2>Content Rotator Administration</h2>

      <?php print $msg; ?>

      <form action="" method="post" id="content_rotation_admin_
options_form">
         <h3><label for="separator">Separator</label></h3>
         <p>This separates units of content. It can be simple like a
comma, or complex like &lt;!--SEPARATOR--&gt;<br/>
```

```
        <input type="text" id="separator" name="separator"
value="<?php print esc_attr( get_option('content_rotation_content_
separator') ); ?>" /></p>

        <h3><label for="content_block">Content Block</label></h3>
        <p>
        Use the separator above to separate blocks of content,
e.g. <code>man, bear, pig</code><br/>
        or <code>&lt;a href="http://mysite.com/"&gt;MySite.
com&lt;/a&gt;&lt;--SEPARATOR--&gt;
        &lt;a href="http://yoursite.com/"&gt;YourSite.com&lt;/
a&gt;</code><br/>
        <textarea rows="5" cols="50" id="content_block"
name="content_block"><?php print get_option('content_rotation_content_
block'); ?></textarea>
        </p>
        <p class="submit"><input type="submit" name="submit"
value="Update" /></p>
        <?php wp_nonce_field('content_rotation_admin_options_
update','content_rotation_admin_nonce'); ?>
    </form>
  </div>
```

Notice that we're using WordPress' `get_option()` function to supply values to our form elements. Also, have a gander at the `wp_nonce_field()` function. What is a *nonce*? A nonce is a "number used only once", and it is an important security feature. By including a nonce as a hidden field on your forms, you can reduce the risk of your form being hijacked by a cross-site request forgery (CSRF). WordPress generates a unique value for this form which gets validated when the form is submitted. This makes it harder to post malicious data to your form. The full explanation of this technique is beyond the scope of this book, but you should use it for security reasons.

Any time we create a form, we also must handle the submission of that form. We need to program some code that handles the form data after it has been submitted. Let's do that next.

We need to save the form values if they were properly submitted. We do this by updating our controller function inside of `ContentRotator.php`:

```
/**
 * Controller that generates admin page
 */
static function generate_admin_page()
{
    $msg = ''; // used to display a success message on updates

    if ( !empty($_POST) && check_admin_referer('content_rotation_admin_
options_update','content_rotation_admin_nonce') )
```

```
    {
        update_option('content_rotation_content_separator',
            stripslashes($_POST['separator']) );
        update_option('content_rotation_content_block',
            stripslashes($_POST['content_block']) );
        $msg = '<div class="updated"><p>Your settings have been
    <strong>updated</strong></p></div>';
    }
    include('admin_page.php');
}
```

If you have built PHP form handlers in the past, you may be more familiar with a big `if-else` statement which decides whether it displays the form or processes the form based on whether or not it has been submitted. Our approach here is simpler. The `check_admin_referer()` function will terminate the script if the submission was not authentic, so we can't use an `if-else` construct. Instead we use a simple `if-statement`.

It's important to summarize the exact syntax that needs to be used for the `wp_nonce_field()` and the `check_admin_referer()` functions because they need to match up. Some of the official documents for these functions are confusing, so here's the short syntax:

```
wp_nonce_field($action_name, $nonce_name);

check_admin_referer($action_name, $nonce_name);
```

Where `$action_name` is the name of the action and `$nonce_name` is the name of the nonce. If you have a page with multiple forms on it, it's important that you give unique values to each instance of the `wp_nonce_field()` function. However, the most important thing to remember here is that the arguments passed to the `check_admin_referer()` function must match **exactly** the values passed to the `wp_nonce_field()` function. If they do not match, WordPress will exit with a message. Oddly the message reads "Are you sure you want to do this?" which gives little inkling as to the root cause.

We use WordPress' `update_option()` function to store the options in the database, and we are using PHP's `stripslashes()` function to help sanitize the data. Note that the option names here match the names used by the `get_option()` functions in the `admin_page.php` page. So once again we have a pair of functions whose inputs must match.

Lastly, we are using a simple `$msg` variable to store a message to show whether or not the options have been updated. We are using some standard WordPress styling information by using a `<div class="updated">` block here, and we encourage you to do the same.

Save your work and refresh your manager page. You should now be able to save custom configuration details and have them persist when you revisit the configuration page. For testing, we recommend that you use a comma separator and a simple comma-separated list. Enter in some text now before proceeding.

Randomizing content from the database

The stars are in alignment—we have custom content in the database, we have a widget that displays content, and choosing the random content all depends on a single function: `ContentRotator::get_random_content()`. Let's update that function, so it pulls our content from the database:

```
static function get_random_content(){
    $separator       = get_option('content_rotation_content_
separator');
    $content_block    = get_option('content_rotation_content_block');

    // Ensure that the user has entered valid settings
    if ( empty($content_block) )
    {
        return '';
    }
    elseif (empty($separator))
    {
        return $content_block;
    }
    // Get an array of non-empty chunks
    $content_array = explode($separator, $content_block);
    $sanitized_array = array();
    foreach ($content_array as $chunk)
    {
        $chunk = trim($chunk);
        if (!empty($chunk))
        {
            $sanitized_array[] = $chunk;
        }
    }
    $chunk_cnt = count($sanitized_array);
    if ( $chunk_cnt)
    {
        $n = rand(0, ($chunk_cnt - 1));
        return $sanitized_array[$n];
    }
    else
```

```
        {
            return '';
        }
    }
```

This all relies on the WordPress `get_option()` function and PHP's `explode()` function (make sure you use same option names that you used in the `generate_admin_page()` function). We are using PHP's `trim()` function to do some cleanup in the event that someone entered in some empty content, but it's a fairly straightforward function. If you needed to test its ability to pick one item out of the list, you could simply supply static values to the `$separator` and `$content_block` variables.

When you save your work now, your initial draft of this widget is complete. Congratulations!

Review of PHP functions used

The following is a list of some of the PHP functions and constants used:

- `__CLASS__`: PHP constant that contains the name of the PHP class in which it appears.

- `__FILE__`: PHP constant that contains the name of the file in which appears.

- `parent::__construct()`: A convenient way to run the `__construct` in the parent class. This statement is only used in a child class.

- `trim()`: Removes whitespace from the beginning and end of a string.

- `rand(x,y)`: Picks a random number between x and y.

- `explode($separator, $str)`: Separates a string `$str` into an array by splitting it at each instance of `$separator`.

- `stripslashes()`: Removes backslashes from form-submitted data.

Summary

We have created a total of seven files to build this plugin:

- `includes/admin_page.php`
- `includes/ContentRotator.php`
- `includes/ContentRotatorWidget.php`
- `index.php`
- `tpls/readme.txt`

- `tpls/widget.tpl`
- `tpls/widget_controls.tpl`

If you made it to this point, give yourself a pat on the back. You've now created your first widget along with a custom manager page. These are important tools to have in your toolbox as you continue to develop WordPress plugins.

When you're ready, let's move on to the next chapter, in which we will explore WordPress' capabilities as a content management system by utilizing custom fields.

6

Standardized Custom Content

In this chapter you are going to learn about customizing your WordPress content. We will show you how to do this by adding custom fields to your posts and how to standardize them so the same fields appear on each post.

WordPress has been a magic egg of blogging platforms, but with version 3.0 it is starting to crack out of its shell. In our opinion, WordPress is still not entirely ready to take flight as a full-featured content management system, but with a little help from some additional plugins, we can get this chick hatched and airborne.

We have the following goals in this chapter:

- To ensure that the same custom fields appear on every post
- To allow for different input types in those custom fields, for example, checkboxes and drop-down lists
- To modify your templates so that this custom data can be displayed in your theme

What WordPress does for you: custom fields

Let's take a moment to look at how you can add custom fields to a WordPress post. Log in to the **Dashboard** and create a new post. Have a look at the bottom of the page. There is a form there that allows you to add **Custom Fields**:

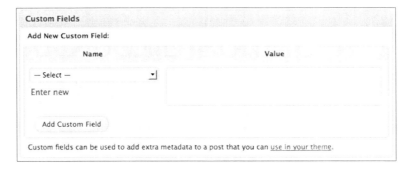

You can create a new custom field, or you can choose from an existing one. Either way, when you save your post, this custom field is saved along with it.

Looks simple, right? Well, yes and no. Let's look a bit closer and see what WordPress doesn't do for you.

What WordPress doesn't do for you

If you start using custom fields more than just occasionally, you will notice a few areas where WordPress isn't helping you. Firstly, if you use the same custom fields on multiple posts, you have to add them one-by-one to each post. Secondly, the custom fields are always text fields. The WordPress admin user interface does not provide a way for you to add drop-down lists, rich text, or checkboxes. Thirdly, your theme may not even display this custom information.

These shortcomings present us with an opportunity. As you may have guessed, in this chapter, we will remedy these shortcomings with a plugin that will meet the goals we have set for this chapter.

Does that whet your appetite? Good. Let's get started.

Standardizing a post's custom fields

In order to ensure that each post automatically uses the same custom fields, we need to shepherd WordPress' behavior using a plugin that makes use of WordPress' `remove_meta_box()` and `add_meta_box()` functions. The "meta box" is where you interact with your custom fields (a.k.a. your post meta). Specifically, we are going to remove the default meta box and replace it with our own. You know the drill by now. Let's create a new plugin.

Creating a new plugin

Create a new plugin folder named `standardized-custom-content` inside the `wp-content/plugins` folder. Next, create an `index.php` file and add an information header to it. If you have forgotten the format, just modify the one from the *Hello Dolly* plugin. The following is our information header:

```
/*
Plugin Name: Standardized Custom Content
Plugin URI: http://www.tipsfor.us/
Description: Forces post-types to use a standard list of custom fields
with options for checkboxes, dropdowns, and various text fields.
Author: Everett Griffiths
Version: 0.1
Author URI: http://www.tipsfor.us/
Based on work by Steve Taylor:
http://sltaylor.co.uk/blog/control-your-own-wordpress-custom-fields/
*/
```

Save your work and then try to activate the plugin. Remember, test early, test often! The next step is to create a folder called `includes` inside the `standardized-custom-content` folder. Within the `includes` folder, create a new file named `StandardizedCustomContent.php`.

Next, declare a new class inside of `StandardizedCustomContent.php`:

```php
<?php
/**
 * StandardizedCustomContent
 *
 * A class designed to standardize WordPress' custom fields and allow
for
 * checkboxes, dropdowns, etc.
 */
class StandardizedCustomContent {
}
/*EOF*/
```

The last step to complete our new plugin's foundation is to update your `index.php` file so that it includes your newly created class file:

```
include_once('includes/StandardizedCustomContent.php');
```

Save your work, and then refresh the manager to ensure that everything works. Congratulations! We've laid the simple foundations for our new plugin. This is a fairly straightforward plugin, and we are only going to use the `index.php` and the `StandardizedCustomContent.php` files to hold our code.

Removing the default WordPress form for custom fields

The first step in handling custom fields our way is to get WordPress' handling out of the picture. To do this, we need to make use of the `remove_meta_box()` function. The secret here is tying into the `do_meta_boxes` action, which is called when the meta box is being created.

Update your `index.php` file so it ties into the `do_meta_boxes` action.

```
add_action( 'do_meta_boxes', 'StandardizedCustomContent::remove_
default_custom_fields', 10, 3 );
```

You can see that we are planning on calling a static function named `remove_
default_custom_fields` (more on that in the next step), but this is the first time we have used the third and fourth arguments to the `add_action()` function. We're throwing the third argument a default value (10) because what we really care about is the fourth argument. The function triggered by the `do_meta_boxes` action accepts three arguments. How did we know that? Well, unfortunately, it's not from any of WordPress' documentation. Adam Brown is our savior here (http://goo.gl/wEHo).

We can have a look inside the `wp-admin/edit-form-advanced.php` file to see where this action is called:

```
do_action('do_meta_boxes', $post_type, 'normal', $post);
```

`do_action()` is the magic function that makes all of our action events happen, so it can be useful to see how it triggers an event. From that call, we can see that there are three additional arguments passed after the name of the action, therefore, we know that if we hook into this action, we need to include 3 as the fourth argument to `add_
action()`. See the official documentation for the `add_action()` function if you need more clarification (http://goo.gl/77Os).

If this seems fantastical that we somehow knew of this action and how to use it, it is. The actions and filters are currently lacking in documentation, so sometimes figuring out which one to use can be a laborious process. The following is a tip on how to find which actions and filters are firing:

- Look at the file being called in your URL (`wp-admin/post.php`, in this case)

- Search for any instances of the `do_action()` or `apply_filter()` functions in that file

- Look for any calls to `include()`, `require()`, `include_once()`, or `require_once()` — from this we know that `edit-form-advanced.php` is included on that page

- Check the included files for the `do_action()` or `apply_filter()` functions

It's not an easy process, but it is one that you can use to help find events (actions or filters) that you can hook into.

An amazingly useful tool available for finding text is the command line tool `grep`, which is standard in any Unix shell (that is Linux and Mac OS X). You can recursively search an entire directory for any files containing a certain string:

`grep -rl 'search-term-here' .`

Where "`.`" is short for the current directory.

Our next task is to update the `StandardizedCustomContent.php` file so that it contains the following two functions along with the public static variable `$content_types_array`:

```
/**
 * Which types of content do we want to standardize? Here you can
list WP
 * built-in content types (aka post-types) e.g. 'page', 'post', or
 * any custom post-types you define.
 */
public static $content_types_array = array('post');

/**
 * This plugin is meant to be configured so it acts on a specified
list of content
 * types, e.g. post, page, or any custom content types that are
registered.
 * FUTURE: read this from the database.
 * @return array   Array of strings, each string being the name of a
WP post-type
```

```
    */
    private static function _get_active_content_types() {
        return self::$content_types_array;
    }

    /**
     * Remove the default Custom Fields meta box. Only affects the
    content types that
     * have been activated. All inputs are sent by WP.
     * @param    string    $type    The name of the post-type being
    edited, e.g. 'post'
     * @param    string    $context    Identifies a type of meta-box, e.g.
    'normal', 'advanced', 'side'
     * @param    object    $post    The current post, with attributes e.g.
    $post->ID and $post->post_name
     */
    public static function remove_default_custom_fields( $type, $context,
    $post ) {
        $content_types_array = self::_get_active_content_types();
        foreach ( array( 'normal', 'advanced', 'side' ) as $context ) {
            foreach ( $content_types_array as $content_type ) {
                remove_meta_box( 'postcustom', $content_type, $context );
            }
        }
    }
```

From the `remove_default_custom_fields()` function we are calling the `_get_active_content_types()` function. If you noticed our comments, you can see that we are anticipating future development of this plugin beyond what we will complete in this chapter, but it brings up an important architectural point: there are times when you should use `getter` and `setter` functions instead of accessing class variables directly.

For the record, we could have bypassed the `_get_active_content_types()` function entirely by using the following line in our `remove_default_custom_fields()` function:

```
    $content_types_array = self::$content_types_array;
```

However, we are anticipating that we will eventually read that value from the database, so we will route all requests for that variable to a `getter` function, which we can later rewrite so it gets its data from the database. When time comes for us to rewrite the next version of this plugin, it will be much easier if we know our edits will be isolated to this particular function. Until then, the function will remain a one-liner that simply returns our class variable.

Understanding $this vs. self

We are once again using static functions in our class. Nothing in this plugin requires objects, so we have opted to create a class of static functions that requires no instantiation. In static classes, `self::` takes the place of `$this->`, and it is used to refer to class variables and methods, for example, `self::$my_var` or `self::my_function()`. Static functions are not allowed to use `$this->` because it refers to a specific instance of the class, and the whole point of using static functions is that there are no instances of the class. In fact, if you use the `$this->` construct anywhere outside of an instantiated class, PHP will die with a fatal error: *Fatal error: Using $this when not in object context.*

Save your work and refresh the WordPress **Dashboard**. The functions here are simple enough for you to be able to quickly track down errors. Remember what we said in *Chapter 1* about keeping your "units" of code small? If your functions are too long, they become more difficult to understand and debug.

Edit the post you created previously that contained custom fields. Notice that the whole section for custom fields is now gone from the **Dashboard**. We have successfully removed it from the post edit page. To prove this, you can temporarily deactivate the plugin and try viewing this post again—the custom fields should be visible once more. Please reactivate the plugin before you continue.

Creating our own custom meta box

Now that we have successfully removed the default custom fields, we need to supply our own handling for custom fields. First, add the following action hook to your `index.php` file:

```
add_action( 'admin_menu', 'StandardizedCustomContent::create_meta_box' );
```

Next, we need to create the static function we just referenced. Create a function named `create_meta_box` inside of `StandardizedCustomContent.php`:

```
/**
 * Create the new Custom Fields meta box.
 */
public static function create_meta_box() {
    $content_types_array = self::_get_active_content_types();
    foreach ( $content_types_array as $content_type ) {
        add_meta_box( 'my-custom-fields'
            , 'Custom Fields'
            , 'StandardizedCustomContent::print_custom_fields'
```

```
            , $content_type
            , 'normal'
            , 'high'
            , $content_type
        );
    }
}
```

This is where we utilize the `add_meta_box()` function. Its arguments are a bit lengthy, so it helps to read its documentation to better understand its use (`http://goo.gl/WoKEK`). Notice that we are again tying into the `_get_active_content_types()` function for easier expansion in the future.

Even though we haven't coded it yet, we are already anticipating a function named `print_custom_fields`, and we are taking advantage of the `add_meta_box()` function's optional seventh argument so that we can send it some additional data. We are passing it each content type defined in the `$content_types_array` so that we can influence the custom fields of other content types (for example, pages). Since we referenced yet another function, `print_custom_fields()`, we need to go and create it.

 WordPress offers a few different types of content in a default installation, namely, pages, posts, and attachments. Each has its own unique attributes and each is used for different scenarios. The official WordPress term for these types of content is "post types", probably because they are all stored in the `wp_posts` database table. That said, we feel that the term "content types" is more descriptive. Throughout this chapter, we use the terms "post types" and "content types" interchangeably.

Inside of `StandardizedCustomContent.php`, create another public static function named `print_custom_fields`. Notice that it takes two arguments; that's just how it gets called by the `add_meta_box()` function. For the record, we figured that out by using the `func_get_args()` function.

```
public static function print_custom_fields($post, $callback_args='') {
    print 'Custom fields go here...';
}
```

For now, let's just ensure that this works. Once it's working, we will flesh out this function to generate some real form fields. Go ahead and save your work, refresh your browser, and then edit your post that contains custom fields. You should see the message you printed in the `print_custom_fields()` function.

Custom Fields

Custom fields go here...

Defining custom fields

Before we can print the custom fields for our posts, we first need to define them in our code. We need to generate a form with multiple elements depending on what custom fields we define for our posts. Form generation is tricky, and it has a lot of edge cases. We want to present something usable without going too far deep down the rabbit hole. First, let's come up with a way to define fields.

What do we need to describe a custom field? We came up with four different attributes:

- *name*: Something to uniquely identify this field in the $_POST array and in the database.

- *title*: The human readable name.

- *description*: Any additional description of this field's purpose.

- *type*: What type of input should this be? Text? A checkbox?

The question now becomes how to describe that in PHP code. Any time we have key/value pairs like we just did while defining attributes, it bespeaks an associative array (a.k.a: a "hash"). However, we need to have a hash for each custom field because we might have multiple fields. So, what we need is a data structure that contains an array of hashes. Here's what we came up with, commented for your convenience:

```
public static $custom_fields =   array(
     array(
          // name and id of the form element & as the meta_key in the
wp_postmeta table.
          // Should contain lowercase letters, "-", and "_" only. Names
beginning with "_"
          // will be hidden from built-in WP functions, e.g. the_meta()
          'name'           => 'my_name',

          // used in the element's <label>
          'title'          => 'This is the bold Text that appears above
the Form Element!',

          // optional text will be wrapped in a <p> and appear below
the element
          'description'    => 'Shh... this is extra italic text...',

          // one of the supported element types: checkbox,
dropdown,text,textarea,wysiwyg
          'type'           => 'dropdown',

          // Include this ONLY when type = dropdown!!
          'options'        => array('one','two','three'),
     ),
   );
```

We are deciding right now that we want to support a limited number of input types which correspond to various HTML form input types: checkboxes, dropdowns, regular text inputs, text areas, and WYSIWYG (What You See Is What You Get) — this is the same as a text area, but it will include formatting controls.

Notice that we need to add one more option for drop-down lists. We need to specify a list of options that appear in the list. Just from this simple exercise, you should start to get an idea how subtly complicated form generation can be. Let's define some custom fields for our posts by using the format we have outlined.

Add the following to `StandardizedCustomContent.php`. For testing purposes, we want to use each of the field types that we plan to support.

```php
public static $custom_fields_for_posts =   array(
    array(
        'name'          => 'my_text',
        'title'          => 'Simple text input',
        'description'    => '',
        'type'          => 'text',
    ),
    array(
        'name'          => 'short_text',
        'title'          => 'A short bit of text',
        'description'    => 'This is a textarea, without any
formatting controls.',
        'type'          => 'textarea',
    ),
    array(
        'name'          => 'gender',
        'title'          => 'Gender',
        'description'    => 'Sample dropdown menu',
        'type'          => 'dropdown',
        'options'        => array('Male','Female'),
    ),
    array(
        'name'          => 'formatted_text',
        'title'          => 'Formatted Text',
        'description'    => 'This uses jQuery to add the formatting
controls.',
        'type'          => 'wysiwyg',
    ),
    array(
        'name'          => 'my_checkbox',
        'title'          => 'Do You Like This Checkbox?',
```

```
            'description'   => 'Checkboxes are tricky... they either have
a value, or they are null.',
            'type'          => 'checkbox',
        )
    );
```

Even if we were going to retrieve this array in the database immediately, it's useful to have a local copy of the data structure for testing.

Up next, let's add a `getter` function for this data. In the future, we can rewrite this function to pull data from the database. Add the following static function to `StandardizedCustomContent.php`:

```
/**
 * Get custom fields for the content type specified.
 *
 * FUTURE: read these arrays from the database.
 *
 * @param   string $content_type   The name of the content type,
e.g. post, page.
 * @return mixed   array of associative arrays defining custom
fields to use
 *   for the $content_type specified.
 */
private static function _get_custom_fields($content_type) {
    return self::$custom_fields_for_posts;
}
```

Next, expand the `print_custom_fields()` function to reference the function we just created. We're outlining this so it can handle all the various input types that we want to support, and we're structuring it all using a `switch` statement:

```
    public static function print_custom_fields($post, $callback_
args='') {
        $content_type = $callback_args['args']; // the 7th arg from add_
meta_box()
        $custom_fields = self::_get_custom_fields($content_type);
        $output = '';

        foreach ( $custom_fields as $field )
        {
            $output_this_field = '';
            switch ( $field['type'] )
            {
                case 'checkbox':
                    $output_this_field .= "<p>I'm a checkbox!</p>";
                    break;
```

```
                case 'dropdown':
                    $output_this_field .= "<p>I'm a dropdown!</p>";
                    break;
                case 'textarea':
                    $output_this_field .= "<p>I'm a textarea!</p>";
                    break;
                case 'wysiwyg':
                    $output_this_field .= "<p>I'm a WYSIWYG!</p>";
                    break;
                case 'text':
                default:
                    $output_this_field .= "<p>I'm a text input!</p>";
                    break;
            }
            // optionally add description
            if ( $field['description'] )
            {
                $output_this_field .= '<p>'.$field['description'].'</p>';
            }

            $output .= '<div class="form-field form-required">'.$output_
    this_field.'</div>';
        }
        // Print the form
        print '<div class="form-wrap">';
        print $output;
        print '</div>';

    }
```

There's some concatenation going on in there that ties into the recommended WordPress div's and styles, but hopefully nothing too "squirrelly". We now have a structured function to handle all the various input types. Please save your work, check for errors, and then refresh the WordPress **Dashboard**. You should see your message displayed where we intend to put the actual form elements:

Generating custom form elements

Here's where we have to dive into some form generation functions. Each type of form element requires slightly different behavior, a fact which unfortunately makes many PHP-generated forms sloppy. Our plan is to keep things clean by creating a private static function for each input type. They are all fairly simple, so we can add them quickly, but before we do that, we are going to add our simple parsing function that we've used in the previous chapters.

Add the parse function to `StandardizedCustomContent.php`:

```
/**
 * parse
 *
 * A simple parsing function for basic templating.
 *
 * @param $tpl    string    A formatting string containing
[+placeholders+]
 * @param $hash    array    An associative array containing keys and
values e.g. array('key' => 'value');
 * @return    string        Placeholders corresponding to the keys of
the hash will be replaced with the values the resulting string will be
returned.
 */
public static function parse($tpl, $hash) {
    foreach ($hash as $key => $value) {
        $tpl = str_replace('[+'.$key.'+]', $value, $tpl);
```

```
        }
        return $tpl;
    }
```

Now let's add five static functions that correspond to the five different input types we will support. Notice that the checkbox and the drop-down functions are the most complex, whereas the text input function is the simplest. Can you guess why the built-in WordPress custom fields only use text inputs?

Add these one at a time, then save your work and refresh your browser to check for errors after each function! Don't go too fast!

```
    //! Private
    /**
    * The following '_get_xxx_element' functions each generate a single
form element.
    * @param    array $data    contains an associative array describing
how the element
    *     should look with keys for name, title, description, and type.
    * @return    string    An HTML form element
    */
    /**
    * Note: the checked value is hard-coded to 'yes' for simplicity.
    */
    private static function _get_checkbox_element($data)
    {
        $tpl ='<input type="checkbox" name="[+name+]" id="[+name+]"
value="yes" [+is_checked+] style="width: auto;"/>
        <label for="[+name+]" style="display:inline;"><strong>[+tit
le+]</strong></label>';
        // Special handling to see if the box is checked.
        if ( $data['value'] == "yes" )
        {
            $data['is_checked'] = 'checked="checked"';
        }
        else
        {
            $data['is_checked'] = '';
        }
        return self::parse($tpl, $data);
    }

    /**
    * The dropdown is special: it requires that you supply an array of
options in its
    * 'options' key.
```

```
     * The $tpl used internally here uses a custom [+options+]
placeholder.
     */
    private static function _get_dropdown_element($data)
    {
        // Some error messaging.
        if ( !isset($data['options']) || !is_array($data['options']) )
        {
            return '<p><strong>Custom Content Error:</strong> No options
supplied for '.$data['name'].'</p>';
        }
        $tpl = '<label for="[+name+]"><strong>[+title+]</strong></
label><br/>
            <select name="[+name+]" id="[+name+]">
            [+options+]
            </select>';

        $option_str = '<option value="">Pick One</option>';
        foreach ( $data['options'] as $option )
        {
            $option = htmlspecialchars($option); // Filter the values
            $is_selected = '';
            if ( $data['value'] == $option )
            {
                $is_selected = 'selected="selected"';
            }
            $option_str .= '<option value="'.$option.'" '.$is_
selected.'>'.$option.'</option>';
        }

        unset($data['options']); // the parse function req's a simple
hash.
        $data['options'] = $option_str; // prep for parsing

        return self::parse($tpl, $data);

    }
    //----------------------------------------------------------------
    private static function _get_text_element($data)
    {
        $tpl = '<label for="[+name+]"><strong>[+title+]</strong></
label><br/>
            <input type="text" name="[+name+]" id="[+name+]"
value="[+value+]" /><br/>';
```

```
        return self::parse($tpl, $data);
    }

    //-------------------------------------------------------------
    private static function _get_textarea_element($data)
    {
        $tpl = '<label for="[+name+]"><strong>[+title+]</strong></
label><br/>
            <textarea name="[+name+]" id="[+name+]" columns="30"
rows="3">[+value+]</textarea>';
        return self::parse($tpl, $data);
    }

    //-------------------------------------------------------------
    private static function _get_wysiwyg_element($data)
    {
        $tpl = '<label for="[+name+]"><strong>[+title+]</strong></label>
            <textarea name="[+name+]" id="[+name+]" columns="30"
rows="3">[+value+]</textarea>
            <script type="text/javascript">
                jQuery( document ).ready( function() {
                    jQuery( "[+name+]" ).addClass( "mceEditor" );
                    if ( typeof( tinyMCE ) == "object" && typeof( tinyMCE.
execCommand ) == "function" ) {
                        tinyMCE.execCommand( "mceAddControl", false,
"[+name+]" );
                    }
                });
            </script>
            ';
        return self::parse($tpl, $data);
    }
```

Whew, that's a lot of busy work! Congratulations on working your way through it.

Next, let's add a static variable to `StandardizedCustomContent.php`. This is merely a preparation for printing the form elements:

```
    /**
     * This prefix helps ensure unique keys in the $_POST array by
appending
     * this prefix to your field names. E.g. if your prefix is 'my_' and
your
     * field name from the $custom_fields_for_posts array is 'field',
then
```

```
   * your form element gets generated something like <input name="my_
field"/>
   * and when submitted, its value would exist in $_POST['my_field']
   *
   * This prefix is *not* used as part of the meta_key when saving the
field
   * names to the database. If you want your fields to be
   * hidden from built-in WordPress theme functions, you can name them
individually
   * using an underscore "_" as the first character.
   *
   * If you omit a prefix entirely, your custom field names must steer
clear of
   * the built-in post field names (e.g. 'content').
   */
   public static $prefix = 'custom_content_';
```

Read the comments there; it's important to understand that we're taking the trouble here to avoid collisions in the $_POST array. You shouldn't need to change this value—we set it up as a class variable because many functions will access it.

Now that you have written functions that generate each type of form input, you can update the print_custom_fields() function once more so that it references these newly created functions. Like we did in a previous chapter, we are also going to add a nonce to the end of the form to make it more secure:

```
   public static function print_custom_fields($post, $callback_
args='') {
      $content_type = $callback_args['args']; // the 7th arg from add_
meta_box()
      $custom_fields = self::_get_custom_fields($content_type);
      $output = '';
      foreach ( $custom_fields as $field ) {

         $output_this_field = ''

         $field['value'] = htmlspecialchars( get_post_meta( $post->ID,
$field['name'], true ) );
         $field['name'] = self::$prefix . $field['name']; // this
ensures unique keys in $_POST

         switch ( $field['type'] )
         {
            case 'checkbox':
               $output_this_field .= self::_get_checkbox_
element($field);
               break;
            case 'dropdown':
```

```
                    $output_this_field .= self::_get_dropdown_
element($field);
                break;
            case 'textarea':
                $output_this_field .= self::_get_textarea_
element($field);
                break;
            case 'wysiwyg':
                $output_this_field .= self::_get_wysiwyg_
element($field);
                break;
            case 'text':
            default:
                $output_this_field .= self::_get_text_element($field);
                break;
        }
        // optionally add description
        if ( $field['description'] )
        {
            $output_this_field .= '<p>'.$field['description'].'</p>';
        }

        $output .= '<div class="form-field form-required">'.$output_
this_field.'</div>';
        }
        // Print the form
        print '<div class="form-wrap">';
        wp_nonce_field('update_custom_content_fields','custom_content_
fields_nonce');
        print $output;
        print '</div>';

    }
```

Please save your work, and then refer back to the post you previously edited. When you edit your post, you should see an example of each type of custom field type as pictured below:

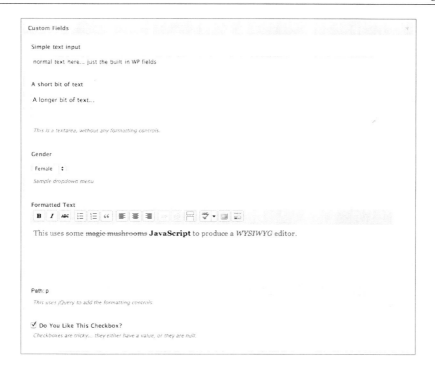

Now that we can generate each type of content, we need to handle the saving of that content.

Saving custom content

Knowing how to generate content for custom fields does us little good unless we can also save it. Remember, dealing with forms requires that you display the form, and that you handle the data after the form has been submitted. Update the `index.php` file to hook into a third action. When finished, the code in your `index.php` should read as follows:

```
include_once('includes/StandardizedCustomContent.php');

add_action( 'admin_menu', 'StandardizedCustomContent::create_meta_box' );
add_action( 'save_post', 'StandardizedCustomContent::save_custom_fields', 1, 2 );
add_action( 'do_meta_boxes', 'StandardizedCustomContent::remove_default_custom_fields', 10, 3 );
```

Next, add a public static function to `StandardizedCustomContent.php`. The name matches the function name we just referenced in the `index.php` file:

```
/**
 * Save the new Custom Fields values. This function reads from the
$_POST array
 * and stores data to the database using the update_post_meta()
function
 *
 * @param    integer $post_id    id of the post these custom fields
are associated with
 * @param    object    $post        The post object
 */
public static function save_custom_fields( $post_id, $post ) {

    // The 2nd arg here is important because there are multiple
nonces on the page
    if ( !empty($_POST) && check_admin_referer('update_custom_
content_fields','custom_content_fields_nonce') )
    {
        $custom_fields = self::_get_custom_fields($post->post_type);
        foreach ( $custom_fields as $field ) {
            if ( isset( $_POST[ self::$prefix . $field['name'] ] ) )
            {
                $value = trim($_POST[ self::$prefix . $field['name']
]);
                // Auto-paragraphs for any WYSIWYG
                if ( $field['type'] == 'wysiwyg' )
                {
                    $value = wpautop( $value );
                }
                update_post_meta( $post_id, $field[ 'name' ], $value );
            }
            // if not set, then it's an unchecked checkbox, so blank
out the value.
            else
            {
                update_post_meta( $post_id, $field[ 'name' ], '' );
            }
        }

    }
}
```

Remember that the arguments to the `check_admin_referer()` function must match exactly with the arguments used in the corresponding `wp_nonce_field()` function that we used back in the `print_custom_fields()` function. If you don't use this function correctly, you may get that strange error: **Are you sure you want to do this?**

Are you sure you want to do this?

Please try again.

If you are plagued by this type of warning, double check the spelling of your arguments to the `wp_nonce_field()` and `check_admin_referer()` functions. As we mentioned before in the chapter on widgets, there are other ways to validate nonces, so if you get stuck, see the official documentation (`http://codex.wordpress.org/ WordPress_Nonces`).

At this point, save your work, and then try adding some custom content to a post and saving it.

Is everything working as expected? Congratulations! You are now standardizing the custom fields for your posts. If you are feeling brave, you can try modifying the `$custom_fields_for_posts` variable to generate your own custom fields.

Having trouble saving data?

If the data vanishes from your custom fields after saving your post, there are a few things you should check. Have you correctly hooked into the `save_post` action in your `index.php` file and are you passing it the correct arguments? Without your customized save function, WordPress will ignore the data in your custom fields.

When editing your post with custom fields, view the source HTML. Search for your `$prefix` that you defined in your class. Are your form elements using this as part of the field names? You should see elements with names prefixed, for example:

```
<input type="text" name="custom_content_my_text" id="custom_content_
my_text" value="" />
```

Next, you should see what's coming through after the form is posted. At the top of your `save_custom_fields()` function, try printing the contents of the `$_POST` array:

```
print_r($_POST);
```

Be sure to add some values to your custom fields and then resubmit the form. WordPress and won't be happy about it, but you can see if your values are coming through.

```
Array
(
    [_wpnonce] => f7b02b18fa
```

```
            [_wp_http_referer] => /wp-admin/post.php?post=7&action=edit&messa
    ge=1
        [user_ID] => 1
        [action] => editpost
    // ...
        [custom_content_fields_nonce] => ac2d7cd5cb
        [custom_content_my_text] => asdf
        [custom_content_short_text] => asfd
        [custom_content_gender] =>
        [custom_content_formatted_text] => afds
    // ...
    )
```

That should help you isolate the problem.

Displaying custom data in your Templates

Thankfully, the hard part is over. You are now able to save custom content using various input types. Now we need to display this information to the users on the frontend. This process should give you a better understanding and an appreciation of how the data from the database is delivered to your site's theme. Third-party themes are developed differently, but if you can wrestle the default theme into submission, then you should be able to deal with others.

If you are using the default WordPress 3 theme, "Twenty Ten", then you may have noticed right away that your custom fields do not appear on your posts when you visit them on the frontend.

Post with Custom Fields

Posted on September 11, 2010 by everett

Post with custom fields yo... do you see them? Is this theme displaying them?

This entry was posted in Uncategorized. Bookmark the permalink. Edit

← Another Post of Mine

In order to fix this problem, let's make a copy of the theme so we can work on the copy without fear of damaging the original.

Copying a theme

As a plugin developer, you need to have some familiarity with how themes work. You should be familiar with some of the concepts that apply to themes, after having dealt with plugins.

Duplicate the `twentyten` folder and place a copy alongside the original in `wp-content/themes/`. We are naming our copied folder `twentyten_v2`.

Open up the `style.css` file inside of the `twentyten_v2` folder and modify the information head so you can distinguish between the two copies of this theme. Specifically, you must be sure to modify the name of the theme in order to distinguish it from the original in the Dashboard.

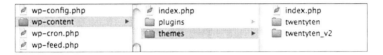

Just as with plugins, there is an information head that needs to be present in your WordPress theme in order for it to show up in the theme administration area. A WordPress theme stores this information inside its `style.css` file.

The following is what our modified information header looks like inside `style.css`:

```
/*
Theme Name: Twenty Ten v2
Theme URI: http://wordpress.org/
Description: Copy of the Twenty Ten theme with modifications to
display custom content.
Author: the WordPress team (mostly)
Version: 1.2
Tags: black, blue, white, two-columns, fixed-width, custom-header,
custom-background, threaded-comments, sticky-post, translation-ready,
microformats, rtl-language-support, editor-style
*/
```

Inside the WordPress Dashboard, head over to **Appearance | Themes**. You should see the new copy listed under **Available Themes**. Go ahead and activate it.

Now that we have safely copied and activated the theme, let's modify the copy.

Modifying the theme

There are a lot of PHP files inside of the theme's sub-folder, but the one we need to concern ourselves with first is `single.php`. As the good folks over at WordPress have commented, this is "the template for displaying all single posts".

After taking a look at `single.php`, we are obligated to pause again to restate our strong recommendation to keep PHP and HTML as separate as possible. In a perfect world, your templates would be devoid of logic and loops and the headaches that accompany them. However, our fantasy world has little to do with the reality of WordPress themes—they are almost always a sticky mixture of PHP and HTML that can easily devolve into chaos. You may be tired of our pretentious warnings against this type of coding, but it is our strong opinion that even though the status quo here is functional, it should not be earmarked for emulation.

Another warning here is regarding WordPress terminology: functions that are used inside theme files, such as `the_title()` or `the_content()`, are often referred to as "tags", even officially (`http://codex.wordpress.org/Template_Tags`). This is a confusing misnomer that would probably not be tolerated in other development circles. Those so called "tags" are in fact PHP functions: they execute, some of them may take arguments, and most of them return a value.

That's enough brow-beating. Let's get back to work and add a function that will print out the data from our custom fields. First, search for `the_content` in `single.php`. It should live somewhere around line 30.

Just after that, call the `the_meta()` function, like this:

```
<?php the_content(); ?>
<?php the_meta(); /* <----------- Custom Fields */ ?>
```

Save your work and then point your browser to the post on your site that uses custom fields. Remember, it must be the full page that displays the full post, not a page that summarizes all recent posts or an archive page.

Post with Custom Fields

Posted on September 15, 2010 by everett

Is this theme displaying my custom fields? I'm going to use **the_meta()** function in my theme's *single.php* file...

- my_text: My sample text input
- short_text: A little textarea never hurt no one...
- gender: Male
- formatted_text:
  Then I got *formatted...*

- my_checkbox: yes

This entry was posted in Uncategorized. Bookmark the permalink. Edit

Congratulations! You have successfully displayed your post's custom fields! If you look at the source HTML, you will notice that WordPress created an unordered list, and each custom field appeared as a list item using the following format:

```
<ul class='post-meta'>
    <li><span class='post-meta-key'>name_of_my_field:</span> Value
of my field</li>
    <!-- [... more fields here...] -->
</ul>
```

Remember, `the_meta()` is a simple formatting shortcut that will only print meta data with names that do not begin with an underscore ("_"). If your field names start with an underscore, `the_meta()` function will skip them. Likewise, the Dashboard will ignore field names starting with an underscore because it will consider them "private". Remember how we named private functions inside of our classes? This is exactly the same naming convention.

Using `the_meta()` function is a viable solution for some people, but what if you want more control? What if you need one custom field to appear at the top of your page and the other at the bottom? That requires a bit more work and help from WordPress' `get_post_meta()` function.

Granular display of custom fields

Before we show you how to extract a post's custom fields into separate places in your theme, make sure you have added a couple of custom fields to one of your posts for the purpose of demonstrating this. For our example, we are using the form fields that we built out previously in the chapter: `my_text`, `short_text`, `gender`, `formatted_text`, and `my_checkbox`. Let's write a simple function that retrieves each field individually.

Inside your theme folder, open up the `functions.php` file. This is where the theme typically stores functions that are used to control its behavior. In this book, we have generally strived to create plugins that are "theme agnostic", that is plugins that will work regardless of which theme is currently in use, so we have avoided placing functions inside theme files. However, this is an occasion where our philosophy breaks down out of necessity. We will explain ourselves momentarily, but for now, paste in the following function:

```
/**
 * Prints the 1st instance of the meta_key identified by $fieldname
 * associated with the current post. See get_post_meta() for more
 details.
 *
 * @param string    $fieldname    Name of custom field from the wp_
 postmeta table.
 * @return none   No value returned; this function prints the value of
 the first field
 *    named $fieldname associated with the current post.
```

```
*/
    function print_custom_field($fieldname)
    {
        // the_ID() function won't work because it *prints* its output
        $post_id = get_the_ID();
        print get_post_meta($post_id, $fieldname, true);
    }
```

Note that we are printing directly from this function instead of returning a value. This is a fairly simplistic way to do this. Take a look at the official documentation for the get_post_meta() function if you want more details (http://goo.gl/m3G0).

Next, edit the single.php page so that it calls the newly created print_custom_field() function. We are going to print a couple of custom values in different places on our page. The following is the relevant part of the updated single.php:

```
<div class="entry-content">

    <p><strong>Simple Text Input:</strong> <?php print_custom_
field('my_text'); ?></p>

    <?php the_content(); ?>

    <p><strong>Gender:</strong> <?php print_custom_field('gender');
?></p>
```

We could also add calls for printing the other custom fields — all we need to pass to the function is the name of the field.

So why did we put the print_custom_field() function inside of our theme instead of inside a plugin? Arguably, because it belongs there. This function prints data into a specific location in an HTML layout. It was designed as a slave to the template. The final resting place for the output of this function is always going to be inside one of the HTML template files — this is where the rubber meets the road. The relationship between the theme and the print_custom_field() function may be subtle, but it is intimate, so it makes sense to store the function along with the theme. This is not uncommon in other CMS's. For example, MODx goes as far as to name these custom fields "Template Variables" in an attempt to emphasize this relationship.

Now that we have extended our post's custom fields in a standardized fashion and we've figured out a way to print these values into our theme, you may want to update your theme files to make the most of these customized values. Your page layouts can now include specific HTML and CSS for each custom field, and this allows for some serious flexibility in your themes.

Bonus for the MySQL curious

We haven't looked under the hood to see how WordPress is actually storing this meta data. The post itself is stored in the `wp_posts` table. Using your MySQL client, you can have a look at the structure of the `wp_posts` table by using the "describe" function. If you are using a GUI tool such as phpMyAdmin, you can usually click on the table name to see its structure. On the MySQL command line, you'd execute the following command:

```
mysql> describe wp_posts;
```

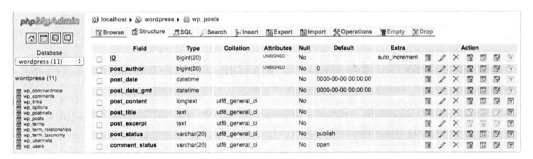

You can look through the list of columns and you can see where your post data is stored: `post_title`, `post_content`, `post_excerpt`, and so on. The problem faced when adding custom fields is that we run out of columns. It's rare that an application changes the column structure of a database table, and WordPress is no exception. In order to store the custom fields, WordPress instead writes rows of data to the `wp_postmeta` table. Essentially, that table stores simple key:value pairs and it associates them back to the parent post.

Have a look at the metadata for one of the posts we created in this chapter. In our database, the `post_id` happened to be 92. The following is the command and the output from the MySQL command line:

```
mysql> select * from wp_postmeta where post_id='92';

+---------+---------+-----------------+------------------------------------+
| meta_id | post_id | meta_key        | meta_value                         |
+---------+---------+-----------------+------------------------------------+
|     136 |      92 | _edit_last      | 1                                  |
|     137 |      92 | my_text         | My sample text input               |
|     138 |      92 | short_text      | A little textarea never hurt no one.. |
|     139 |      92 | gender          | Male                               |
|     140 |      92 | formatted_text  | <p>Then I got <em>formatted</em>..</p> |
|     141 |      92 | my_checkbox     | yes                                |
|     144 |      92 | _wp_old_slug    |                                    |
|     145 |      92 | _edit_lock      | 1284569248                         |
+---------+---------+-----------------+------------------------------------+

8 rows in set (0.25 sec)
```

You can see our custom field names and values in there, and you can see that WordPress is using this table to store some additional information about the post. Those are hidden values, whose names begin with an underscore.

The `meta_id` is this table's "primary key". Each row in this table gets a unique `meta_id`, which uniquely identifies that row. The `post_id` is a "foreign key". That means it references the primary key from another table. In this case, it is referencing the primary key in the `wp_posts` table. The `wp_posts` table simply names its primary key, "ID"; it would have been clearer if it had been named `post_id`, but it is a common naming convention to name your primary key simply "id" or "ID".

Known limitations

Even though the solution presented in this chapter offers some nice possibilities, it is incomplete. For one, our custom field definitions rely on configurations in our plugin files, so they are not accessible to the average user. We did not build out an options page in the Dashboard—we showed you how to do that in the previous chapter, so if you want to add a manager page for updating this plugin's options, please review the previous chapter and give it a try. Check the plugin's page on `www.tipsfor.us` if you want to see some more discussion on this plugin or how to design a manager page for it. As it is right now, you have to define your custom fields in code.

If you look a bit harder, there are a few other limitations here. Form generation is really its own level of hell, and it's difficult to capture all the myriad edge cases that arise. We've been there and done that, and we sneakily side-stepped some of the pitfalls in our presentation. For example, what if you wanted your checkbox to be checked by default? Alternatively, what if your text input needed to have a default value? Ah, tricky....

We also avoided the checking of permissions; instead we relegated that responsibility to WordPress. Effectively, we assumed that if the user could edit the post, then they should be allowed to edit the custom fields. A more thorough solution would use WordPress' `current_user_can()` function to check permission on a per-field level.

There are other limitations here, but this should serve as a good introduction to custom content, and it offers a nice segue into the next chapter that deals with custom post-types.

Summary

We have taken an important step in realizing WordPress' potential as a content management system. We are now able to standardize custom fields on our posts, and we're able to use a handful of different input types to simplify the job of administering them. Next we will talk about custom post-types, where we take the idea of customizations even further.

7
Custom Post Types

This chapter ties together several of the core concepts from previous chapters, while investigating WordPress' capabilities as a CMS. It also covers a few extra tricks, including shortcodes, creating a link to your plugin's settings page, and how to clean up when someone uninstalls your plugin.

The task before us is to tap into WordPress' CMS abilities by using the `register_post_type()` function. Judging by the difficulties tracked in the SVN repository as WordPress 3.1 got ready for launch, it seems that we weren't the only ones who experienced difficulties in wrestling with WordPress' CMS capabilities.

A word of warning: this function is difficult to use and lacks good documentation, and exploring its full capabilities is beyond the scope of this chapter. If you want to examine a fuller implementation of custom post types and what they can do, have a look at one of our plugins (`http://goo.gl/cgJDU`) — this is the plugin we wrote for early drafts of this chapter, but the code quickly grew too complex for educational purposes. Our aim here is to demonstrate one use case of the `register_post_type()` function, so you can see how it works. We want a plugin that allows users to create their own reusable chunks of content that we can reference in other posts via WordPress shortcodes, denoted by square brackets, for example, `[example-shortcode]`. This is a great way to reuse content across many posts or pages.

For example, you could create chunks containing your signature information, or a link to the latest travel deals.

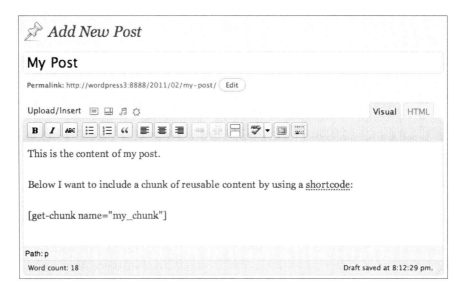

The preceding screenshot is what we're aiming for. We have a lot of ground to cover, so let's get started.

Background: What's in a name?

Out of the box, WordPress offers several primary types of content: *posts*, *pages*, and *attachments*. WordPress refers to all of these as "post types". Why is a page a type of post? Well, our best guess is that the naming convention stems from the fact that *posts*, *pages*, and *attachments* are all stored in the wp_posts table in the database. Examine the contents of that table by issuing the following query in your MySQL client:

```
SELECT * FROM wp_posts;
```

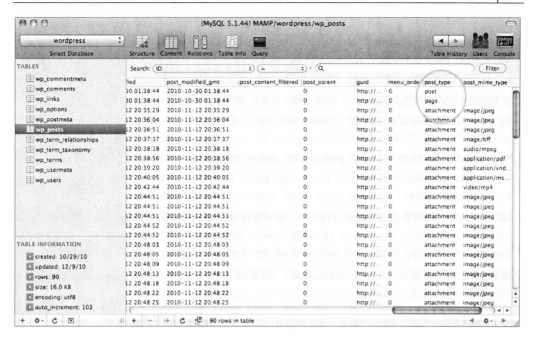

The contents of the post_type column will tell you the type of any given "post". Whether it is a post, a page, or an attachment, the data is stored in the wp_posts table and it all has the same attributes (that is columns). Perhaps a more descriptive name for this table would have been wp_content, but for the sake of uniformity, we will defer to WordPress' naming conventions as much as possible.

You may have even spotted a few other post types in your database, such as "revision", but don't worry about them too much for now. In this chapter, we are primarily concerned with post-types that represent *text content*.

Understanding register_post_type()

WordPress uses built-in post types for normal everyday use, but you can extend the list of available post types by using a pivotal function: register_post_type(). It is this function that allows WordPress to fulfill more traditional CMS roles. For example, you could create a custom post type for "movies" with custom fields for "plot", "genre" and "rating". The important thing to realize is that any custom post types will be visible to WordPress only if you register them using the register_post_type() function, and as you may have guessed, the only way for you to do that is inside a plugin.

To really understand what this complex function does, we really need to get our hands dirty and try using it ourselves. You guessed it, it's time for you to create another plugin.

We are naming this plugin "Content Chunks", so our first step is to create a folder named `content-chunks` in the `wp-content/plugins` folder, and then create our `index.php` with a valid information header.

```php
<?php
/*
Plugin Name: Content Chunks
Plugin URI: http://tipsfor.us/
Description: Display Chunks of Content from a custom post type "chunk"
Author: Everett Griffiths
Version: 0.1
Author URI: http://tipsfor.us
*/

include_once('includes/ContentChunks.php');
add_action( 'init', 'ContentChunks::register_chunk_post_type');

/*EOF*/
```

You can see we have already added the action we intend to use, so the next step should be no surprise; create an `includes` folder, and in it create a file named `ContentChunks.php`:

```php
<?php
/**
 * ContentChunks
 *
 */
class ContentChunks {

    /**
     *
     */
    public static function register_chunk_post_type()
    {
        register_post_type( 'chunk',
            array(
                'label' => '0. Chunks',
                'labels' => array(
                    'add_new'          => '1. Add New',
                    'add_new_item'     => '2. Add New Chunk',
                    'edit_item'        => '3. Edit Chunk',
                    'new_item'         => '4. New Chunk',
                    'view_item'        => '5. View Chunk',
                    'search_items'     => '6. Search Chunks',
                    'not_found'        => '7. No chunks Found',
                    'not_found_in_trash'=> '8. Not Found in Trash',
```

```
                        'parent_item_colon'    => '9. Parent Chunk Colon',  /*
        ??? */
                        'menu_name'            => '10. Chunks',   /* ??? */
                    ),
                'description' => 'Reusable chunks of content',
                'public' => true,
                'publicly_queryable' => true,
                // 'exclude_from_search' => false,  /* optional */
                'show_ui' => true,
                'show_in_menu'   => true,
                'menu_position' => 5,
                //'menu_icon'    => '', /* optional string */
                'capability_type' => 'post',
                //'capabilities' => array(), /* optional */
                //'map_meta_cap' => false, /* optional */
                'hierarchical' => true,
                'supports' => array('title','editor','author','thumbnail'
        ,'excerpt','trackbacks','custom-fields','comments','revisions','page-
        attributes'),
                'register_meta_box_cb' => '', /* optional callback */
                // 'taxonomies' => array('category'), /* optional */
                // 'permalink_epmask' => EP_PERMALINK, /* optional */
                // 'has_archive' => false,
                'rewrite' => false, /* optional - can be an array */
                'query_var' => false, /* boolean or string */
                'can_export' => false,
                'show_in_nav_menus' => true,

            )
        );
    }
}
/*EOF*/
```

As always, we begin by mocking things up so that we have a functional outline to test. Save your files and then refresh your browser while logged into the Dashboard and correct any typos in your code. Here we will give you all possible parameters to the `register_post_type()` function, even the optional ones.

We have to pause to remind you not to write functions like this. It has a ridiculous number of inputs that are very difficult to keep straight. To make matters worse, the official documentation at present is rather poor (http://goo.gl/LtE3). Our final gripe is that the data types of many input options are inconsistent. It should be a red flag if your functions have inputs like "boolean *or* string"—that usually is an indication of a poorly architected function. At a minimum, such functions are more demanding on you (the developer) because you have to sanitize the input parameters. We get the feeling that this function is half-baked, and we are hoping that future versions of WordPress will include a better implementation, or at least more-thorough documentation. In our opinion, this function should have been broken down into several more manageable object methods, but WordPress tends to favor the all-in-one approach, and in this case, it seems to have been the wrong approach.

Congratulations for making it through all of that—you should now have your very own custom post type. If you were successful, once you activate your plugin, you should see **Chunks** listed in the left-hand administration menu alongside the other post types.

One of the most confusing areas of the register_post_type() function is the labels. These labels are part of an optional parameter, but it makes for a nicer user experience if you take the time to provide them. We have numbered our parameters in our code to help demonstrate where each label will appear.

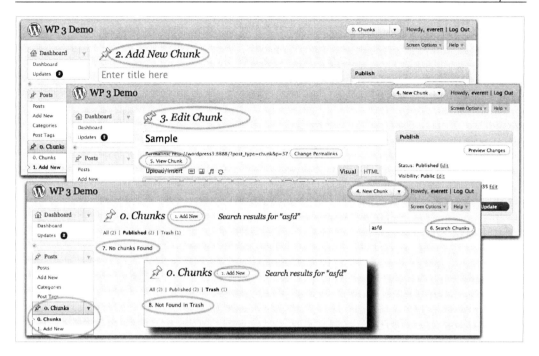

We could not locate the `parent_item_colon` or the `menu_name` labels.

We encourage you to play around with the `$supports` array and watch how each setting affects the manager. Try creating a new Chunk and look at all the different parts of the editing page. Almost every component of the editor can be changed by the `$supports` array.

We have outlined the components here as a reference:

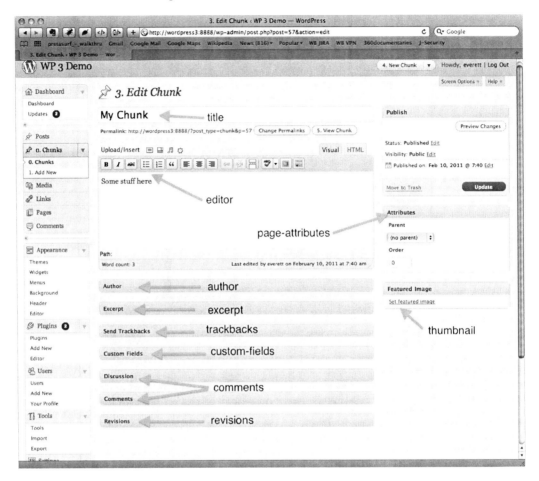

Note that the thumbnail image option requires that you enable thumbnail support for each content type by including the `add_theme_support()` function. Typically this function appears in the active theme's `functions.php` file, but you can put it immediately after the `register_post_type()` function in the `ContentChunks.php` file, just so you see how it works:

```
add_theme_support( 'post-thumbnails', array('chunk') );
```

Without that line, the "Featured Image" meta box would not be visible.

The thing you might not realize when looking at these options is that several of them are interconnected in unforeseen ways, and unless you are extremely patient, it is difficult to figure out how to use all of them. It's no accident that there are practically no tutorials out there for how to accomplish certain tasks related to custom post types. The reality is that the documentation is lacking or absent, and figuring out how to accomplish some of the tasks is beyond the average developer. Again, if you want to see this in a fuller implementation, take a look at our Custom Content Type Manager plugin (`http://goo.gl/cgJDU`); it doesn't qualify as "easy to understand", but it can help you get a sense of what custom post types can do.

Now that we know how to control the appearance of the manager by altering the inputs to the `register_post_type()` function, let's configure them so our new "chunk" post type will have the attributes we want.

Customizing our post type

Remember that our intent is to create reusable chunks of content, so we don't need all the bells and whistles that are available to us. Let's scale this down to something simple that meets our needs. Here is our simplified `register_chunk_post_type()` function:

```
public static function register_chunk_post_type()
{
    register_post_type( 'chunk',
        array(
            'label' => 'Chunks',
            'labels' => array(
                'add_new'           => 'Add New',
                'add_new_item'      => 'Add New Chunk',
                'edit_item'         => 'Edit Chunk',
                'new_item'          => 'New Chunk',
                'view_item'         => 'View Chunk',
                'search_items'      => 'Search Chunks',
                'not_found'         => 'No chunks Found',
                'not_found_in_trash'=> 'Not Found in Trash',
            ),
            'description' => 'Reusable chunks of content',
            'public' => false,
            'show_ui' => true,
            'menu_position' => 5,
            'supports' => array('title','editor'),
        )
    );
}
```

The `show_ui` option refers to the WordPress Dashboard, and this will be set to `true` nearly all the time. It is difficult to imagine how you might use a post type that is not visible in the Dashboard.

The `public` option affects whether or not a public visitor could view a chunk. Another way to think about it is whether or not you need a URL associated with this bit of content. If our post type was `movies` or `store_locations` where we envisioned a page on our website that would house information about that movie or store, then `public` would have to be true. However, we don't want that behavior—we instead want to keep the chunks visible only in the Dashboard, and then we can access them via shortcodes in our existing posts and pages.

 Remember that if the `public` option is set to `false`, you won't be able to preview your post, so the preview links will generate a 404 page.

When you're all done, the Dashboard page should simply have fields for the title and for the main content. That's all we need. Create a few sample chunks before continuing.

Using shortcodes

Shortcodes were introduced to WordPress in version 2.5 and they offer a simple way of adding macros to a post's content. You may have already seen them used by other plugins. For example, the Viper's Video Quicktag plugin (`http://goo.gl/ofe0K`) is a great plugin that adds videos to your posts via shortcodes that look like the following:

```
[youtube]http://www.youtube.com/watch?v=stdJd598Dtg[/youtube]
```

Given this shortcode macro, the plugin renders the appropriate embed code so the YouTube video is included inside your post without you having to write the necessary HTML.

We are going to do something similar. We want a macro that lets us specify the name of a chunk by its title, like the following:

```
[get-chunk title="my_title"]
```

In order to make this work, we need to do two things: we need to register the shortcode's name so WordPress is aware of it, and secondly we need to write the function that will handle the retrieval of the chunk.

To start, we use WordPress' `add_shortcode()` function, and the syntax is fairly similar to the now familiar `add_action()` and `add_filter()` functions:

```
add_shortcode('name-of-shortcode', 'your_callback_function');
```

We are going to register our shortcode in a separate function, so create the following function inside of `ContentChunks.php`:

```
/**
 * Register the shortcodes used
 */
public static function register_shortcodes()
{
    add_shortcode('get-chunk', 'ContentChunks::get_chunk');
}
```

This function basically says that if a shortcode named `[get-chunk]` is found in a post's content, then you have to call the `ContentChunks::get_chunk()` function. In a moment we will show you how the shortcode's parameters are passed.

In order to execute our `register_shortcodes()` function we are going to tie it to a WordPress action, so add another `add_action()` to your `index.php` so it looks like the following:

```
include_once('includes/ContentChunks.php');

add_action( 'init', 'ContentChunks::register_chunk_post_type');
add_action( 'init', 'ContentChunks::register_shortcodes');
```

At this point, we are registering the shortcode, but we don't yet have a valid callback function—ContentChunks::get_chunk() doesn't exist yet. Let's create that callback function now. Add the following to ContentChunks.php:

```
/**
 * Returns the content of a chunk, referenced via shortcode, e.g.
put the
 * following in the content of a post or page:
 *    [get-chunk title="my_title"]
 *
 * See http://codex.wordpress.org/Function_Reference/get_page_by_
title
 *
 * @param    array   $raw_args   Any arguments included in the
shortcode.
 *                          E.g. [get-chunk x="1" y="2"] translates to
array('x'=>'1','y'=>'2')
 * @param    string  $content   Optional content if the shortcode
encloses content with a closing tag,
 *                          e.g. [get-chunk]My content here[/get-
chunk]
 * @return    string   The text that should replace the shortcode.
 */
public static function get_chunk($raw_args, $content=null)
{
   $defaults = array(
      'title' => '',
   );

   $sanitized_args = shortcode_atts( $defaults, $raw_args );

   if ( empty($sanitized_args['title']) )
   {
      return '';
   }

   $result = get_page_by_title( $sanitized_args['title'], 'OBJECT',
'chunk' );

   if ( $result )
   {
      return $result->post_content;
   }
}
```

Pay attention to the input parameters of the callback function—they were described in the function's documentation. So let's look at this shortcode.

```
[get-chunk x="1" y="2"]Some content here[/get-chunk]
```

It would produce the following `$raw_args`:

```
Array ( [x] => 1, [y] => 2 )
```

If in doubt, try using `print_r()` to print the contents of the incoming parameters. The second parameter, `$content`, is optional, but you will use it if your shortcode uses the full opening and closing tags. Anything found between the opening and closing tags will be passed to this second `$content` parameter, or "Some content here" in our example.

> Be careful when using the full opening and closing tags. In our experience, the `$content` was not correctly passed unless the closing tag followed the content immediately—putting it on a new line caused the input to fail. Another thing to be aware of is that shortcodes are only parsed when they appear inside a post's main content block. They are not parsed if you try to use them inside any other field.

WordPress has dedicated a function to help you sanitize the inputs to your shortcode functions: `shortcode_atts()`. Without this function, you'd find yourself writing the same type of code to clean up the inputs over and over again. Basically, to use the `shortcode_atts()` function, you define the values that you want to "listen" for and provide some default values, and then WordPress will do the rest. Have a look at the official documentation if you need some more information: `http://goo.gl/xCnZE`.

WordPress has several functions devoted to retrieving posts, and we landed on one that can retrieve a post by its title: `get_page_by_title()`. That's the final function we need to make this whole thing work. See the function reference for more information: `http://goo.gl/tcflU`.

> The WordPress API is a bit bewildering when it comes to retrieving posts. There is the `get_posts()` function, the `get_post()` function (to retrieve a single post by its ID), the `query_posts()` function, and the `WP_Query` object, all of which give you some control over which posts you want to retrieve. Unfortunately each of these has limitations, and most of them require different syntaxes. The quality of the documentation for these functions is as varied as the functions themselves, so take a deep breath if you need to use one these in your plugins.

We have added a couple of checks here to handle the possibility that no chunk of the specified title was found. We should also point out that if two or more chunks share the same title, the first one will be returned. "First" in this case means the one with the smallest ID (that is first in the database).

Testing our shortcode

Now that we have put together all the parts, let's test this out. Make sure you have a few chunks created. Inside a new or existing post, try using the shortcode that references one of your chunks by its title. Remember, we are adding the shortcode to an ordinary post, under the **Posts** menu. The limitation here is that you have to remember the title of your chunks in order to use them, so keep your titles simple.

You can see that only the shortcode in the post's content was parsed; the shortcode in the post's title was ignored.

Congratulations, if you got this all working! You now have a good way of reusing content. If you are experiencing problems, double-check the spelling of your shortcode and make sure it matches the name used in the add_shortcode() function.

Customizing our plugin

Now that we have the basic functionality in place, you might realize that the success of this plugin depends on the uniqueness of your shortcode. If another plugin happened to use the same name for their shortcode, your plugin could break. It's not a likely scenario, but it's one we're going to address by creating an administration page to let the users control the name of the shortcode.

We've created a manager page before, but let's review the process now. In order to have a manager page for this plugin, we need three things: a function that defines the menu item, a function that generates the page when that menu item is clicked, and finally an `add_action()` hook to ensure that the other two functions are executed.

Let's begin by creating the function that will add the menu item. We are going to do something new here by demonstrating how you can create a dedicated menu item. It's not at all necessary for this plugin, but we wanted to show you how to do it. Add the following function to your `ContentChunks.php` file:

```php
// Used to uniquely identify this plugin's menu page in the WP manager
const admin_menu_slug = 'content_chunks';

/**
* Create custom post-type menu
*/
public static function create_admin_menu()
 {
    add_menu_page(
        'Content Chunks',                  // page title
        'Content Chunks',                  // menu title
        'manage_options',                  // capability
        self::admin_menu_slug,             // menu slug
        'ContentChunks::get_admin_page' // callback
    );
}
```

Using the `add_menu_page()` function instead of the `add_options_page()` allows us to create a dedicated menu item, although the options are quite similar. We have omitted the last two options; see the official documentation if you want to try your hand at including a custom icon and a custom location in the menu tree: `http://goo.gl/OZ8CW`.

We are making use of a class constant here, named `admin_menu_slug`. Note that you reference it without the use of a dollar sign, for example, `self::admin_menu_slug`. This is similar to how you reference normal PHP constants. We are using a constant here because this is a value that should not ever change during runtime. Just to be pedantic, if you needed to reference this value from somewhere outside of the `ContentChunks` class, you would have to use the fully qualified name, for example:

```
print ContentChunks::admin_menu_slug;
```

> Inside of a class you can retrieve static class variables and constants using the self keyword, but outside the class, you need to specify the full class name. In code, this is analogous to when we use the `self::` or $this-> constructs. We can use them inside the class, but outside the class, we must be more verbose.
>
> Imagine being in a hotel and calling for room service. It would be exceedingly odd if you told the receptionist the name of the hotel in addition to your room number: the receptionist already knows that you are staying in this hotel. On the other hand, if you called for pizza delivery, you would have to include the hotel name — you couldn't just tell them your room number and expect them to find you.

You may have noticed that we've already defined a callback function, `ContentChunks::get_admin_page()`, so let's create that next. Add the following function to your `ContentChunks.php` file:

```
/**
 * Prints the administration page for this plugin.
 */
public static function get_admin_page()
{
    print 'testing...';
}
```

We will add something more substantial to this function once we have verified that it works, but for now, we want something simple we can test.

Finally, you need to add an action to make this code execute. In your `index.php` file, add the following action:

```
add_action('admin_menu', 'ContentChunks::create_admin_menu');
```

Save your work and try refreshing the manager. You should see this menu item appear in the menu hierarchy on the left-hand side of the WordPress Dashboard.

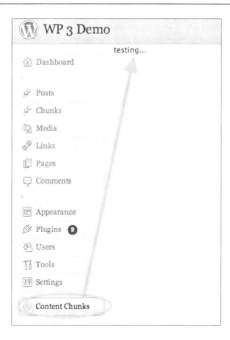

Once you have verified that this is working, let's customize the manager page by creating a form that will allow users to change the name of the shortcode. It's a simple form with only one input, so we can follow the example from the previous chapter on widgets. Create a file named admin_page.php, and save it inside your includes folder. The following is what our admin_page.php looks like:

```
<div class="wrap">
    <?php screen_icon(); ?>
    <h2>Content Chunks Administration</h2>

    <?php print $msg; ?>

    <form action="" method="post" id="content_chunks_form">
        <h3><label for="shortcode_name">Shortcode Name</label></h3>
        <p>Define the shortcode that will be used to trigger the
retrieval of a Chunk, e.g. [get-chunk title="My Title"]<br/>
        <input type="text" id="shortcode_name" name="shortcode_name"
value="<?php print $shortcode_name ?>" /></p>

        <p class="submit"><input type="submit" name="submit"
value="Update" /></p>
        <?php wp_nonce_field('content_chunks_options_update','content_
chunks_admin_nonce'); ?>

    </form>
</div>
```

We are again using the built-in WordPress `screen_icon()` function to give our page a default icon, and once again, we are wrapping our form with `<div class="wrap">` so we can take advantage of WordPress' styling.

Now that we have a viable form, we need to use it. Update the `get_admin_page()` function inside the `ContentChunks.php` file so it includes and processes the form:

```
public static function get_admin_page()
{
    if ( !empty($_POST) && check_admin_referer('content_chunks_
options_update','content_chunks_admin_nonce') )
    {
        update_option( self::option_key,
            stripslashes($_POST['shortcode_name']) );
        $msg = '<div class="updated"><p>Your settings have been
<strong>updated</strong></p></div>';
    }
    $shortcode_name = esc_attr( get_option(self::option_key,
self::default_shortcode_name) );
    include('admin_page.php');
}
```

As before, we use the `check_admin_referer()` to check whether we need to process the form or simply display it. Notice that the path to the `admin_page.php` file is relative to the `ContentChunks.php` file, so as long as `admin_page.php` is in the same directory, no further path information is required.

At the top of the `ContentChunks.php` file, add the following two class constants:

```
const default_shortcode_name = 'get-chunk';
const option_key = 'content_chunks_shortcode';
```

We need these values to define the default value of chunk, and to define the name of the option key we will use in the `wp_options` table when we store our plugin's settings. Both of these constants are used when we invoke WordPress' `get_option()` function, just as we did in the chapter on widgets. As a reminder, this function either retrieves the option requested or it returns the default value.

Save your work and verify that you can edit the value.

Remember that it is vital that your inputs to the `admin_referer()` function *exactly* match the inputs you passed to the `wp_nonce_field()` function, otherwise you won't be able to correctly submit your form.

The only thing we need to do now is update our `register_shortcodes()` function so it uses the dynamic value from the database instead of the one we hardcoded. Update the function so it looks like the following:

```
public static function register_shortcodes()
{
    $shortcode = get_option(self::option_key, self::default_
shortcode_name);
    add_shortcode($shortcode, 'ContentChunks::get_chunk');
}
```

To test this, try saving a new value for the shortcode name on the administration page, then verify whether posts using this shortcode behave as expected. For example, if you change the shortcode name to "chunk" instead of "get-chunk", your shortcode must reflect that change: `[chunk title="testing"]`.

Congratulations! You now have a dynamic plugin that can be configured, and you have more experience under your belt when it comes to creating administration forms. Let's demonstrate another trick that's useful for creating a good user experience.

Creating a settings shortcut link

One of the problems encountered by users is that a plugin's settings may be difficult to locate. It's not immediately clear if a new menu item has been added when a user first activates a plugin. That's the problem we are going to solve by adding a **Settings** link that takes us to our plugin's administration page.

How did we do that? Well, it turns out that the information for each plugin is printed via a process that we can modify using a WordPress filter. The name of one of these secret filter hooks is `plugin_action_links`. How did we know that? Thanks to the nature of open-source code, we saw it used in Viper's Video Quicktag plugin, and then we looked through his code to figure out how Mr. Viper007Bond pulled this off. We could use that same filter here, but the thing to remember is that this filter is called for each plugin listed, so if we used that filter, we would have to check to ensure that we were filtering the data for our plugin, and not another plugin, otherwise we would end up modifying the links for some other plugin. We want the **Settings** link to appear under our plugin, not under the "Hello Dolly" plugin.

Let's demonstrate one option for tackling this. First, add the filter to your `index.php` file:

```
add_filter('plugin_action_links', 'ContentChunks::add_plugin_settings_
link', 10, 2 );
```

This is one of the few times when we need to pass additional parameters to the `add_filter()` function: the `10` is merely a default value for `$priority`, but pay attention to the fourth argument, which specifies that two arguments will be passed to the callback function. This is something that's simply inherent with this particular event, and the only way to learn that is to see examples like this one or to browse the WordPress source code.

Now, we must add the callback function to `ContentChunks.php`:

```
    /**
     * The inputs here come directly from WordPress:
     * @param   array    $links - a hash in theformat of name =>
    translation e.g.
     *        array('deactivate' => 'Deactivate') that describes all links
    available to a plugin.
     * @param   string   $file   - the path to plugin's main file (the
    one with the info header),
     *        relative to the plugins directory, e.g. 'content-chunks/
    index.php'
     * @return   array    The $links hash.
     */
    public static function add_plugin_settings_link($links, $file)
    {
        if ( $file == 'content-chunks/index.php' )
        {
            $settings_link = sprintf('<a href="%s">%s</a>'
                , admin_url( 'options-general.php?page='.self::admin_menu_
    slug )
                , 'Settings'
            );
            array_unshift( $links, $settings_link );
        }

        return $links;
    }
```

The incoming `$file` parameter contains the name of each plugin's main file (the one containing the information header). Remember that the file name is relative to the `wp-content/plugins/` directory, so you can see how we tested it. Alternatively, we could have dynamically determined the name of our plugin's folder using some combination of `basename()`, `dirname()`, and the `__FILE__` constant.

We know the URL for this plugin's settings page, so we use PHP's `array_unshift()` function to put this link first in the `$links` array, and then we return the result.

Save your work, then try refreshing the WordPress Dashboard and viewing the Plugins administration area. You should see a new **Settings** link that takes you directly to the administration page we created in the previous section. Very nice.

There is another filter hook we could have used, and we had to poke around in the WordPress source code to find it. If you search through the codebase for where `plugin_action_links` appears, you will find it in the `wp-admin/plugins.php` file, called by the `apply_filters()` function. Only by examining the source code did we realize that each plugin's action links has its own filter event, corresponding to the name of the plugin's main file. Following is the alternative filter event that you can use in your `index.php` file:

```
add_filter('plugin_action_links_content-chunks/index.php',
'ContentChunks::add_plugin_settings_link', 10, 2 );
```

In other words, we prefix `plugin_action_links_` to the name of the plugin's main file, relative to the `wp-content/plugins/` directory. The resulting filter name is a bit unexpected, but it is legitimate. Now that you have a filter event that is dedicated to your plugin, you no longer need to check the plugin file name in the callback function. If you use the `plugin_action_links_content-chunks/index.php` filter, update your `add_plugin_settings_link()` function so it omits the if-statement:

```
public static function add_plugin_settings_link($links, $file)
{
    $settings_link = sprintf('<a href="%s">%s</a>'
        , admin_url( 'options-general.php?page='.self::admin_menu_
slug )
        , 'Settings'
    );
    array_unshift( $links, $settings_link );
    return $links;
}
```

The results for using this filter should be exactly the same as using the more general `plugin_action_links` one.

Congratulations again! You now have in your arsenal a way to enhance the user experience for anyone using your plugin. The only thing left to do in this chapter is to show you how to clean up if someone "uninstalls" your plugin.

Cleaning up when uninstalling

It could happen to any developer: a user decides to uninstall your plugin. It's a scenario that you should prepare for, especially if your plugin performs any database modifications. You should consider it a bit rude if your plugin makes custom modifications to the database or file system and does not clean up its mess when asked to leave. Cleaning up is just being considerate. Unfortunately, many plugin authors fail to do this, and who can blame them when the process is so poorly documented? Let's show you how to do this relatively simple task.

When you choose to delete a plugin, WordPress will look for a special file, named uninstall.php, located at the root of your plugin's directory. In it, you can place all the code necessary to clean up whatever modifications you made. However, you must also consider the insidious possibility that a nefarious user navigates directly to this file, for example, by visiting http://yoursite.com/wp-content/plugins/your-plugin/uninstall.php.

WordPress has a solution for this potential pitfall, it defines a special constant named WP_UNINSTALL_PLUGIN, and you can check whether or not it is defined before proceeding with your cleanup.

Let's demonstrate a simple uninstall script for your plugin. Create the uninstall.php file and add the following text to it:

```php
<?php
/**
 * This is run only when this plugin is uninstalled. All cleanup code
goes here.
 *
 * WARNING: uninstalling a plugin fails when developing locally via
MAMP or WAMP.
 */
if ( defined('WP_UNINSTALL_PLUGIN'))
{
    include_once('includes/ContentChunks.php');
    delete_option( ContentChunks::option_key );
    global $wp_rewrite;
    $wp_rewrite->flush_rules();
}
/*EOF*/
```

It's a relatively short script, because we made relatively few modifications. In fact, the only thing we really need to clean up is the custom option we created. Since we defined the name of that option inside of the ContentChunks.php file, we first include it, and then read the name of the value using the full name of that class constant: ContentChunks::option_key. This ensures that the row we created in the wp_options database table is removed. You can see how we tested for the WP_UNINSTALL_PLUGIN constant before taking any action; that constant is only defined when someone clicks on the link to delete your plugin.

The other thing that we are demonstrating here is overkill for this example, but we thought it was relevant because we are dealing with custom post types and they potentially deal with custom URLs. We use the flush_rules() method to clear out any stored URLs. In this chapter, our custom chunks were private, so they were not viewable via a URL, but if your custom post type was public, then your uninstall process should include these steps to flush the rewrite rules.

As pointed out in the comments, this process fails if you are developing on a local server in the same way that automatic plugin installation fails. Be sure to upload your plugin to a public web server to test your uninstall process, but be sure to make a backup of your plugin before you test deleting it.

With that, you have another powerful tool in your arsenal for creating professional WordPress plugins.

Summary

Congratulations! You have taken some big steps in understanding how WordPress works as a CMS, and you have seen some of the things that the `register_post_type()` function can do, and hopefully you have glimpsed at what is possible with custom post types. Frankly, we found dealing with this function to be rather frustrating, but we trust that its usability and documentation will improve with future releases of WordPress. You have also learned a couple of useful tricks for constructing user-friendly plugins, and these are valuable tools as you consider releasing your plugins to a wider audience.

With that in mind, it's time to start talking about getting our plugins off the ground and available to the general public. To get us started down that path, our next topic is versioning our code with SVN.

8

Versioning Your Code with Subversion (SVN)

By the end of this chapter, you will know what Subversion is, what it does, and how to use it to effectively manage your software development projects. Even if you are already familiar with Subversion, this chapter is a useful reference of how to complete common tasks and how to fix common problems. Throughout this chapter, we will be referencing the shell commands used to perform various actions; although there are a number of graphical clients available, they all make use of the underlying command-line utilities. Once we show you how to accomplish these tasks on the command-line, you should have no trouble figuring out the comparable actions within a GUI application.

By now, you should be familiar with the process of code development and you should be able to recognize the need to back up different versions of your files. You have certainly encountered situations where the "undo" button could no longer save you. You may have also had files that got inadvertently overwritten when multiple people were working together on the same project. This is where a version control system can save you.

Subversion (or any version control system) does three things for you:

- It stores multiple versions of your files so you can easily roll back to a previous version at any time
- It backs up your code in a remote location (unless you've configured your own local server)
- It allows multiple contributors to work on the same set of files without tripping over one another

From the official on-line documentation (`http://svnbook.red-bean.com`):

> *Subversion is a free/open source version control system. That is, Subversion manages files and directories, and the changes made to them, over time. This allows you to recover older versions of your data or examine the history of how your data changed. In this regard, many people think of a version control system as a sort of "time machine".*

Indeed, any serious software development project would be virtually impossible to manage without a system like this. Every application on your computer was probably developed using some kind of version control.

Why Subversion?

Subversion, often abbreviated as SVN, is not the only or best version control software available, but since it is used by WordPress to manage user-contributed plugins we have to talk about it specifically. However, we aren't bowing in blind obeisance here: SVN has earned its place as one of the standard version control applications because it is reliable, it has a good set of features, and it is relatively easy to use.

Understanding the terminology and concepts

Before we get into details on how to accomplish specific tasks, let's take a moment to discuss some of the terms and concepts so you can see the forest for the trees.

The first concept to introduce is that of the "repository", or the repo. An SVN repository holds all of a project's files and folders and all of its incremental revisions. You can set up a repository anywhere, but it is commonly set up on a remote server separate from your development environment. At any time, you can download the latest version of your project from the repository. Even though you can set up an SVN server locally on your own computer, we find it helpful to think of the repository as existing somewhere "out there", far away from your local machine.

The next concept is that of the working copy. That folder on your desktop containing your project's myriad PHP and HTML files will become a "working copy", but it's not a working copy yet. The word "copy" should ask the question: "a copy of what?" The answer should be, it is a copy of the repository. A folder cannot be an SVN working copy until you make a copy of the repository using the SVN checkout command, which we will show you in a moment. It's a bit like training to be a Jedi—your project's folder has to be subjected to special SVN treatment before it gets superhuman powers to track changes. Until your folder gets schooled in "the ways of the force", it's just another folder.

In a moment we will show you how to get this all started, but it's important to recognize the distinction between a regular vanilla folder and an SVN working copy. A working copy contains a series of hidden directories (named ".svn") that store information about the parent repository and its files and folders. These hidden folders are how SVN gets its Jedi powers to track changes between revisions.

Before we get too far ahead of ourselves, let's get our hands dirty and learn by doing.

Checking out a local working copy

The local working copy is a copy of a repository, so the repository must exist before you can have a copy of it. Creating a working copy is done by using SVN's `checkout` command (sometimes abbreviated to `co`). The checkout command creates a local working copy of the repository it references, even if that repository is empty. An important part of running the `checkout` command is establishing the connection between the repository and a local folder on your computer.

Have you ever wondered how some people download the cutting edge versions of software before they are officially released? Often it's simply a matter of checking out a working copy of the software's repository. For example, if you want to download the latest version of WordPress, navigate to an empty folder on your computer and use the following command from your command line:

```
svn checkout http://core.svn.wordpress.org/trunk/
```

You should see a list of files streaming by as they are downloaded into the current directory. When finished, you should have a `trunk` directory inside your current folder and you should have gotten a message like this:

Checked out revision 17369.

You have just downloaded the latest development version of WordPress. Now you too can see what's in store in the next version of WordPress! See `http://wordpress.org/download/svn` for more details.

Congratulations! You have created a working copy on your local computer! If you move into the `trunk` directory and view the hidden files, you should see all of WordPress' files as well as a directory named `.svn`. Each directory in your working copy will have a `.svn` directory — that's how Subversion tracks which files you've added or modified. Do not touch these directories! Damaging them could cripple your local working copy!

We are going to introduce you to a simple helper function here:

```
svn info
```

That command will tell you about the working copy, including the repository URL. It can be a useful way to look up your repo's URL if you can't remember it.

Now that you have a local working copy, you may be wondering why you have a `trunk` folder. Well, the answer to that question could be quite lengthy depending on whom you ask, but it all has to do with how versions of code are typically organized, so we need to explain a bit about SVN's folder structure.

SVN folder structure

Technically speaking, SVN doesn't know or care about directory structures, it simply cares about deltas, or differences between two versions of a file. In practice, however, it is common to organize your files into a couple of extra folders to help you distinguish public versions of your project from the ongoing development revisions. This folder structure is what WordPress expects if and when you commit your plugin code to their repository.

The `trunk` folder will be used to store the latest saved version of your project. A couple more directories may also come into play, which means your code base will be organized into at least two folders, but possibly all three of the following:

- `/trunk/`: Contains the private "development" version of your code
- `/tags/`: Contains "snapshots" of the trunk, made when the development of trunk has reached a significant point
- `/branches/`: Used for more complex development scenarios

There are several main philosophies that describe how you should interact with these folders, but we are going to focus on only one of them, known as the "Never Branch" method, since it is easier to understand and it agrees with WordPress' plugin submission process. Our explanation of these folders pertains to this "Never Branch" development method, but if you are curious about some of the alternatives, have a look at Jean-Michel Feurprier's nice article on the topic: `http://goo.gl/y5ox`.

In short, the `trunk` folder is like a tree, and it contains multiple folders and files that collectively represent your project in development. This is where you will be editing files—it is really the heart of your local working copy.

The `tags` folder contains named copies of the trunk. If your trunk is like a tree, then the tags folder will contain "snapshots" of your tree at times when you thought it was looking particularly good. **You will never commit code directly into the tags folder.** The only way code will end up in that folder will be if you copy the entire contents of the trunk into a new subfolder inside of the `tags` folder. This is how you identify significant versions or milestones in your project. You may have saved and committed hundreds of different versions of the trunk before you are ready to officially label it as a separate tag, but once you are ready to make that distinction, you will use SVN to copy the trunk wholesale into a named subfolder inside of tags, such as: `tags/beta` or `tags/rc-2.3` or `tags/public-version-1.0`. For WordPress plugins, your releases must contain **only** numbers and periods, for example, `tags/0.6.1`.

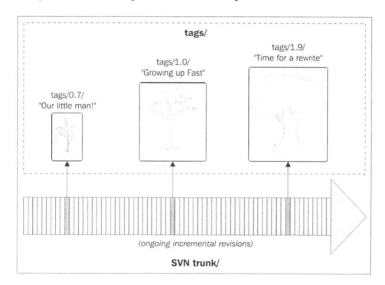

You need not worry about the `branches` folder because our simple development methodology here doesn't require its use. Again, SVN does not know nor does it care about how you structure your directories; this is just how a majority of developers have agreed to do it, and considering its effectiveness and popularity, you should be aware of it. WordPress offers its own explanation about using SVN with your projects (`http://goo.gl/QeGm`).

Now we have an understanding of how we are planning to organize our files and folders inside our repository, so let's bring the point home by trying to checkout an older version of WordPress.

Checkout, revisited

The checkout command has an optional second argument, and your checkouts can get a bit sloppy if you omit it. The optional second argument specifies a local path, and if you omit it, the basename of the URL will be used as the destination. In our example, we ended up with a directory named `trunk` because that was name of the folder in the repository's URL. Try making another folder, and then moving into it, and this time modify the command to add a period at the end (in the shell, a period represents "this folder", so we are telling SVN to checkout a working copy "here"):

```
svn checkout http://core.svn.wordpress.org/trunk/ .
```

You will still see the same message about "Checked out revision xxxx", but this time, all the files and folders downloaded directly into the current folder, so you didn't end up with a `trunk` folder at all. Depending on what you're doing, there are times when you may want to see the `trunk` folder, and there are times when you might want to omit it. Now you know how.

Before, when you omitted the period, the files you checked out were downloaded into a newly created `trunk` directory:

- A   `trunk/wp-admin/user/admin.php`
- A   `trunk/wp-admin/user/index-extra.php`
- A   `trunk/wp-feed.php`

Whereas if you added the period as your second argument, the files were checked out into the current directory:

- A   `wp-admin/user/admin.php`
- A   `wp-admin/user/index-extra.php`
- A   `wp-feed.php`

Make sense? We are going to drive the point home here as we show you how to download an older version of WordPress. Create yet another directory and navigate to it before issuing the following command:

```
svn checkout http://core.svn.wordpress.org/tags/3.0.4/ .
```

Can you guess what this will do? This command will download a working copy of WordPress 3.0.4 to the current directory. This lets you see how the `tags` directory is used to store snapshots of the trunk, and it gives you more practice using the checkout command.

Hopefully this gives you some confidence in your abilities to use Subversion, but checking out the WordPress code has some limitations. Unless you have been invited to submit changes to the WordPress code base, your access to the repository is read-only. In order for us to continue our SVN education, we need to create our own repository so we can practice submitting our own changes and start versioning our own code. Let's create a repo.

Setting up an SVN repository

If we are going to version our own code, then we need to start with finding a suitable SVN host to house our repository. There are a lot of SVN hosting providers that are free to use, but they often come with limitations regarding the number of users and the amount of disk space offered. You may have to read the fine print before you find one that suits your needs.

For this example, we are going to make use of Google's free code repository at `http://code.google.com/hosting` (read more information about the project at `http://code.google.com`). Anyone with a Google account can get a 2048 MB repository quota, as well as a wiki and a ticketing system, but it is a requirement that any submitted code be compatible with an open-source license. This is a free public service, so it's perfect for an open-source project. Anyone can "check out" the code (just like we did earlier when we checked out the WordPress code), but only members you invite to your project will get privileges to commit changes to the repository—this is, by the way, more or less how WordPress' plugin repository works. If you do not want to use Google Hosting for your project, you can sign up for a free repository with any number of other sites; many of those sites also offer project management features that help you identify milestones and track errors. We recommend `http://unfuddle.com` as a nice scalable versioning and management solution.

No matter where your repository is hosted, the most important thing for this chapter is that you become familiar with all the SVN commands you'll need.

Go to `http://code.google.com/hosting`, sign in with your Google account (or create one), and click on **Create a New Project**. You need to enter a unique name, summary, description, and make sure you choose **Subversion** as the version control system. If you are going to store code meant for a WordPress plugin, you can use the GNU General Public License v2 as your license, because that's what WordPress uses.

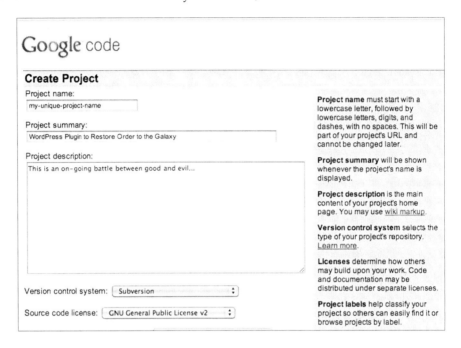

Once you have completed this, a special password will be generated and you will be given some commands to use when connecting to your repository. We will use those commands in the next section.

At this point, our repository is completely empty. It literally contains nothing. We will add files to it later, but first we need to establish the connection between the repository and a local working copy, so let's use those commands Google provided to check out a local working copy!

Checking out a local working copy of our repo

The commands used to check out code from our Google repository are more or less the same as the ones we saw previously while checking out code from WordPress' repository.

A bit later, we will start adding your project's files to the repository, but leave them alone for now. Create a fresh new directory on your computer. Move into the new directory and then try running this command to check out a working copy:

```
svn checkout https://my-unique-project-name.googlecode.com/svn/trunk/
--username mygoogleid
```

Google requires an additional parameter because you need to validate before connecting, but once finished, you should see something like the following as output:

```
svn checkout https://my-unique-project-name.googlecode.com/svn/trunk/
--username mygoogleid
Checked out revision 1.
```

If you view hidden files in that directory, you should now see the hidden `.svn` folder. Remember: do not touch anything in the `.svn` folders! You could irreparably damage your local working copy!

> Do not immediately try to check out your repository into the same folder as your project! Your first checkout should always be into a blank new folder. Always keep a backup of your files separate from SVN just in case something goes wrong with the SVN setup!

Congratulations! You have created a working copy for your project and you can now start adding files and folders to it to bring them under version control.

You can see that Google required a username to check out the code. Some repositories do require authentication. SVN will often store the necessary username and password, so you usually don't need to type them again when updating or committing your changes.

Adding files

The normal workflow is that we add files to our local working copy before they get added to the repository. Our local working copy is like the launch-pad where we rocket our code into that far away repository. You probably already have files sitting in a folder somewhere that you're dying to bring under version control, but first we are going to try this out using some test files, just to make sure that it will work. Hey, the Russians blasted Laika the dog into space aboard Sputnik 2 long before they tried it with a human being.

To begin, try saving a copy of a file into your working copy folder. We're naming this file `laika.php`. The process here is always going to be two-part: you do your regular coding work, and then you come back to SVN and do your versioning. After saving `laika.php` to your working copy, head back to the command line to see what SVN thinks about it. We use SVN's `status` command to get a rundown of the changes that have happened in this folder:

```
svn status /path/to/your/working/copy
```

Alternatively, if you are already inside your working copy:

```
svn status
```

Which produces the following output:

```
?        laika.php
```

The question mark signifies that SVN doesn't know what this file is—it's not being tracked. It turns out that you always have to tell SVN about what you're doing inside your working copy. It wants to know who is invited to the party. We do this using SVN's `add` command:

```
svn add laika.php
```

Which produces the following output:

```
A        laika.php
```

The `A` shows us that the file has been added to SVN's list. You can add files one by one, or you can use the common filename wildcards, for example, `svn add *.php`. See the help page for more options:

```
svn help add
```

Next, we have to upload this file to the repository—right now it's still just sitting on the launch-pad, waiting to blast off to the big repository in the sky.

Committing changes to the repository

This is how we really add files to the repository, we commit them. To jump right to it, we use the `commit` command like this:

```
svn commit . -m "Testing our first commit"
```

It produces some output like the following:

```
Sending        laika.php
Transmitting file data ......
Committed revision 2.
```

The dot after the `commit` symbolizes this directory, so as written, the command assumes that you are inside the root of your working copy. You could run that command from elsewhere on the file system simply by specifying the full path and it would have the same effect:

```
svn commit /full/path/to/my-working-copy -m "Testing our first commit"
```

The `-m` is short for `--message`, and it allows us to describe this particular commit. These messages are searchable and they can help you track down when particular changes were made, so it's good to describe each commit in a meaningful way so that you can search for those changes later.

The rest of the output shows us which files were transmitted to the repository and it gives us a new revision number. That number will increase sequentially each time you make a commit. Sometimes software projects include a "revision number" in their "about" page; often that comes directly or indirectly from the version control system. For more information, have a look at the help page:

```
svn help commit
```

Overcoming errors

You may run into an error when trying to commit, such as the following:

> *svn: Could not use external editor to fetch log message; consider setting the $SVN_EDITOR environment variable or using the --message (-m) or --file (-F) options*
> *svn: None of the environment variables SVN_EDITOR, VISUAL or EDITOR are set, and no 'editor-cmd' run-time configuration option was found*

What in the world does that mean? Well, number one, it means that you ignored our advice and did not to include an `-m` option with a description of your commit. Secondly, it means SVN did not know which editor to pop open for you in order to make you provide a description. You can either always include the `-m` option with a description each time you make a commit, or you can set an environment variable that specifies which editor to use.

In Linux and Mac OS X systems, you can run the following commands on the command-line which will set the value of the `SVN_EDITOR` environment variable:

```
SVN_EDITOR=pico
export SVN_EDITOR
```

You can also paste those lines into your ~/.profile or ~/.bash_profile files so your settings don't go away when you log out. On Windows, you can set the editor environment variable by navigating to **Environment Variables** in your **System Properties** (right-click on **My Computer**, choose **Properties**, choose **Advanced**, and then look for the **Environment Variables** button).

From there, you can define a new variable called SVN_EDITOR and a value that is the system path to your text editor (such as C:\Windows\notepad.exe).

Verifying the new state of your repository

If you're doing this for the first time, we encourage you to double-check the action here by downloading another copy of your repository to a new location on your computer, or you could even go as far as to checkout your repository on a whole other computer using the same commands we learned before. Create a new folder for your local working copy, and then issue the SVN checkout command, for example:

```
svn checkout https://my-unique-project-name.googlecode.com/svn/trunk/ .
```

The latest version of the repository (known as the head) should download to your current directory and you should have a clean copy of the `laika.php` file. The files you committed in the preceding section should appear in the new location. Unlike Laika the dog, who died shortly after entering orbit, `laika.php` should have survived the trip to the repository and back. Are you starting to get the hang of this?

Adding more files to your repository

Now that you have fired a test shot and verified that your machinery is working, you can add some more files and folders to your repository. You can add files directly to the repository using SVN's `import` command—they can come from anywhere on your hard-drive; they don't have to be inside your working copy.

```
cd /path/to/non-versioned/files

svn import . http://yourrepo.com/ -m "Priming the pump: submitting
directly to the repo"
```

Then, over in your working copy, run the `update` command to pick up those changes made to the repository:

```
cd /back/to/your/working/copy

svn update .
```

Alternatively, in one line:

```
svn update /back/to/your/working/copy
```

The `import` command is primarily used when you are setting up your repository for the first time. For more information, look at the help page:

```
svn help import
```

You can also continue to use the previous add/commit method we outlined before, but you'll find it more and more useful to specify multiple files using wildcards, for example:

```
svn add *
```

This will throw some warnings when you try to add files that are *already* under version control, but usually they are harmless warnings that you can ignore. You might see something like this:

```
svn: warning: 'test.php' is already under version control

A        other.php
```

The command threw some warnings, but it succeeded in adding new files to SVN's special list. Now you commit your changes and the new files will be added to the repository.

```
svn commit . -m "Added some more files!"
```

Removing files from the repository

Hopefully you are getting the hang of this. Once you're ready, you can start adding some of your "real" files to the repository, but sooner or later you'll want to delete files too.

 Remember: You cannot just delete the file! It will pop right back in there the next time you update your working copy.

You *must* use the SVN equivalent command:

```
svn delete test.php
```

Sometimes you may get an error, such as:

```
svn: 'test.php' has local modifications
```

What does that mean? **You can only delete files that have been committed.** If you are trying to delete a file that has been edited since you checked it out or if you are trying to delete a file that you added but never committed, you will get this error. If you accidentally added the file and haven't committed it yet, you can "delete" it by using the `revert` command. The usage here is a bit odd, but remember that the `revert` command discards local changes. In this case the change is that you added the file to your working copy, so sometimes you need to revert a file before you can delete it. If you need some more guidance, refer to the help page:

```
svn help delete
```

Updating your working copy

The final command necessary to maintain basic version control is the `update` command. You will generally use the `checkout` command only once when you first connect to a repository, whereas the `update` command you will use frequently. You will use it to sync your local working copy with the most recent copy from the repository. In SVN nomenclature, the most recent version is called the "head" and it contains the most recent changes committed to the repository.

To try this out, run the update command from any working copy:

```
svn update
```

The `update` command assumes that you want to update the current directory, but it's equally valid to specify the full path:

```
svn update /path/to/your/working/copy
```

If anyone has made new changes to the repository, this will ensure that your copy is in sync. This command is absolutely vital if you have other people working on your project. You want to make sure that your local working copy has all the new changes that they may have committed. Even if you are working solo on your project, it's a good habit to get into running the `update` command periodically.

Tagging a version

After you have gone back and forth editing and committing revisions, you will eventually come to a major revision that you want to "tag". All that's involved here is making a copy of your trunk and putting it into a named folder inside your tags folder. Again, you can't just copy the trunk; you have to use SVN's equivalent `copy` command. We take this a step further because we don't need to create a *local* copy of the code at all; we just want to take a snapshot of the repository and store it in the repository.

The following is what your tagging command could look like:

```
svn copy https://my-unique-project-name.googlecode.com/svn/trunk https://
my-unique-project-name.googlecode.com/svn/tags/0.0.1
```

Remember that this command must appear on one line. Just like the normal shell `cp` command, the `svn copy` command takes two arguments. The first specifies the source, and the second specifies the destination. Every time you create a tag, you will copy the trunk into a named directory, named `0.0.1` in our example.

The example above may not play nicely with how WordPress expects your plugin to look, in particular the readme.txt file. WordPress' official documentation for using SVN demonstrates how you create a tags directory locally: `http://wordpress.org/extend/plugins/about/svn/`. Their solution plays nicer with the readme.txt file, but it requires that you dedicate a separate directory outside of your WordPress install to act as a launchpad to the WordPress repository. See our article on the topic for more information: `http://goo.gl/r2ebz`.

SVN doesn't care what you name your tags, but WordPress does. Get into the habit of naming the subdirectories in the tags folder using only numbers and periods, like typical WordPress version releases. As you will see later, these numbers relate to your plugin's `readme.txt` file.

As always, consult the help page if you need more guidance:

```
svn help copy
```

Let's cover a few more scenarios that you may encounter.

Reverting an entire project

Oh no! You just realized that your project is hopelessly screwed up and you want to rollback to a previous version. Given that SVN is built for precisely this scenario, it's a bit surprising how tricky this option can be. One thing that may seem baffling to you is that SVN really only moves forward. It lets you pull up older versions of code, but any revisions still get saved on top of the stack so you have a full record of every commit you've ever made, including those bug-plagued ones you made at 3 AM from a net bar in Tijuana.

One option is to create a new folder, then check out an entire working copy from a previous date. Use the `--revision flag` (or the `-r` abbreviation) to specify a date. SVN accepts several different formats, but make sure you use quotes if your date includes a space.

```
svn checkout --revision {"2010-11-15 15:30"} http://your-repo.com/trunk/ .
```

Remember that this gives you the most recent version of the repository as of the date you specified. If the most recent commit that occurred on or before 2010-11-15 was actually a revision that was committed on Halloween two weeks prior, then that's what this command will check out. Trick or treat!

It may seem strange to check out the entire code base into a separate folder, but it can be easier to compare the two versions and paste the necessary changes into your current working copy when you have them isolated into separate locations. The important thing is that you get your current working copy repaired so you can commit the necessary fixes.

You can also use the `--revision` flag to check out revisions by their number:

```
svn checkout --revision 567 http://your-repo.com/trunk/ .
```

This is how you can flip through open source software projects to see the iterative process of development, but it's not very readable by humans.

Please refer to SVN's included help by issuing the following command:

```
svn help checkout
```

You may have noticed that this command does more or less exactly what we did previously when we demonstrated how to check out older versions of WordPress. Normally, the `checkout` command grabs the most recent version of the files in the repository, but by using the extra parameters, you can grab older versions of the files.

Reverting a single file

If you don't want to check out a complete working copy, you can rollback a specific file too. Oddly, this requires that you use the `update` command, not the `revert` command! You can think about it like this: just like the `checkout` command, the `update` command can take additional arguments that specify a date or a revision.

```
svn update test.php --revision {"2010-10-31"}
```

In this example, we are "updating" the `test.php` file to its last known state as of Halloween 2010. This option can be more complicated than checking out an older version to a separate directory. However here's how you should go about performing a rollback to a previous version of a file.

First, commit your existing code:

```
svn commit . -m "BROKEN! Preparing to roll back!"
```

This may seem crazy if you know that it is in fact broken, but you have to move forward. Simply indicate in your commit message (the `-m` option) that this version is broken. If you don't do this, you may encounter an error when you try to update the broken file in question:

```
svn update myfile.php --revision {"2011-01-01"}
Conflict discovered in 'myfile.php'.
Select: (p) postpone, (df) diff-full, (e) edit,
        (mc) mine-conflict, (tc) theirs-conflict,
        (s) show all options:
```

All that is to say that the file you are trying to roll back has local modifications. You can press *Ctrl+c* to escape out of this option. Make sure you commit your local copy before continuing.

Next, use the `update` command to specify a date or revision number of your file that you want to roll back to. You should see some output like the following:

```
svn update myfile.php --revision {"2011-01-01"}
```

The output will be as follows:

```
U    myfile.php
Updated to revision 42.
```

Now that you have the older version of the file, go ahead and make the necessary changes to it. Once you're done, you can commit your changes as you would normally:

```
svn commit . -m "I fixed the problem with myfile.php"
```

If you need more options, don't forget to have a look at the help page:

```
svn help update
```

When you fix up your current working copy using bits and pieces of an older working copy, you are manually merging the two versions. SVN does have a merge command, but it is a bit more complicated to use, so we recommend that you get comfortable manually patching things together before you try it.

Moving files

One of the easiest ways to break your working copy is to move or rename files without telling SVN about it. It's a surefire way to get SVN coughing up a stream of errors. Any time you need to move or rename a file, remember to use SVN's move command:

```
svn move oldname.php newname.php
```

Exporting your working copy

The final task we want to demonstrate for you is how you can take a working copy and turn it back into a bunch of normal files and folders. If you need to send a copy of your project to a friend or a client who is not an SVN user, you don't want to include all those .svn folders. Another scenario is maybe you need to change repositories, and you need to purge all the .svn folders that associate the code with a particular repository. In this chapter, we have been submitting code to the Google repository, so how do we transition this code so that we can store it in the WordPress repository? We'll show you how to publish your plugin in *Chapter 10*, but you'll need to first extract the raw files and folders from your local copy using the export command:

```
svn export /path/to/my/working/copy /path/to/backup/destination/my-export
```

Or you can use the following if you are in the root of your current working copy:

```
svn export . /path/to/backup/destination/my-export
```

Just like the `copy` command, the first argument specifies the source, while the second argument specifies the destination. The thing to be aware of when using the `export` command is that it *must* create a new folder at the destination, so don't try exporting to an existing folder. In our example, we are assuming that the `my-export` folder doesn't yet exist. If it does already exist, SVN will throw an error. So, just remember to always provide the `export` command the name of the folder that you want created.

After completing the export, the new folder will contain a vanilla copy of the working copy, without any of the magical `.svn` directories.

Sometimes SVN cannot complete the export due to errors. Usually the errors result from you having accidentally deleted files and folders without telling SVN about it (that is deleting a file instead of using `svn delete`). Regardless of the cause, sometimes it is easier to use humble `rsync` to make a copy of the directory. This is a powerful command-line utility available in Linux and Mac OS X systems. All we need it to do is to filter out the `.svn` directories and we will end up with a vanilla copy of our working copy:

```
rsync -arvz /path/to/my/working/copy/ /path/to/backup/destination/my-
export --exclude=".svn"
```

Don't forget the trailing slash after the source argument: `/path/to/my/working/copy/` — if you omit that trailing slash you will recreate unwanted sub folders in your target directory. Just like the export command, `rsync` will create a folder of the name specified in your second argument. The SVN export command is easier, but if you're dealing with a corrupted working copy, `rsync` can be a lifesaver.

Quick reference

Here's a brief summary of all the commands we covered in this chapter in one place. We are demonstrating these in an order that's plausible for a normal workflow. Sometimes the official documentation for utilities like Subversion are terse and confusing, so we're going to give you full examples here, using `http://repo.com` as our imaginary repository:

- `svn checkout http://repo.com/trunk/ .`
  Run this command only once, when you first establish a connection with the repo to the current folder. This will also download the latest version of the repository to your local folder:

  svn checkout --revision {"2010-11-15 15:30"} `http://repo.com/trunk/ .`

  Add the `--revision` flag with a date to check out an older version of the repository indicated.

- `svn status`

  Run this command from inside your working copy to get a summary of which files were added (A), modified (M), deleted (D), or ones that need to be added (?).

- `svn info`

  Run this command from inside your working copy to get basic information about your working copy, most importantly the repository URL.

- `svn update`

  Run this command from inside your working copy to update your files to the latest versions. This will not overwrite any files that you are working on. It is important to run this command frequently if other collaborators are committing changes to the repo:

  svn update somefile.php --revision {"2010-11-15 15:30"}

  Add the `--revision` flag to specify that you want to download an older version of the file indicated.

- `svn add *`

  Run this command from inside your working copy to add new files to the repository. You can specify the files by name, or you can use the standard wildcard characters. The files will be added to the repo on the next commit.

- `svn delete somefile.php`

  Run this command to delete the referenced file. It will be deleted from the repository on the next commit. The next version of the repository will remove the file, but the file will still be there in older versions of the repo.

- `svn revert otherfile.php`

  Run this command to restore this file to where it was before you modified it. This is similar to the "revert to saved" function available in applications like Photoshop, except this reverts the file to its condition when you last performed an `svn update`.

- `svn commit . -m "My descriptive message goes here"`

  Run this from the root of your working copy to commit all pending changes to the repository with a message. This will upload all changes to the repository and create a new revision number.

- `svn copy http://repo.com/trunk http://repo.com/tags/2.0`

  Run this command to create a tagged version of your code in the repository.

- `svn export . /path/to/new/folder`

  Run this command from within your working folder (or specify a full path instead of the period) to create a clean version of your working copy without all the myriad hidden `.svn` directories. Use this command if you need to send someone a clean version of your code base.

- `svn move oldfilename.php new/filename.php`
  Use the move command to move a file or change its name.

Summary

Congratulations on learning these valuable commands! Knowing how to version your code gives you peace of mind and it could potentially save you from catastrophic loss of work. It's also a great *résumé* bullet point since almost any developer shop will expect you to have familiarity with versioning your code.

Now you are poised for serious development, and you'll be ready to work with WordPress' repository once you are ready to publish your plugin. However, before you publish your plugin, you will have to make sure it is clean enough to be released to the public. We'll help you make sure your bases are covered in the next chapter.

9

Preparing Your Plugin for Distribution

In this chapter you will learn how to groom your plugin in preparation for publishing it to the official WordPress repository. This chapter is **not** about the mechanics of how to apply for a login or how to use Subversion to commit your code; those are all covered in other chapters. This chapter is all about making your plugin as good as it can be before you go through those mechanics. Specifically, we will discuss how to test and document your plugin so all your hard work may be a benefit to others.

A word of warning:

You should be aware that submitting your plugin for any public use requires some degree of responsibility. One of the worst things you can do as a developer is to distribute shoddy, untested code. It is one thing if you have thousands of lines of useless code inside the privacy of your own computer (and we have lots of that), but it's another thing entirely if you push this problematic code onto the unwitting public. Make sure your code is clean and functional before distributing it for public use.

Public enemy number one: PHP notices

If you have followed our recommendations in this book, then you have developed every line of your PHP code while having PHP errors, warnings, and notices verbosely printed. As a result, you knew *immediately* if at any time your code had so much as a hiccup. If you have somehow gotten to this point of the book without enabling PHP notices and errors, then do us all a favor and **do not** submit your plugin for public use. That may sound harsh, but under no circumstances should untested code be distributed to the public.

Hands down, this is the single worst problem that infests the third-party plugins in the WordPress repository. During the course of writing this book, we tested hundreds of plugins and it was shocking how many of them had errors that caused PHP notices to print. The majority of these notices came down to a simple pattern that looked something like this:

```
$x = $my_array['x']
```

That statement will work *only* if x is defined in the array. It will throw a notice if it is *not* defined. The correct way to handle this condition is to test the array beforehand using the isset() function:

```
$x = '';
if ( isset($my_array['x']) )
{
    $x = $my_array['x'];
}
```

Clearly, plugins with that type of problematic construct were developed in an environment that hid PHP notices from the plugin authors, so they never knew that their code was coughing and wheezing behind the scenes. We have alerted many authors to this type of code using the feedback pages on the WordPress site, and usually the authors complied with our recommended corrections, but one author chided back that "notices aside, my plugin is working perfectly". Wrong! Don't for a second think that notices can be ignored—even a notice can break your plugin. Depending on where they occur, they could end up printing into form fields or polluting XML data feeds and cause your plugin to critically fail, just to name two examples.

The other way notices might "break" your plugin isn't really technical, but it is realistic. No sane user is going to continue using your plugin as soon as it starts printing freaky messages all over their website. Having unhandled notices in your code is a sure-fire way to doom your plugin to the trash-heap, and all of your hard work will be wasted.

The bottom line is to clean up any code that causes notices before submitting your plugin for public use.

PHP short tags

The other horrible bad habit that you should avoid is using PHP short tags. We mentioned this specifically at the beginning of this book—it's a horrible idea because you can never be sure if a given server will support them, and there are good reasons why your server *should not* support them. Before your plugin can be considered ready for publication, you must remove any instances of short tags: always use `<?php` in favor of the short tag `<?`. The best way to check for these is to disable support for them in your `php.ini` file, reboot Apache, and see if any errors crop up.

Those two problems plagued about 80% of the plugins we evaluated for this book. That means only one in five is potentially usable. Those are great odds! If you are being diligent about cleaning your code and you avoid these two pitfalls, your plugin immediately stands far in front of the pack! All you have to do is not screw up! However, we can do even better—let's look at a few more subtle tests for your plugin.

Conflicting names

PHP as a language is particularly vulnerable to naming collisions, and this is especially prevalent in WordPress plugins where many authors are not particularly aware or sensitive about this problem. If your site is running a lot of plugins, you are increasing the odds that a naming conflict might occur. While debugging a plugin, one of the first things that you should do is disable **all** of your other plugins so you can isolate problems.

We have seen a lot of useless attempts to prevent naming collisions when plugin authors wrap their function definitions in a big if-block:

```
if ( !function_exists('myfunction') )
{
    function myfunction()
    {
        // Do stuff
    }
}
```

Do not think that your plugin is safe if you use if-blocks like this! This is **not** guaranteed to solve the problem! The only time where this type of wrapping is effective is when you are wrapping a stand-alone function (for example, a theme function) that is not interdependent on the other functions in your plugin. If your plugin defines 10 interrelated functions, and you wrap their declarations in this way, can you imagine the erratic behavior that might occur if even *one* of your function definitions deferred to someone else's existing definition? What are the odds that their function will do exactly what you need it to do? Seriously, it would be a miracle. You need to go further than these simple checks in order to prevent naming collisions.

Throughout this book, we have used a single `index.php` file to act as the main file for your plugin: it contains the information head, your `includes`, and hopefully all the events (that is actions and filters) that it ties into. This makes it easy for anyone to see how your plugin interacts with WordPress and which resources it requires. However, we are about to switch this up a little so you can be sure that your plugin gracefully avoids naming conflicts.

Naming conflicts can occur in three places: function names, class names, and constant names. Thankfully, PHP gives us a way to easily list all declared functions, classes, and constants, so we are going to test for potential collisions in all three places. The first step is to move the contents of your `index.php` file into a separate file named `loader.php`, but leave the information head in the `index.php` file. That is critical because we need WordPress to load `index.php` first. We are going to put our tests into `index.php`, and if those tests pass, only then will we include the `loader.php` file and proceed normally.

The following is what our `index.php` file looks like now:

```php
<?php
/*
Plugin Name: My Plugin Name
Description: My description
Author: My Name
Version: 0.0.0.1
Author URI: http://tipsfor.us/plugins/
Plugin URI: http://tipsfor.us/plugins/
*/

/**
 * CONFIGURATION:
 *
 * Define the names of functions and classes used by this plugin so we
can test
 * for conflicts prior to loading the plugin and message the WP admins.
 *
 * $function_names_used -- add any function names that this plugin
declares in the
 *     main namespace (e.g. utility functions or theme functions).
 *
 * $class_names_used -- add any class names that are declared by this
plugin.
 *
 * $constants_used -- any constants defined using the "define"
function.
 */
```

```php
$function_names_used = array('my_naked_function','other_template_
function');
$class_names_used = array('MyClassName','SomeOtherClass');
$constants_used = array('MY_PLUGIN_PATH','MY_PLUGIN_URL');

$error_items = '';

function some_unique_function_name_cannot_load()
{
   global $error_items;
   print '<div class="error"><p><strong>'
   .__('The "MyPlugin" plugin cannot load correctly')
   .'</strong> '
   .__('Another plugin has declared conflicting class, function, or
constant names:')
   ."<ul>$error_items</ul>"
   .'</p><p>'
   .__ ('You must deactivate the plugins that are using these
conflicting names.')
   .'</p></div>';
}

/**
* The following code tests whether or not this plugin can be safely
loaded.
* If there are no name conflicts, the loader.php is included and the
plugin
* is loaded, otherwise, an error is displayed in the manager.
*/// Check for conflicting function names
foreach ($function_names_used as $f_name )
{
   if ( function_exists($f_name) )
   {
      $error_items .= '<li>'.__('Function: ') . $f_name .'</li>';
   }
}
// Check for conflicting Class names
foreach ($class_names_used as $cl_name )
{
   if ( class_exists($cl_name) )
   {
      $error_items .= '<li>'.__('Class: ') . $cl_name .'</li>';
   }
}
// Check for conflicting Constants
foreach ($constants_used as $c_name )
```

```
{
    if ( defined($c_name) )
    {
        $error_items .= '<li>'.__('Constant: ') . $c_name .'</li>';
    }
}
// Fire the error, or load the plugin.
if ($error_items)
{
    $error_items = '<ul>'.$error_items.'</ul>';
    add_action('admin_notices', 'some_unique_function_name_cannot_
load');
}
else
{
    // Load the plugin
    include_once('loader.php');
}
/*EOF*/
```

We aren't feeding this to you bit by bit anymore, but by now you should be able to follow how this code snippet works. If your plugin includes three classes named `Larry`, `Curly`, and `Moe`, you should list those in the `$class_names_used` array. Likewise, if you use any "naked" functions declared in the main namespace (outside of a class), you should list them in the `$function_names_used` array. It's the same procedure for the constants using the `$constants_used` array. All that this requires of you is that you diligently list each of your classes, functions, and constants so they can be tested against whatever may have already been declared when your plugin loads. All the grunt work is done by PHP's `function_exists()`, `class_exists()`, and `defined()` functions. We have also used WordPress' localization function `__()`, which helps you translate messages. We will cover that in the next chapter.

Can you see the advantage of using classes? You don't have to double-list every function that exists in a class—if the class name is available, then all of the class' functions and methods are guaranteed to work because their definitions exist only within that class, **not** in the main namespace.

This code gathers error messages into the $error_items array, and if it's not empty, it hooks into the admin_notices action. This action only fires when a user is inside the Dashboard. The idea here is that we want to display a message to an admin user only; we don't want to bring the whole site to its knees and publicly announce to the world that we had a bit of an "accident". So we create a single callback function, in this example, we name it some_unique_function_name_cannot_load. That function is hooked to the admin_notices action, and it only executes if your plugin encounters any problems with name collisions. In that case, the admin will be notified, and the rest of your plugin's files will wait in the sidelines—the loader.php file will not load unless the coast is clear, as illustrated in the following screenshot:

Congratulations! Now you can be sure that your plugin isn't bumping into anyone else out there on the dance floor, but still it could have problems. Just because your classes, functions, and constants can get declared safely doesn't mean that your plugin is guaranteed to work. You may also need to test PHP, MySQL, or WordPress itself. Sometimes you have to get creative about what you should test, but we are going to show you a handful of tests and one way of implementing them.

Checking for naming conflicts only ensures us that our loader.php and all of our plugin's files *can* load, but there are still plenty of things that can go wrong, and we need a second tier of tests to check for them. Next, we are going to show you how to integrate additional tests to ensure that your plugin has the version of PHP, MySQL, or WordPress that it requires.

Modifying loader.php

We have set this up to use a dedicated class containing all the tests we need our plugin to run:

```php
<?php
// loader.php

// Required Files
include_once('includes/MyPlugin.php');
include_once('tests/MyPlugin_tests.php');

// Run Tests.
MyPlugin_tests::test1();
MyPlugin_tests::test2();
// ... more tests go here ...

// If there were no errors, load our plugin normally
if ( empty(MyPlugin_tests::$errors) )
{
    add_action( 'init', 'MyPlugin::do_stuff');
    // ... other actions here ...
}
// There were errors!
else
{
add_action( 'admin_notices', ' MyPlugin_tests::print_notices');
}

/*EOF*/
```

Can you see how we're setting this up? In addition to including our standard includes for our plugin, now we're going to also include a special class that contains tests for this plugin. Create a new directory inside your plugin's main folder and create a new file with a name corresponding to the name of your plugin. In our example, the file is named tests/MyPlugin_tests.php.

The flow will go like this: The `loader.php` file loads from the top down, we include the testing class, and then we put in a line for each test we need to run, such as `MyPlugin_tests::test_function1();`. If any test fails, we will add a message to an array `MyPlugin_tests::$errors`. If any errors are detected, we print some messages to the admin users via a function named `MyPlugin::print_notices`. If the `MyPlugin_tests::$errors` comes out clean after running the gauntlet of tests, then our plugin loads normally. Makes sense? The following is what our `MyPlugin_tests.php` file looks like:

```php
<?php
class MyPlugin_tests
{
    public static $errors = array(); // Any errors thrown.

    public static function print_notices()
    {
        if ( !empty(self::$errors) )
        {
            $error_items = '';
            foreach ( self::$errors as $e )
            {
                $error_items .= "<li>$e</li>";
            }
            print '<div id="my-plugin-error" class="error"><p><strong>'
            .__('The &quot;My Plugin&quot; plugin encountered errors! It
cannot load!')
            .'</strong> '
            ."<ul style='margin-left:30px;'>$error_items</ul>"
            .'</p>'
            .'</div>';
        }
    }

    // Add as many testing functions as you need...
    public static function test1()
    {

    }
}
/*EOF*/
```

You can now add as many testing functions as you need to this class, then call them by referencing them in your `loader.php` file just like we did in the example. In practice, you would change the function names from "test1" to something more descriptive. Have a look at the tests below for some examples of how to test various aspects of your environment.

Testing WordPress version

We demonstrated this in our chapter about Social Networking, but here it is again, this time adapted for use in a testing class. You can add this to your plugin's dedicated testing class and reference it by name in your `loader.php` file:

```
/**
 * Tests that the current version of WP is greater than $ver.
 *
 * @param string $ver   the version of WordPress your plugin requires
 * in order to work, e.g. '3.0.1'
 * @return none       Registers an error in the self::$errors array.
 */
public static function wp_version_gt($ver)
{
    global $wp_version;

    $exit_msg = __("MyPlugin requires WordPress $ver or newer.
        <a href='http://codex.wordpress.org/Upgrading_WordPress'>Please
update!</a>");

    if (version_compare($wp_version,$ver,'<'))
    {
        self::$errors[] = $exit_msg;
    }
}
```

Back in your `loader.php`, you would reference this test by name and pass it a minimum required version of WordPress:

```
// Run Tests.
MyPlugin_tests::wp_version_gt('3.0.1');
```

You can create variables to hold these types of settings instead of writing them directly into your function call; it really depends on how you have set up your tests.

Testing PHP version

The following is how you test your what version of PHP looks like:

```
/**
 * @param string    the minimum version of PHP required to run, e.g.
 '5.2.14'
 */
public static function php_version_gt($ver)
{
```

```
$exit_msg = __("MyPlugin requires PHP $ver or newer.
    Talk to your system administrator about upgrading");

if ( version_compare( phpversion(), $ver, '<') )
{
    self::$errors[] = $exit_msg;
}
}
```

Again, you would add a corresponding function call to your `loader.php` file:

```
// Run Tests.
MyPlugin_tests::wp_version_gt('3.0.1');
MyPlugin_tests::php_version_gt('5.2.14');
```

Testing MySQL version

It's the same pattern to test the database version, but we rely on the global `$wbdb` object and its `get_results` method. We are using a simple MySQL statement: `'SELECT VERSION()'` to return the MySQL version. (The `'as ver'` part of the query merely specifies how MySQL should name that particular column in its results).

```
// INPUT: minimum req'd version of MySQL, e.g. 5.0.41
public static function mysql_version_gt($ver)
{
    global $wpdb;

    $exit_msg = CustomPostTypeManager::name . __( " requires MySQL $ver
or newer.
    Talk to your system administrator about upgrading");
    $result = $wpdb->get_results( 'SELECT VERSION() as ver' );
    if ( version_compare( $result[0]->ver, $ver, '<') )
    {
        self::$errors[] = $exit_msg;
    }
}
```

Testing PHP modules

Sometimes, your plugin may require the use of non-standard functions that are only available if PHP was compiled using special options. You can use PHP's `get_loaded_extensions()` function to list all loaded extensions on the server you developed on, and you can then test against this list on the production server. This is a bit more advanced than the standard tests, but it can really help ensure that the environment is set up correctly before someone tries to run your plugin.

```
/**
 * PHP might have been compiled without some module that you require.
Pass this
 * function an array of $required_extensions and it will register a
message
 * about any missing modules.
 *
 * @param   array $required_extensions   an array of PHP modules you
want to
 *     ensure are installed on your server, e.g. array('pcre', 'mysqli',
'mcrypt');
 * @return   none   An error message is registered in self::$errors if
the test fails.
 */
 public static function php_extensions($required_extensions)
 {

    $loaded_extensions = get_loaded_extensions();

    foreach ( $required_extensions as $req )
    {
       if ( !in_array($req, $loaded ) )
       {
          self::$errors[] = __("MyPlugin requires the $req PHP
extension.
          Talk to your system administrator about reconfiguring PHP.");
       }
    }

 }
```

Testing WordPress installed plugins

A slightly more complicated test involves seeing whether or not another plugin
is installed. This can be useful if you have one plugin that depends on another, or
perhaps you just need to test whether or not a site has all of the plugins you expect it
to. We took this a step further. The following function lets you specify the required
plugins *and* the required versions of those plugins:

```
/**
 * This relies on the output of WP's get_plugins() and
 * get_option('active_plugins') functions.
 *
 * @param array   $required_plugins   An associative array with
 *     the names of the plugins and the required versions, e.g.
```

```
*    array( 'My Great Plugin' => '0.9', 'Some Other Plugin' => '1.0.1'
)
* @return    none    An error message is registered in self::$errors if
the
*    test fails.    There are 2 errors that can be generated: one if
the
*    plugin's version is too old, and another if it is missing
altogether.
*/
public static function wp_required_plugins($required_plugins)
{
    require_once(ABSPATH.'/wp-admin/includes/admin.php');
    $all_plugins = get_plugins();
    $active_plugins = get_option('active_plugins');

    // Re-index the $all_plugins array for easier testing.
    // We want to index it off of the name; it's not guaranteed to be
unique, so this
    // test could throw some illegitimate errors if 2 plugins shared
the same name.
    $all_plugins_reindexed = array();
    foreach ( $all_plugins as $path => $data )
    {
        $new_index = $data['Name'];
        $all_plugins_reindexed[$new_index] = $data;
    }

    foreach ( $required_plugins as $name => $version )
    {
        if ( isset($all_plugins_reindexed[$name]) )
        {
            if ( !empty($all_plugins_reindexed[$name]['Version']) )
            {
                if (version_compare($all_plugins_reindexed[$name]
['Version'],$version,'<'))
                {
                    self::$errors[] = __("MyPlugin requires version
$version of the $name plugin.");
                }
            }
        }
        else
        {
            self::$errors[] = __("MyPlugin requires version $version of
the $name plugin. $name is not installed.");
        }
    }
}
```

The input for this test is slightly more complicated. In your `loader.php` file, you might have something like this:

```
$required_plugins = array('Party to the Max'=>'2.0', 'Random stuff' =>
'0.7.3');
MyPlugin_tests::wp_required_plugins($required_plugins);
```

Also note you would replace the messaging with the correct name for your plugin.

Custom tests

Hopefully the sample tests listed here got your imagination going. Some software projects rely heavily on tests, and in general, we fully condone this practice. If you can identify "fail" points in your code and then write functions which test for them, you will save both yours and your users' time and frustration.

If you have ever had problems deploying a development site to a live production server, then these types of tests can save you a lot of hassle. For example, if you told your client to provide a server with exact specifications, this can ensure that the server meets those requirements.

Basically, any time your project starts to have any requirements that deviate from what's normally available in a WordPress installation, you should consider writing some tests to ensure that those conditions are being met. Don't assume that your client will understand the technical requirements or that a new server environment will meet them.

Unit tests

We would be remiss if we did not mention unit tests in this chapter. Unit testing is a method by which individual units of source code are tested to determine if they are fit for use. Remember from the beginning of the book how we recommended that you write your code in "units"? This is where it all comes together: units of code should be a size that makes them easy to test.

There are a couple of testing frameworks available for PHP that help you write unit tests. It's beyond the scope of this book to demonstrate their use, but we encourage you to look into them if your plugin is getting complicated and difficult to maintain. Unit tests are a real lifesaver because they help you catch any place where your code has failed. All of the tests that we have demonstrated in the book could be easily rewritten as unit tests.

If you want to learn about writing unit tests, we recommend having a look at the SimpleTest library. The code base may have been abandoned, but the site has some good examples and it is a suitable introduction to some of the concepts and code patterns that you will encounter while writing unit tests. `http://www.simpletest.org/`.

A more common library is PHPUnit, but its documentation is harder to follow and it is short on the phrasebook style definitions, so we don't recommend it unless you are already familiar with unit testing. You can download it at: `http://phpunit.de` and read its manual at: `http://www.phpunit.de/manual/current/en/`.

Just like any serious software project uses version control, any serious software project should also implement some kind of unit testing.

WordPress limitations

Unfortunately, WordPress does not yet have a good way for you to reference common files between plugins. In the case of these tests, it would be more efficient to put them into some sort of global WordPress library so that multiple plugins could use the tests contained in a single testing class file. However, until our testing scripts get integrated into the WordPress core, you have to work with a couple of options.

The first option is that you can copy all your testing functions into a dedicated class used by only your plugin (as we did in the previous examples). The upside here is that this is guaranteed to work, but the downside is that it's inefficient—imagine if 100 plugins each copied the *exact* same tests. It would take up 100 times more space, and it would be a nightmare to maintain—even the most trifling change in one of the tests would require that you make the same alterations to the other 99 copies.

As part of a second option, you can put all of these tests into a separate plugin, and then reference the functions from your other plugins. This is certainly more efficient, but it does create some dependencies between plugins that could easily be broken. You might have a hard time distributing your plugin if it requires that the users download a second plugin to make the first one work. It's possible, but not ideal.

Health check page

One drawback of what we have outlined here is that these tests execute during *every* WordPress page request. If you have written a long series of tests, they may incur some significant overhead and they can really slow down your site performance. One option is to move all your tests into a separate file that you must navigate to directly.

Perhaps you have heard of a "health check" page—all it does is run a series of tests, and if everything looks good, it prints out an "Ok" message. There are many different monitoring applications out there (for example, Nagios—http://nagios.org/) that can be configured to take quick looks at these health check pages and verify that they are seeing the "Ok" message. If a test hits a snag, it will generate and error, and the monitoring software will notice it.

To set up a health check page, you can remove all the tests from your loader.php file and construct a new file like the following:

```php
<?php
// Sample Health Check page
require_once( realpath('../../../').'/wp-config.php' );

include_once('includes/MyPlugin.php');
include_once('tests/MyPlugin_tests.php');

// Run Tests.
MyPlugin_tests::some_long_and_difficult_test();
MyPlugin_tests::another_long_and_difficult_test();

if ( empty(MyPlugin_tests::$errors) )
{
    print 'Ok';
}
else
{
    $error_items = '';
    foreach ( MyPlugin_tests::$errors as $e )
    {
        $error_items .= "<li>$e</li>";
    }
    print '<div class="error"><p><strong>'
    .__('The &quot;MyPlugin&quot; plugin encountered errors! It cannot load!')
    .'</strong> '
    ."<ul style='margin-left:30px;'>$error_items</ul>"
    .'</p>'
    .'</div>';
}
/*EOF*/
```

If the file were named healthcheck.php, you would navigate to it directly in a browser and look for the "Ok" message (for example, http://yoursite.com/wp-content/plugins/myplugin/healthcheck.php).

This is a great way to run your tests "on demand", instead of bogging down the normal users with repeated testing, but the downside is that the users wouldn't have any idea that the plugin was causing problems until someone bothers to look at the health check page.

Storing test results in the database

Another option to help reduce the overhead caused by slow tests is to store test results in the database. Each time a page is requested, you would pull up a specific record from the `wp_options` table where you stored the results of the last test. Based on the result, you could decide whether or not you needed to run tests again. Querying the database does incur some overhead, but it may be significantly less overhead than running through an entire gauntlet of testing functions.

There are many different options available to you when choosing how to test your plugin. The requirements really vary depending on the nature of the code you have used, but we've given you a good starting toolbox for how to test for some of the most common conditions.

However, valid tests are not the only thing your plugin needs before it is cleared for launch. You need to examine your configuration and the documentation before you push your plugin out of the nest.

Death to clippy: Use sensible configurations

One of the overlooked aspects of prerelease preparations is how you should set up your default configurations. Remember Clippy, the insistently annoying animated paperclip that greeted users when they opened older versions of Microsoft Word? Clippy was both well known and well hated, and that annoying little paperclip is a vivid representation of one of the most notorious failures of configuration defaults. What made Clippy so aggravating? By default, the user was assumed to be inept and in dire need of hand-holding at every turn. We have no objection to Clippy's existence—some people may actually want that kind of help—but it is absurd to think that the majority of users should be assaulted by his incessant speech-bubbles *by default*. Instead of assuming that the average user was half-way competent, by leaving those settings on by default, Microsoft assumed that the average user was nearly a computer illiterate.

If you or your users are constantly editing the configuration settings of your plugin, then it's probably time to re-examine your defaults and set them to something that better matches what your users need. Do not assume that **you** as the plugin's author represent an average user. Figure out what **their** needs are and cater to them.

Double check your interface

Going into round two with our previous punching bag, Clippy the Office assistant was doubly bad because disabling it required jumping through a few unnecessary hoops. In Office 2k/XP, killing Clippy required at least four mouse clicks, and in Office 97, it was nearly impossible to disable the eager assistant. Many people found it easiest to bypass the user interface entirely and just rename the appropriate folder on the hard drive (it was "Actors" for those of you having a nostalgic flashback).

If your users are having trouble finding their way around your plugin, then you should consider some other ways of implementing the user interface. You could switch the brake pedal with the accelerator pedal and your car would still work, but anyone who drove it would be more likely to have an accident. It takes time and intuition to figure this out, but try to put options and menus where the user expects to see them. This is one of the last chances you have to adjust your plugin's interface—once your plugin gets published, it can be really disruptive to alter it.

Documentation

One of the problems that plague open source projects (and the WordPress plugin repository) is a lack of effective documentation. There are a lot of books about how to write good code, but there are precious few on how to write good documentation. Since documentation is a critical part of your plugin, we would be remiss if we neglected to give you some guidelines on how to write it effectively. Nothing is worse than pushing a good plugin on the public and not telling them what they need to know in order to use it. Think of it from a business standpoint: good user documentation means fewer client support requests and lower support costs.

Identify the purpose

The very first thing you need to do when writing documentation is identify the purpose of the given area that you are trying to document. The purpose in documenting a function, for example, is to educate the developer, whereas the purpose of the plugin's `readme.txt` file is to educate the plugin user. The following are the three main areas of the `readme.txt` file and their purposes:

- **Description**: Its purpose is to answer the question, "What problem does this plugin solve?" The answer to that question should inform potential users as to whether or not they should download it. Remember, it's all about *what* problem gets solved, and not so much about *how* it gets solved. If you keep drifting into explanations of *how* something was solved, try reframing your definition of the problem.

- **Installation**: Its purpose is to answer the question, "How do I make this work?" or "How can I see this in action?" If your plugin includes a menu item, you should mention its location here. This may be an appropriate place to include a simple common use case that demonstrates how to use the plugin.

- **Frequently Asked Questions**: You may have many FAQs, but each of them should have the goal of instructing the user how to accomplish a specific task.

Your documentation will always be hit or miss if you cannot identify the purpose behind it. No matter what component you are writing about, big or small, the mere act of *identifying* a purpose for each piece of documentation will help guide your writing. If the purpose is to instruct the user on how to complete a certain task, your documentation will look completely different than if the purpose is to define what functions are at work to carry out that task. Having a purpose in mind behind each piece of documentation will give it structure and durability.

> *"If a technical document cannot be used to accomplish the task it was written for, it has no real use and belongs at the bottom of the cat box"*
> *Good documentation and the cat box factor. (Guest Editorial) Technical Communication – February 1, 2004, Kathryn Poe).*

The most important pieces of documentation are those whose purpose it is to *instruct the user in how to accomplish a given task*, so we are going to focus most of our time fielding that particular type of writing. The most frequent examples of this type of documentation are the items in the "Frequently Asked Questions" area.

Learning to drive: Keeping it relevant

The mere act of identifying a task immediately helps you filter out what is and what is not relevant for instructing users on how to complete that task. Try to have some appreciation for what the average person *needs to know* about it. Put those instructions in front of them **first**. The beautiful thing about online documentation is you can always provide the streamlined "Average Joe" instructions first, and then include links so users can "click here to read more".

Can you imagine learning to drive with your dad, but instead of him telling you how to start the car and shift gears, he tells you about how the fuel injectors work? The average driver doesn't *need to know* about fuel injectors, just like the average user doesn't *need to know* about class names, query formats, or that really clever way you overrode the `plugin_action_links` filter, so don't cram your `readme.txt` file with detailed explanations about them. Always strive to give a concise explanation of how to accomplish the task you identified. Fuel injectors might be broadly relevant to driving, but they should take a back seat to the gas pedal and steering wheel.

Phrasebooks vs. dictionaries: Give examples

If you have ever travelled to a foreign country and had to speak a foreign language, you know that one of the first things you learn to say are particular *phrases*. You really don't need to know which word means "toilet" or which word is the reflexive pronoun; all you really need to know is how to get to a bathroom before you have an accident. That's why travelers carry phrasebooks more than dictionaries. Technically, the dictionary is more thorough, and technically, it contains everything you need to know, but it's put together in a completely inefficient way if you are trying to construct entire sentences.

Tying this into our previous example, imagine learning to drive if your dad gave you instructions like this:

- **release** –*verb (used with object)*: To free from confinement
- **the** –*definite article*, used, esp. before a noun
- **clutch** –*noun*: A mechanism for readily engaging or disengaging a shaft with or from another shaft or rotating part

That's a seriously relevant chunk of information from your old man, but it's just ridiculous and completely ineffective. Your documentation should include phrasebook-style examples instead of dictionary definitions. Instead of explaining every trifling detail, you first need to give the bigger picture, as in "if you are trying to accomplish X, then do Y". Again, you can always include links to more detailed explanations after you have fielded a few examples.

Analogy: The three bears

Documentation is like porridge in the story of Goldilocks; some documentation is too short, some is too long, and some is *just right*. You want to aim for that sweet spot and write enough to tell people how to accomplish the given task. Avoid terse instructions that offer no details and avoid longwinded explanations because no one will bother to read them — massive verbiage is no substitute for clarity. In our experience, sometimes the longest documentation is the worst because despite their best efforts, the authors were not able to clearly identify purposes and tasks.

Analogy: PC load letter

Messaging to the user should be clear and detailed. Detailed error messages can be time consuming to construct and translate, but they make for a much better user experience. Look at our previous example in this chapter about conflicting names:

The Custom Post Type Manager plugin cannot load correctly! Another plugin has declared conflicting class, function, or constant names:

> ** Function: really_common_function_name*

> *You must deactivate the plugins that are using these conflicting names.*

This alerts the user about an error, and it tries to identify the cause, and it gives the user some idea of how to correct the problem. No, it's not perfect, but it's a lot more informative than the fatal PHP error that would have popped up in this situation:

Fatal error: Cannot redeclare really_common_function_name() in /path/to/wordpress3/html/wp-content/plugins/your-plugin/index.php on line 88

Anyone who has seen the cult-classic comedy "Office Space" can relate to the distinctly unhelpful "PC Load Letter" printer error that befuddled and angered one of the main characters to the point of destroying the printer with a baseball bat. It pays to go the extra mile and try to make your messages to the user as specific and helpful as possible. What does "PC Load Letter" mean, anyway?

The decalog of documentation

The following is a checklist of actions for you to go through to help ensure that your plugin's documentation is reasonably sound.

1. Include full examples. Short little code fragments are only relevant *after* you've demonstrated a full example. Zoom out a little bit and include a couple of lines of code before and after your example—they are invaluable in helping to put your examples into context. Take the time to demonstrate a few use-cases, and don't be cheap. If people repeatedly ask you how to do something related to your plugin, you should thank them for the interest and demonstrate a viable solution. Remember that they are asking you for a *phrase*, not a definition—an example demonstrates how to perform a specific task in its entirety. Assume that your audience is knowledgeable, but pretend they have had five or six beers, so you have to be extra clear in your explanations.

2. At the top of each file, include a brief description that identifies what it is and what it does. How does it fit into the larger picture? What problem is this file solving? What is an example of how it gets used? Which files use it? What is the expected input? What is the expected output? We've included this type of basic documentation throughout this book, so you have numerous examples to pull from. For example:

```
/**
* This file is included by the index.php file when the Live-Search
plugin is loaded.
```

```
* This class contains static functions that manipulate date
formats.
*/
```

Your target audience here is other developers, including your future self in three months after you've forgotten everything you know about this plugin. The purpose of these little comments is to identify the lay of the land for other developers.

3. Include a summary of each function and class describing its input and output. Avoid the perfunctory descriptions that are just copies of the function or class name. If it makes more sense to provide documentation for a group of similar functions rather than for individual ones, then do that. Include a simple example if you can't think of anything else. The point of this is so that a developer can quickly see how each function is used. This can be done effectively in one line, and that's fine so long as it is clear:

```
/**
* Converts incoming date, e.g. '2010-10-31' to human readable
'October 31, 2010'
*/
function convert_yyyymmdd_to_human_date($yyyymmdd) {
    /* code */
}
```

4. Take some time to review the names of your variables, functions, and classes. Do they make sense? It can be a tricky find-and-replace operation to change these after you're wrapping up a round of development, but those names are the key to understanding your code, so descriptive names can save you a lot of time debugging later on.

5. In technical and end-user documentation, remove any instances of the following words: "obviously", "clearly", "of course", or any other word or phrase that assumes that the user will have any idea what you're talking about. Any time you are tempted to use one of those key words or phrases, it should be a blistering red light that you need to stop your short-hand shenanigans and include a full example of what you're talking about because it's virtually guaranteed that your conception of "obvious" is a viewpoint shared by you alone.

6. Sleep on it: Take a break from working on your plugin, and when you return, see if your descriptions and examples make any sense.

7. Avoid pronouns. This is just to remind you to be super clear in your sentences. You can literally do a "find all" operation in your documentation and replace any instance of "it" or "them". Unless you say the noun specifically, it may not be clear to the user what you were talking about.

8. Clearly list the requirements of your code (for example, versions of PHP/ MySQL/WordPress) and give a detailed description of how to install and configure it. If you are not sure which versions of PHP/MySQL/WordPress your plugin requires, then list the versions on which you tested it—don't assume that it works on anything else unless you have specifically tested it on other systems and versions. Your tests from the previous section should correspond to these version numbers *exactly*.

9. Find an editor. Although you are the author, in a way, you are the person *least* qualified to explain your creation to the outside world because more than anyone else, your view is from the inside out. It takes time and practice to learn how to write good documentation from the *outside* point of view. It really is a skill that is entirely separate from writing good code, so don't beat yourself up if you are having some trouble or if some confused forum goons flame you for having poor explanations. Ask for help. Sometimes the people who have the most trouble with your code can offer the best explanations for others in how to use it. Remember that it is a separate skill, so even if someone is a horrible coder, they may run circles around you and your ability to effectively document your code.

10. Be sure your documentation separates the "phrasebook" style tutorials that show users how to accomplish specific tasks from verbose "dictionary" style definitions. The "phrasebook" style tutorials are absolutely required, whereas the "dictionary" style definitions are optional in most cases.

Summary

Writing a plugin is always more work than it seems. You thought that you were done when you first got the thing to work, but really there is a lot more that goes into it. Collectively, that's all part of the process of creating well-crafted and high-quality plugins for the masses. Take pride in it.

Up next, we'll tell you about the mechanics of getting your plugin published to the WordPress repository.

10
Publishing Your Plugin

In this chapter, we are going to deal specifically with the mechanics of submitting your plugin to the WordPress repository for public distribution. Previous chapters dealing with testing and documentation would broadly apply no matter where you deployed your plugin, but this chapter deals wit the things that are specific to deploying your plugin on the WordPress platform. It includes how to handle internationalization, using the WordPress SVN repository, and writing the readme. txt file that is required for all WordPress plugins.

Internationalization and localization

In the context of plugin development, internationalization is the process of *preparing* software so that its messages can be translated into a specific regional dialect, whereas localization refers to the actual *translating* of those messages. These two terms sometimes blur together because they are so closely related, but to be clear, we are focusing on internationalization in this section. The goal is to ensure that your plugin's messages can be easily translated (that is "localized").

See the official documentation on internationalization (`http://goo.gl/fGXQ`) as well as the documentation for translating WordPress (`http://goo.gl/Mlbf`) for more information on this topic. Although it is not technically required, it is highly recommended that you internationalize your plugin so that users from different countries can localize it.

Giving you a heads up on the following sections, the process works in several stages:

1. First, you internationalize your plugin by adding special functions that will process each message. Perhaps you've spotted them already. `__()` and `_e()` are the primary functions WordPress uses to facilitate translation. They don't translate (that is localize) anything *yet*, but they will, once you provide some valid language files.

> **Remember**
> Internationalization is about *preparing* your plugin for translation.

2. Second, you can use Poedit, a free tool that will extract these messages into a portable object template (POT) file.

3. Third, you will provide translations for each message—even if your messages are already in English, you actually have to "translate" the message identifier in the POT file into a localized (that is translated) message. After providing a translation, you will end up with ".po" and ".mo" files for each locale that you translate those messages into.

4. Lastly, you will ensure that WordPress loads your *textdomain* and its associated files when your plugin needs to display messages to the user. Don't worry if it all sounds Greek to you—we will explain each step in more detail as we come to it.

We should add that for most intents and purposes, the terms translate and localize are equivalent. Likewise, a POT file and a .pot file refer to the same thing: a portable object template that contains all the translatable messages gleaned from your plugin.

Processing each message

WordPress uses the GNU *gettext* localization framework to provide localization infrastructure. The most important thing you need to know about it while internationalizing your plugin is that *gettext* uses message-level translations—each message might be a single word, a phrase, or several sentences. There are two primary localization functions that you will be using:

    __($message)

This first function searches the localization module for the translation of $message, and passes the translation to the PHP return statement. If no translation is found for $message, it just returns $message.

    _e($message)

The second function above is shorthand for echo __().

These function names are hardly descriptive, but they are easy to use because they are so short. There are a few other related functions, too, but these two are the most important.

The basic idea here is truly simple. Scan through your plugin for messages that are displayed to the user, and wrap them using the functions above. For example, if your plugin contains the following HTML/PHP:

```
<?php $label = 'Click to search the database.'; ?>
<p><?php print $label; ?></p>
<input type="submit" value="Search" />
```

Then you might end up with something like the following:

```
<?php $label = __('Click to search the database.'); ?>
<p><?php print $label; ?></p>
<input type="submit" value="<?php _e('Search'); ?>" />
```

Any message passed to the __() function will be looked up in the localization module and a translation will be returned if possible. So if you have the locale set to Germany, __('Yes') would return "Ja", and if you have it set to Mexico, it would return "Sí".

It makes sense, but it's a little too good to be true. Don't go changing all of your messages just yet because there is a bit more to learn first. Just because the locale has been defined does not mean that there is only one viable definition of a message. In the same way that "football", "fag", or "weed" have *very* different meanings in American and British locales, a term such as "stoned" might mean something very different depending on whether the context of your conversation was biblical adulterers or drug-using hippies.

So in addition to specifying the locale, the __() translation function and its cousins can accept an optional second argument for a *textdomain* that identifies a proper context for the translation. We'll show you how to load a *textdomain* in a moment, but you can already grasp how it can be used:

```
__('stoned', 'biblical-textdomain'); // translates to being pelted by
rocks
__('stoned', 'drug-slang-textdomain'); // translates to being
intoxicated or dazed from drugs
```

Once you have adjusted your plugin's messages to be piped through the localization functions, you will be ready to scrape them using Poedit or any similar tool.

Choosing a textdomain

Choose a unique textdomain for your plugin—the name should contain only alphabetical characters, hyphens, and underscores. Keeping in line with WordPress parlance, it should match the name of your plugin's folder. Once you have chosen a name, you need to comb through your plugin and ensure that each message is wrapped with the `__()` or `_e()` functions that specify the message and the textdomain:

```
__('This is my message', 'my-unique-textdomain');
```

Usually this isn't difficult, but it may take a while. As always, be careful about apostrophes and periods when concatenating strings. If you encounter some messages that are a bit more complicated, have a look at the following sections for examples of how to handle them.

Some users may find it preferable to include the `__()` and `_e()` functions as soon as they start writing code—it's up to you. We have omitted them from previous chapters so we could keep our examples clean and save the discussion for this chapter. There's no harm in including the localization functions right from the get-go once you know how to use them—they will execute without errors even if the translations or textdomain do not yet exist.

Best practices

It may seem completely counter-intuitive, but you *must* avoid using variables for your message text. Consider the following two examples:

```
_e('This is an Ok message', 'my-textdomain');
$msg = 'This never shows up on the radar';
_e($msg, 'my-textdomain');
```

As far as PHP syntax is concerned, both of those functions are properly formed. However, the second example causes problems down the road when we need to extract translatable messages into a dedicated language file. It's maddening, but the scraping tools rely on simple text parsing, *not* PHP parsing, so they don't attempt to figure out variable values. We will cover the Poedit application and creation language files momentarily, but for now, just make sure you are using *literal* strings in conjunction with the `__()` and `_e()` functions and *not* variables. Don't forget!

In conjunction with the basic "scrape-friendly" syntax, here are a handful of best-practices that WordPress recommends along with a few of our own:

- Use regular, proper English. Minimize slang and abbreviations.

- Use entire sentences: Do not do something like:

  ```
  _e('This is the first line') . '<br/>' . _e('of my really long
  message.');
  ```

- Think of each message as a unit. If you wrote all your messages on pieces of paper and dropped them into a hat, would a translator be able to translate each one if he pulled them out of the hat one by one?

- Use `sprintf()` instead of string concatenation. For example:

  ```
  sprintf(__('Replace %s with %s'), $a, $b); is always better than
  __('Replace ').$a.__(' with ').$b;
  ```

- Split long messages into paragraphs. Merge related sentences, but do not include whole pages of text in one string.

- Avoid unusual markup and unusual control characters. Do not use HTML or URLs in your translation messages unless there is some legitimate reason that they would change with locale (for example, a link to a locale specific help page).

- Do not leave leading or trailing whitespace in a translatable phrase.

- Do not translate variables; translate *literal* strings only; otherwise language file generators will be unable to extract language strings. For example:

  ```
  __('This works'); /* whereas */ $x = 'This'; __($x); // fails.
  ```

Working with formatting

This whole process of internationalization and localization requires some careful doctoring of your messages, and you may find it necessary to dumb-down your HTML formatting. Consider the following message:

```
$msg = 'Determines where this post type should appear in the left hand
admin menu.<br/>
Default: null - appears below Comments.
<ul style="margin-left:40px;">
<li><strong>5</strong> - below Posts</li>
<li><strong>10</strong> - below Media</li>
</ul>';
```

How can we correctly format this message to rely on __() to provide translatable strings? We need to break it down into units, and we don't want to include any HTML as part of our translatable message. The following is what we came up with:

```
$msg = __('Determines where this post type should appear in the left
hand admin menu.','my-textdomain');
$msg .= '<br/>';
```

```
$msg .= __('Default: null - appears below Comments.','my-textdomain');
$msg .= '<ul style="margin-left:40px;">
   <li><strong>5</strong> - ' . __('below Posts','my-textdomain') .'</
li>
   <li><strong>10</strong> - '. __('below Media','my-textdomain') .'</
li>
   </ul>';
```

It's more complicated than the original, but it's now ready for localization!

More advanced messages

Some of you may have realized that there are some messages that need to include additional bits of data, such as a number of records returned:

```
$msg = "3 fields deleted";
```

In the scenario above, "3" is a variable. In this case, you can wrap your messages using the sprintf() function, just like we did in *Chapter 3*:

```
$cnt_fields_deleted = 3;
$translated_msg = sprintf( __( '%s fields deleted', 'your-
textdomain'), $cnt_fields_deleted );
```

This preserves the integrity of the message for translation purposes, and it allows you to better inform the user about what is going on.

Plural vs. singular

Wait! Some of you are already a step ahead. What happens if there is only a single field deleted? The message should then read "field" instead of "fields". Ah, this is tricky. Well, there *is* a function that solves precisely that problem:

```
_n( $msg_single, $msg_plural, $number, $textdomain)
```

This function allows you to provide variations on messages when there are chances of singular or plural versions of the text. It solves one problem, but we discourage its use because it causes another: its translation strings *do not* get picked up by Poedit's radar. Remember, Poedit and the other tools used to generate language files rely on simple text parsing that grabs only the first argument from a defined translation function. In other words, only the message for the $msg_single ends up getting scraped. It's unfortunate that we cannot rely on a WordPress internal, but for cases like this we have to write our own if-statement if we want our POT file to be generated correctly:

```
$msg = '';
if ($cnt_fields_deleted  == 1 )
{
    $msg = __('A single field was deleted','my-textdomain');
}
else
{
    $msg = sprintf( __('%s fields deleted','my-textdomain'), cnt_
fields_deleted);
}
```

These messages are starting to get more and more complex, so you may need to do some shuffling to keep your code clean. Be diligent!

More complex messages

Since we're talking about `sprintf()` and its invaluable assistance in formatting translated messages, we should cover the cases where you want to supply it with more than one bit of data. If you've got your multi-lingual "mojo" going on, you will remember that many languages use a different word order than English (for example, noun and *then* adjective), and this may affect your messages. You can still rely on the `sprintf()` function, but we need to follow `sprintf`'s rules for argument swapping. If we leave translations out of this for a moment, we can see that argument swapping allows us to specify exactly where the additional arguments get placed into the format string:

```
$msg_v1 = 'They were %1$s %2$s.';
$msg_v2 = 'The %2$s were %1$s.';
print sprintf($msg_v1, 'large','dogs');   // They were large dogs.
print sprintf($msg_v2, 'large','dogs');   // The dogs were large.
```

As a mnemonic, the original `%s` is still hidden in there, but now it has `1$` or `2$` sandwiched in between the `%` and `s` to reference the original order of the incoming arguments: `%1$s` references the first argument ("large") and `%2$s` references the second argument ("dogs"). Make sure to use single quotes around your message format string, otherwise the `$s` will get interpreted as a new variable:

```
$msg_v3 = 'The %2$s were %1$s.';    // single quotes are ok
$msg_v4 = "The %2\$s were %1\$s.";    // using double-quotes, you must
escape the '$'
```

It is good to cover the fundamentals here, because little things like syntax can get in your way when what you really want to focus on is the translation of your message.

Let's take a look at how this all fits together in a more complex message. In the following message, assume that "bob" and "12" are both variables:

"User bob is currently editing page 12."

To get this to work, all you need to do is use verbose placeholders that allow argument swapping:

```
$translated_msg =  sprintf(
    __('User %1$s is currently editing page %2$s.', 'your-
textdomain')
  , $user
  , $post_id
);
```

Now you have a message string that is safe to translate into languages that may change the order of your arguments, such as German:

"Seite 12 wird vom Benutzer bob bearbeitet."

If you're wondering how you are supposed to translate a string that contains mysterious instances of "%s" in it, then the next section is for you. There are times when you really need to put in a comment for the translator.

Notes to translators

Sometimes, the usage of your messages may be obscure or fairly complicated (like some of the above examples), and you will want to include a message to translators. This can be done using a simple comment with a pre-defined format. Simply preface your comment with `translators:`, like this:

```
/* translators: this should reflect a localized date format, see
http://php.net/date */
$localized_date_format = __('g:i:s a');
```

This is how you can clarify the usage of strings that contain instances of "%s". It is best to give an example of what the message might read after `sprintf()` has replaced the "%s" with a value.

The Poedit application also has an option to add a comment to each message, but its functionality seems quirky and poorly implemented. The comment does get written to the generated .po files, but once made, the comments are not editable. For that reason, we discourage the use of Poedit's comments function.

These examples should cover the majority of cases that you may encounter while internationalizing your messages.

Language files

Now that we have internationalized our code and prepared it for localization using the __() family of functions, it's time to create a POT file. POT stands for "portable object template", and the .pot file will store all of your translatable messages in one place. The POT file is what translators will typically use to translate your messages into a specific language and locale. It is called a template because it contains **message IDs**. You may have thought that you were typing actual *messages* into your plugin, but take a moment to think of them as IDs. We are all familiar with this type of message ID—we see them all the time in error codes. For example, the copy machine might display "Error Code 7", or you may get a 404 message when you try to visit a web page that no longer exists. Later we translate that code or ID into a message we understand, like "Toner Low" or "Page not Found", but the ID itself is language agnostic.

In other words, you could have written your entire plugin using esoteric message codes for your messages and technically the process would still work—that's a horrible idea, but it is technically possible. This type of architecture means that plugin developers can use *any* language they want when displaying messages—Spanish, Thai, German—and it doesn't matter so long as they can translate those message IDs into other languages. Pretty cool, huh?

From the POT file, we will translate our message IDs into actual languages and create a .po file for each localization. Remember that the message ID in the .pot file should be thought of as being language agnostic *until* it gets translated into a specific locale via a .po file. Thankfully our messages in the POT file are already in our native language, so our first "translation" is nothing more than a copy and paste.

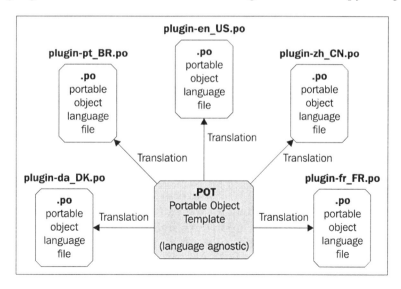

You have several options available to you when creating your POT file, but the one we will be covering next uses a cross-platform application named Poedit (available at www.poedit.net/download.php). Make sure you download and install it before continuing. We've done a lot of explaining so far, but now it is time to get to it!

Creating a POT file

Open up Poedit and choose to create a "catalog". Hopefully the terminology makes more sense to you after our discussions about how the process works. A "catalog" is a list of "message IDs". Poedit's interface is a bit unwieldy (particularly on Mac OS X), but it outperformed the other tools we tested. Follow our instructions and have some patience, and you'll get through it (we wouldn't lie to you). You need to enter data on three tabs: **Project info**, **Paths**, and **Keywords**.

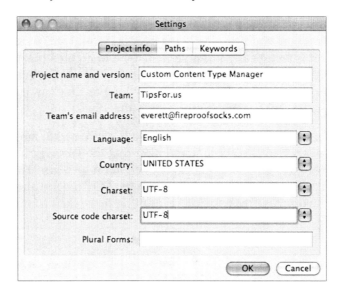

The **Project info** tab is pretty straightforward. Adjust your country and the language used in your messages accordingly. You'll want to use UTF-8 as your **Charset**. However, don't click **OK** yet! You need to edit information on the other two tabs!

It's common for WordPress plugins to include a folder dedicated to holding your localization files. Often this is called "languages", "localizations", "translations" or simply "lang", and that's where you will save your .pot file. We are choosing to name our folder "lang", but what's important for the **Paths** tab is that you include a relative path *from* the dedicated lang folder up to the plugin's base directory, namely: "..". All we are doing is telling Poedit the path from where the language files will be stored. If you stored your translations nested inside two folders, for example, special/ languages, then you would have to use a path of ../../. Make sense?

Do not change the base path, and do not click on **OK** yet! First update your
Keywords tab!

Keywords are used to identify the names of the translation functions. Keep in mind
that Poedit is not made just for WordPress — it can be used to create .pot files for
any application that uses the *gettext* localization framework, so you have to define
which functions (that is keywords) are used when displaying messages. Remove or
edit the defaults so the two keywords are __ and _e. Yes, there are other WordPress
localization functions, but we are omitting them from this example.

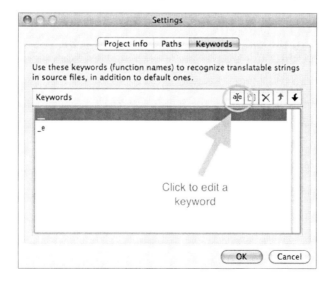

Only after you have configured each of the three tabs, you can safely click on the **OK** button. Save the file into your plugin's `lang` directory (or whatever you chose to call it). Make sure you manually type in the `.pot` extension, and name the file using the same name as your plugin's directory. Oddly, some translation tools require that your `.pot` file uses the same name as your plugin's folder.

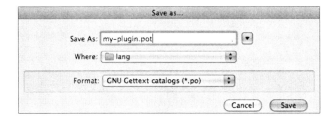

If you received an error when trying to save, it can mean that you accidentally changed the base path from "." in the **Paths** tab—make sure that you *add* a new path named "`../`" and leave the base path alone.

Congratulations! Hopefully that was not too troublesome. You should now have a valid `.pot` file!

Creating translations: .po files

Once you have successfully saved your `.pot` file, it's immediately time to create your first translation. Remember that at this point, the `.pot` file technically contains only language-agnostic message IDs, not yet actual messages. You need to translate those message strings into a specified language and save the resulting `.po` file. Poedit's interface is a bit skimpy on the labeling. Select the term you want to translate from the list, and then type the translation into the text field at the bottom of the window. For your first locale, this is as simple as copying and pasting your original message.

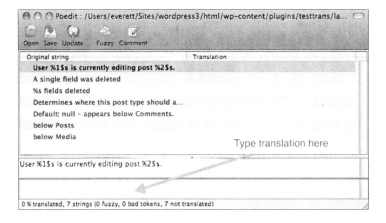

After you have translated all the entries, you should save your work in the original POT file, but you also need to do a **Save As**. The way this works is very similar to how Microsoft Office deals with templates. **Any** Word document or Excel spreadsheet can be saved as a template and its contents stay the same (more or less). With Poedit, your POT template file is essentially identical to your primary language's `.po` file, but the way they are treated by the application is slightly different.

After you've saved your `.pot` file, save a copy as a `.po` file using a naming convention that incorporates your plugin name, the language of the translation, and the locale. For example, if "my-plugin" had been localized for traditional Chinese (Taiwan), you would end up with a file named `my-plugin-zh_TW.po`, whereas if it had been localized for simplified Chinese (China), you would save your file as `my-plugin-zh_CN.po`.

"zh" is a language code as defined by ISO 639-1 (Wikipedia link: `http://goo.gl/yHjM`) whereas "TW" and "CN" are country codes as defined by ISO 3166-1 (Wikipedia link: `http://goo.gl/hUim`). Sometimes the language code and the country code are the same.

In our example, we're going to save the translation as `my-plugin-en_US.po`. This naming convention helps WordPress find the correct file when you specify a locale — your plugin's folder name, *textdomain*, and the prefix to your language files should all be the same. You'll notice that saving a `.po` file also creates a `.mo` file. The `.mo` files are "machine object" files — they are binary reproductions of the `.po` files, and they are not meant to be read by humans. Normally, you don't need to concern yourself with the `.mo` files, but if you ever need to, you can regenerate a `.po` file from its corresponding `.mo` file.

To summarize, WordPress language files come in three flavors:

- POT: A "Portable Object Template", or POT file, saved with a .pot extension. This is the file that will store all of your translatable messages in one place.

- `.po`: "Portable Object" files are created when a POT file is translated into a specific locale. They contain the locale-specific translation of the message strings.

- `.mo`: These are binary versions of the `.po` files which are not intended to be read by humans.

Congratulations! You have now internationalized and localized your plugin!

Loading a textdomain

If you've come this far, you should be ready for a victory lap: you've done a lot of work to internationalize and localize your plugin. The final thing you need to do is to tell WordPress to actually load up your localized translations. The format of the function is as follows:

```
load_plugin_textdomain('your-unique-name','/path/to/your/plugin-name/
location-of-language-files/');
```

Again, for consistency we recommend using the same name for your plugin's folder as for your *textdomain*. We've seen some inconsistent behavior in different plugins and applications that seem to expect this naming convention, so it's best to follow it. To load the language files, all you need to do is to tie into a WordPress action and reference the `load_plugin_textdomain()` function.

Chances are that you've already hooked into WordPress' `init` action somewhere in your plugin, so you can just add the `load_plugin_textdomain()` function to the callback function that you have already defined. If your plugin isn't already hooking into the `init` event, you might add a hook and a function looking something like the following:

```
add_action('init', 'myplugin_load_translation_file');

function myplugin_load_translation_file()
{
    // relative path to WP_PLUGIN_DIR where the translation files will
sit:
    $plugin_path = plugin_basename( dirname( __FILE__ ) .'/lang' );
    load_plugin_textdomain( 'myplugin', '', $plugin_path );
}
```

The trickiest thing here is determining your plugin path. Depending on whether your callback function is in a file at the root of your plugin's directory, in a class in the `includes` directory, or somewhere else entirely, the plugin path may have to be adjusted. When in doubt, print it out — if you can see the path that you are intending to use, you can tell if it is correct.

Save your work, and try browsing through the WordPress manager to ensure that no errors are being thrown.

Updating a translation

Each time you change the messages used in your plugin, you will have to update your POT file and the primary .po file that you created when you first created the POT file. Each time you publish a new version of your plugin, you may end up re-reading this chapter so you can regenerate your translation files. You are familiar with the process now, and Poedit makes it fairly straightforward.

Launch Poedit and open your existing `.pot` file. Double-clicking on the POT file may cause PowerPoint to launch because it too uses the `.pot` extension.

Mac only: We encountered some difficulties using the Mac version of Poedit: it was unable to easily open an existing `.pot` file. You can either drag the `.pot` file onto the Poedit icon while holding down the *option + Apple* keys to force Poedit to open the file, or when you click on the **Open** button inside of Poedit, make sure you enable the **All files (*.*)** option so you can correctly select your `.pot` file.

Once you have opened your POT catalog, you merely need to click on the "Update" icon and your plugin files will be re-scanned for new message strings.

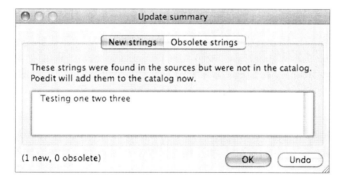

Any new messages will be added to the catalog, and any old ones that are no longer used will be deleted. As before, all you need to do is provide translations of the new message strings. Save your work in the original POT file, and then perform another "Save as" where you update your primary language .po file. Remember: your primary language file is essentially a copy of your POT file.

Format for the readme.txt file

There are only a couple more requirements for you to fulfill before you can submit your plugin to the WordPress repository. One of those requirements is that each plugin *must* be accompanied by a `readme.txt` file, and several of the other requirements can piggyback on its merits once you have written this file. We included information about writing good documentation in the previous chapter — this section has only to do with using the correct format for that documentation.

The `readme.txt` file uses a standardized format to describe a plugin's functionality, installation procedures, and a usage manual. Its contents are automatically parsed by the WordPress plugin repository to display an information page for each plugin — you've already seen many such pages while browsing for plugins (for example, `http://wordpress.org/extend/plugins/vipers-video-quicktags`).

There is a sample `readme.txt` file available here: `http://goo.gl/1kFQ`. We recommend that you copy this into your plugin's directory and customize it. The sample file is fairly descriptive, and it relies on a common markup engine. The only things we will clarify are right at the beginning:

- **Requires at least**: 2.0.2: This refers to a version of WordPress
- **Tested up to**: 2.1: This also refers to a version of WordPress
- **Stable tag**: 4.3: This refers both to a version of your plugin, and a corresponding SVN tags directory (for example, tags/4.3/ inside your plugin's repository)

If you diligently followed our chapter on testing your plugin, it will be easy for you to enforce the use of a minimum version of WordPress. The stable tag is a way for you to continue development and tagging without alerting users that an update is available. You are perhaps already familiar with WordPress' efficient notices about when your plugins have updates available. These messages are triggered when the plugin authors submit new versions of their plugins to the WordPress repository and they update the stable tag in their `readme.txt` files. No messages are sent until the readme's "Stable tag" setting is updated and the repository trunk is copied and named in the `tags` folder. Just remember that the version listed in your plugin's information header should match up exactly with the tagged directories you create in SVN. Versions and tags should *only* contain numbers and periods.

The main sections include:

- Description
- Installation
- Frequently Asked Questions
- Screenshots

You can also add your own sections as needed. This is a perfect time to review the chapter on good documentation and ensure that your explanations are clear and to the point.

Section – installation

WordPress plugins are very easy to install, and they are almost always installed in the same manner. This section should include a reference to any configuration options or manager pages that may have been added—direct the user to those pages so they can see your plugin in action with their own eyes.

Section – Frequently Asked Questions

The Frequently Asked Questions section should include both answers to simple *what* questions such as "what does this button do?", as well as answers to *how* questions such as "how do I make a rainbow in my brain?" The *how* questions are your chance to shine with detailed and full examples, or even provide references to included screenshots or videos.

An often overlooked FAQ is "how do I remove this plugin?" Even though you think your plugin is super-awesome, you should at least let people know if it made any modifications to the database or if it is using any rows from `wp_options`, and so on. If you haven't already done so, you should consider adding some cleanup code that helps uninstall the plugin. Refer back to *Chapter 7* for an example.

Section – screenshots

Your `readme.txt` file can include screenshots of your plugin in action. We highly recommend including a couple. People are very visual, and a picture can speak a thousand words. You can include images in the standard "web-friendly" formats: `.png`, `.jpg` (or `.jpeg`), and `.gif`. Your screenshots should be named `screenshot-1.jpg`, `screenshot-2.jpg`, and so on (or whatever file extension you are using), and you can add a corresponding description simply by updating the Screenshots section in the `readme.txt` file.

Our only pet peeve with this is that WordPress requires the screenshots to be saved in the root of your plugin's directory. All that work we did organizing our plugin's files into classes and folders seemingly goes to waste when the screenshots come to town. Oh well. At least it's not the in-laws.

Quick tip: Taking screenshots

On Mac OS X, you can use the Grab utility to take screenshots and Preview to draw annotations on them (arrows, highlights, or extra text—many of the illustrations in the book were made using the Grab/Preview combo).

On Windows Vista/7, you can use the built-in Snipping Tool to capture screenshots and draw annotations. There are also a number of free third-party utilities available. One of our favorites is Picpick (`www.picpick.wiziple.net`).

On any platform, you can also use the powerful and venerable GIMP photo editor (`www.gimp.org`) to capture and edit screenshots.

New addition – videos

As of 2010, WordPress' `readme.txt` files can also include videos! Directly including object/embed HTML into the `readme.txt` file is not supported, so you have to use these short-tags depending on what service is hosting the video:

- YouTube: [`youtube http://www.youtube.com/watch?v=abcd123`]
- Vimeo: [`vimeo http://vimeo.com/12345`]
- WordPress.com and VideoPress: [`wpvideo 0a1b2c`]

This is a great way for you to add screencasts of your plugin in action. Making an effective screencast is really a topic unto itself, but we recommend keeping it short (under 10 minutes) and focused. Don't try to talk people's ears off by droning on about every component in a single video. Several short and pointed videos are better than a single long one. Young Grasshopper, follow our recommendations from the chapter on good documentation and choose a purpose for any single video, and it will guide you with what you should and should not talk about.

Section – summary

The only thing WordPress cares about at a technical level is that the `readme.txt` file is in the correct format. To assist with that, WordPress offers a validator service (`http://goo.gl/kiSP`). We *highly* recommend that you use it early and often. It will help you catch formatting errors and it will give you a crude preview of your formatting. It will even display the embedded videos.

Unfortunately, it's a lot easier to programmatically verify the format of a `readme.txt` file than it is to test whether or not any of its instructions are actually worth reading. In case you haven't noticed, we are passionate about you including quality documentation for your plugin, so we won't mind a bit if you pause for a moment now to edit your `readme.txt` file one more time for clarity's sake.

Requesting and using SVN access

Are you chomping at the bit? The only thing that is left for you to do at this point is to actually submit your plugin and its code. Before you are granted *commit* access to the WordPress repository, you have to request it on the following page: `http://wordpress.org/extend/plugins/add/`.

One of the things required in your request is a name and a description. This is one of the areas where you can literally copy and paste from your `readme.txt` file. You have already done the hard work by creating the `readme.txt` file, now you get to cash in on that investment.

The other thing you need before SVN access is granted is a dedicated URL for your plugin. Say what? Yes, you need to create a web page somewhere dedicated to your new plugin. We're not sure exactly why this is a requirement for publishing your plugin since WordPress handles the hosting and related forum banter. Perhaps it's some sort of developer hazing or a rite of passage, but if you are developing plugins, you ought to have your own website(s) and you should be able to quickly dedicate a URL to your plugin.

What content should appear on that page? Well, that's up to you, but you already have some viable fodder in your `readme.txt` file, so that is a good starting point. Remember, this is the page that should be referenced in your plugin's information header.

It may take a few days to be granted access — WordPress includes a link about understanding the process: `http://wordpress.org/extend/plugins/about/`. Fairly soon you will receive an e-mail that looks something like this:

plugin-devleoper,

Your plugin hosting request has been approved. Within one hour, you will have access to your SVN repository at:

`http://plugins.svn.wordpress.org/name-of-your-plugin/`

with your `WordPress.org/bbPress.org` username and password (the same one you use on the forums).

Following are some handy links to help you get started:

Using Subversion with the WordPress Plugins Directory

`http://wordpress.org/extend/plugins/about/svn/`

FAQ about the WordPress Plugins Directory

`http://wordpress.org/extend/plugins/about/faq/`

WordPress Plugins Directory `readme.txt` standard

`http://wordpress.org/extend/plugins/about/readme.txt`

`readme.txt` validator:

`http://wordpress.org/extend/plugins/about/validator/`

Enjoy!

Once you have gained access to this new SVN repository, it's simply a matter of committing your code to that repository. Feel free to review our chapter on SVN, but in a nutshell the process will go something like this:

1. Create a new folder on your computer dedicated to the *WordPress* version of your plugin.

2. Establish the link between this folder and the new repository by using SVN's `checkout` command to create a local working copy:

   svn checkout `http://plugins.svn.wordpress.org/name-of-your-plugin/` .

3. If you haven't been "versioning" your code, go ahead and skip to the next step. However, if you *are* versioning your plugin using SVN and a different repository (for example, GoogleCode), then you must first export the latest code to a separate directory on your hard drive using the `svn export` command, for example:

   svn export /path/to/my/versioned/code /path/to/a/new/folder/that/ does/not/exist/yet

Remember: `svn export` *needs* to create a new folder for the export.

4. Take your plugin's files and copy them into the dedicated folder that now contains your working copy of your WordPress repository. Use the `svn add` function to put all these files and directories under version control and schedule them for addition to repository, for example:

```
svn add *
```

5. Commit your code using `svn commit`, for example:

```
svn commit . -m 'My first commit'
```

6. Wait! We're not quite done! You'll want to tag your current version so as to be compatible with the "Stable tag" attribute in your `readme.txt` file. Adjust the `svn copy` command to match the versions you are tagging:

```
svn copy http://plugins.svn.wordpress.org/name-of-your-plugin/
trunk http://plugins.svn.wordpress.org/name-of-your-plugin/
tags/1.2.3
```

It would be a really good idea to check the WordPress repository yourself to see if you can download your plugin. Keep in mind it may take up to an hour for your updates to percolate through the system. Before you cross this item off your to-do list, just make sure that the potential users out there can download your plugin.

Once that is done, the only thing you need to do is tell the world about your shiny new plugin.

Publicity and promotion

We'd like to think that a good plugin will stand on its own merits, but it never hurts to give it a helping hand. If you have written a terrific plugin, don't be shy about it—we want to know about it, and we might never find it if you don't tell us about it!

Here are few places where you can try to let people know about your new creation:

- The WordPress Support Forum (`http://goo.gl/2Tg0`): This should be your first stop. The title and description can more or less from your `readme.txt` file—the important thing here is to let people know about it.

- Weblog tools collection (`http://goo.gl/Mrur`): This is another great place to let people know about your plugin. Use the "New WordPress Plugins" forum to put your project on everyone's radar. Your post here can be about the same as the one on the WordPress forum.

- Facebook (or other social media): If you have friends who might be interested, you can try giving a simple non-technical pitch announcing your plugin and what it does as a Facebook status update or link. Even if your friends don't understand it, they might get excited and help you get the word out. Hooray for friends!

- Your own clients: This one is brilliant. If you wrote a plugin that does something really useful and you managed to do it *while getting paid*, then there's a high possibility that someone else is going to want that functionality. As the plugin's author, **you** will be the point of contact if people have projects requiring the functionality of the awesome plugin you wrote—it can easily lead to other gigs, so although your instinct might be to keep your plugin private for your own personal use, publicizing it might actually bring you more business, and that's more in keeping with the spirit of open source software anyhow. Remember that WordPress plugins are released under the GPLv2 license, so you don't have the same legal rights as you would with a standalone application.

Summary

We have come a long way. You have not only developed a plugin that does something useful, but you have also jumped through the flaming hoops of random requirements in order to get it published as an official WordPress plugin. The responsibility goes beyond this day, however. Be alert to bugs, security problems, or any feature requests. Above all, take a moment to be proud of your accomplishment. Getting a software project out the door is a lot more work than it seems, and if you have persevered, you deserve some praise and a seat in the "authors only" clubhouse.

We hope that this book has been a useful part of your WordPress and PHP education. Code on!

Recommended Resources

Not done learning yet? Excellent! A developer's work is never finished, it seems. Here are some additional resources that we recommend in order to continue your education.

PHP reference

`http://php.net`

This is the official documentation for PHP, and it should be one of your fist stops when determining how to use any PHP function.

Function reference

`http://codex.wordpress.org/Function_Reference`

This is *the* place to look up official documentation for any WordPress function. However, some pages are poorly linked and many functions are sparsely defined. The WordPress community needs your help in making this a better reference, so if you struggle with any of the definitions here, please take a moment to go back and clarify the documentation to help out the rest of us. We added and edited a handful of these pages while writing this book.

The WordPress forums

`http://wordpress.org/support`

We are obligated to mention this site as the official forum for WordPress, but in our own experiences, the forums are not particularly helpful for people with specific programming questions. Generally, only simpler questions are likely to garner responses.

A more active alternative is the WordPress IRC chat rooms using the #wordpress channel:

`http://codex.wordpress.org/IRC`

WebDev Studios

`http://webdevstudios.com`

This is a website run by Brad Williams, a WordPress developer and enthusiast. His name shows up in a number of WordPress articles, podcasts, and events. Look for his plugins in the WordPress repository.

Viper007Bond

`http://www.viper007bond.com`

Alex is an employee of Automatic, and his site and plugins offer some great tips on how to use the software.

Kovshenin

`http://kovshenin.com`

A tech-savvy Russian named Konstantin Kovshenin runs this site. He makes some great observations and has tackled some difficult WordPress issues. Your chances of overcoming a problem are much higher if Konstantin has cleared the way first.

SLTaylor

`http://sltaylor.co.uk`

Steve Taylor lives and works in London, and his blog covers a variety of topics, including WordPress, and the articles are generally good and informative.

XPlus3

`http://xplus3.net`

This is the brainchild of Jonathan Brinley, who runs a web development company with his wife. This site was sometimes the only place where we could find certain difficult topics discussed. If Jonathan has written about something you need to work on, then it's probably hugely educational to see what he has to say about it.

WP Engineer

`http://wpengineer.com`

Here is another useful site with lots of tips and tricks about the inner workings of WordPress.

Other plugins

Honestly, a terrific way to learn more about coding plugins for WordPress is by plowing through hundreds of existing plugins that offer to do something similar to your project idea. Once you find a good plugin author, you know where to get quality stuff. In general, if the plugin throws errors or notices and is a mess to read, then it's likely not worth copying.

This is one of the beautiful aspects of an open source project. If you need to find inspiration from existing code in another plugin, seek the cleanest and best code available.

B

WordPress API Reference

The following is a compendium of functions, actions, and filters referenced within this book.

PHP functions

There are over 700 functions built into PHP. The following are seven that we used, with examples.

dirname

```
string dirname( string $path);
```

Returns parent directory's path. Often this is used to determine the path to the current script.

Example:

```
print dirname(__FILE__); // prints something like '/users/me'
```

file_get_contents

```
string file_get_contents( string $filename [, bool $use_include_path =
false [, resource $context [, int $offset = -1 [, int $maxlen ]]]] )
```

Reads an entire file into a string. This is a useful way to read static, non-PHP files. It can even work for downloading remote files, but it's better to tie into the curl functions for serious downloading.

preg_match

```
int preg_match( string $pattern , string $subject [, array &$matches
[, int $flags = 0 [, int $offset = 0 ]]] )
```

The preceding code performs a regular expression match using Perl-compatible regular expressions.

Example:

```
if ( preg_match('/^wp_/', $post_type) ){
    print 'Post type cannot begin with wp_';
}
```

Special codes are used to signify different things:
- `^` = The beginning of the string.
- `$` = The end of the string.
- `[0-9]` = Any digit, 0-9.
- `[a-z]` = Any lowercase letter, a-z. You can make the search case-insensitive by using the "i" flag.
- `.*` = Shorthand for any character.

preg_replace

```
mixed preg_replace('/[^a-z|_]/', '_', $sanitized['post_type']);
```

Performs a regular expression search and replaces using Perl-compatible regular expressions.

Example:

```
$string = 'The dog ate my homework';
$pattern = '/dog/i';
$replacement = 'bear';
echo preg_replace($pattern, $replacement, $string);
```

Returns:

"The bear ate my homework"

print_r

```
mixed print_r( mixed $expression [, bool $return = false ] )
```

Prints human-readable information about a variable. This is extremely useful for debugging.

Example:

```
$x = array( 'x' => 'Something',
        'y' => array('a' => 'alpha')
);
print_r($x);
```

Output:

```
Array
(
    [x] => Something
    [y] => Array
        (
            [a] => alpha
        )

)
```

sprintf

```
string sprintf( string $format [, mixed $args [, mixed $... ]] )
```

Returns a string produced according to the formatting string format. This function helps to avoid sloppy PHP concatenations. Mostly, we have used only the string types, marked by the %s placeholder, but there are others available. If your format string uses two or more placeholders, you can make use of the syntax for argument-swapping.

Example:

```
$format = 'The %1$s contains %2$s monkeys';
$output = sprintf($format, 'zoo', 'many');
```

strtolower

```
string strtolower( string $str )
```

Makes a string lowercase. This is a simple text formatting tool.

substr

```
string substr( string $string , int $start [, int $length ] )
```

Returns part of a string.

Example:

```
// Get the first 20 characters of a long string:
$short_str = substr($long_str, 0, 20);
```

WordPress Functions

The following are a number of functions within WordPress that we utilized, with examples.

___

```
string __( string $text [, string $domain ])
```

Retrieves the translated string into the current locale. The $domain is "default" by default, but when authoring your own plugin, you should define your own text domain.

Example:

```
print __('Hello', 'my_text_domain'); // Might print "Hola" in a
Spanish speaking locale.
```

_e

```
_e( $text, $domain )
```

Prints the translated string into the current locale. The result is the same as if you had done:

```
echo __('your-string');
```

add_action

```
add_action( $event, $function_to_add, $priority, $accepted_args );
```

Hooks an action event to a user-defined callback function; normally, no values are returned from these callback functions.

Example:

```
add_action('wp_head', 'MyClass::my_static_function');
```

add_filter

`add_filter( $event, $function_to_add, $priority, $accepted_args );`

Hooks a filter event to a user-defined callback function; filter events normally accept a string as input and return a filtered string value.

add_meta_box

`add_meta_box( $id, $title, $callback, $page, $context, $priority, $callback_args );`

Allows plugin developers to add sections to the Write Post, Write Page, and Write Link editing pages. See the chapter on custom fields for an example.

add_options_page

`add_options_page( see below );`

Allows plugin authors to create their own menu page in the WordPress manager. This function is a wrapper function for the `add_menu_page()` function.

Example:

```
add_options_page(
    'Custom Post Types',              // page title
    'Custom Post Types',               // menu title
    'manage_options',                 // capability
    'my_unique_menu_slug',             // menu-slug (should be unique)
    'MyClass::my_static_function'     // callback function
);
```

See `http://codex.wordpress.org/Administration_Menus`

check_admin_referer

`check_admin_referer( $action, $name_of_nonce_field );`

Tests if the current request carries a valid nonce, used to avoid security exploits. This function dies if not referred to from an admin page, returns Boolean true if the admin referrer was successfully validated. Its inputs should line up exactly to the inputs used in the `wp_nonce_field()` function.

Example:

```
if ( check_admin_referer('name_of_my_action','name_of_nonce_field') )
{
   // process form data, e.g. update fields
}
// Display the form
print '<form method="post">';
// other inputs here ...
wp_nonce_field('name_of_my_action','name_of_nonce_field');
print '</form>';
```

esc_html

```
string esc_html($string)
```

Encodes `<`,`>`,`&`, `"`,`'` (less than, greater than, ampersand, double quote, single quote). Very similar to `esc_attr()`.

get_option

```
mixed get_option($option_name, $default)
```

A safe way of getting values for a named option from the options database table. If the desired option does not exist, or no value is associated with it, the `$default` value will be returned. If the value you are trying to retrieve is an array, then an array will be returned; if it's a string, then a string will be returned.

get_post_meta

```
mixed get_post_meta( $post_id, $name, $single )
```

This function returns the values of the custom fields with the specified key from the specified post. Also see `update_post_meta()`, `delete_post_meta()`, and `add_post_meta()`. `$single` is "false" by default, so it's possible to retrieve an array of values. Since this can be unexpected and architecturally awkward, we recommend that you always set `$single` to "true".

get_the_ID

```
integer get_the_ID()
```

Returns the numeric ID of the current post. This tag must be within the Loop.

register_post_type

`register_post_type`(see chapter 7)

Creates or modifies a post type. Do not use `register_post_type` before `init`. This function has a lengthy list of inputs. Be careful about supplying literal Booleans (for example, a literal false instead of zero or "). This is the function that really allows WordPress to have CMS capabilities. Please see *Chapter 7* for examples on how to use this complex function.

remove_meta_box

`remove_meta_box`(`$id, $page, $context`);

Allows plugin developers to remove sections from the Write Post, Write Page, and Write Link editing pages. This is the counterpart to the `add_meta_box()` function.

See `http://codex.wordpress.org/Function_Reference/remove_meta_box`

screen_icon

`screen_icon`()

Simple template function used when generating admin pages. This will print a plugin icon.

the_content

`the_content`(`$more_link_text, $strip_teaser`)

This prints the contents of the current post. This tag must be within the Loop. Remember that this does not return the results, it prints them. You can optionally configure it to output the first part of the content.

the_meta

`the_meta`()

This is a simple built-in function for printing custom fields for the current post, known as the "post-meta" (stored in the `wp_postmeta` table). It formats the data into an unordered list.

update_post_meta

```
update_post_meta( $post_id, $field_name, $value );
```

Updates the value of an existing meta key (custom field) for the specified post.

wp_count_posts

```
integer wp_count_posts($post_type[, $perm]);
```

Outputs a count of the given post type. Setting the $perm option will include private posts that the current user has permission to read. The function doesn't provide any options for more granular control of the count.

wp_die

```
wp_die($msg [, $title, $args] );
```

Kills WordPress execution and displays HTML page with the supplied error message. You can configure how the page is displayed.

wp_nonce_field

```
wp_nonce_field($action, $name_of_nonce_field);
```

Retrieves or displays nonce hidden field for forms. Works hand in hand with the check_admin_referer() function. This function prints its results.

Actions

See the WordPress Codex "Action" reference (http://goo.gl/zo5vY) for a more complete list.

admin_init

Runs at the beginning of every admin page before the page is rendered. If you need to display data to the admin users, this is a great action to hook into.

admin_menu

Runs after the basic admin panel menu structure is in place. Hook into this action when adding your own custom menu items.

Example:

```
add_action('admin_menu', 'ContentRotator::add_menu_item');
```

do_meta_boxes

Runs as meta boxes are being constructed in the manager. Meta boxes are any "extra" bit of data displayed, for example, custom fields on a post edit page.

Example:

```
add_action( 'do_meta_boxes', 'StandardizedCustomContent::remove_
default_custom_fields', 10, 3 );
```

init

Runs after WordPress has finished loading but before any headers are sent.

Example:

```
add_action('init', 'LiveSearch::initialize');
```

save_post

This action is called immediately after a post or page is created or updated.

Example:

```
add_action('save_post', 'StandardizedCustomContent::save_custom_
fields', 1, 2 );
```

widgets_init

Runs in the Dashboard when widgets are registered.

Example:

```
add_action('widgets_init', 'ContentRotatorWidget::register_this_
widget');
```

wp_head

Runs when the template calls the wp_head function.

Example:

```
add_action('wp_head','diggthis_add_js_to_doc_head');
```

Filters

See the WordPress Codex "Filter" reference (http://goo.gl/1UX4U) for a more complete list.

In this book, we have used mostly actions to achieve our goals, but it can be necessary to filter data.

the_content

This is an important one. Triggered when the template file executes the_content() function (that is the tag).

Index

Symbols

Thank you for buying
WordPress 3 Plugin Development Essentials

About Packt Publishing

Packt, pronounced 'packed', published its first book "*Mastering phpMyAdmin for Effective MySQL Management*" in April 2004 and subsequently continued to specialize in publishing highly focused books on specific technologies and solutions.

Our books and publications share the experiences of your fellow IT professionals in adapting and customizing today's systems, applications, and frameworks. Our solution based books give you the knowledge and power to customize the software and technologies you're using to get the job done. Packt books are more specific and less general than the IT books you have seen in the past. Our unique business model allows us to bring you more focused information, giving you more of what you need to know, and less of what you don't.

Packt is a modern, yet unique publishing company, which focuses on producing quality, cutting-edge books for communities of developers, administrators, and newbies alike. For more information, please visit our website: www.packtpub.com.

About Packt Open Source

In 2010, Packt launched two new brands, Packt Open Source and Packt Enterprise, in order to continue its focus on specialization. This book is part of the Packt Open Source brand, home to books published on software built around Open Source licences, and offering information to anybody from advanced developers to budding web designers. The Open Source brand also runs Packt's Open Source Royalty Scheme, by which Packt gives a royalty to each Open Source project about whose software a book is sold.

Writing for Packt

We welcome all inquiries from people who are interested in authoring. Book proposals should be sent to author@packtpub.com. If your book idea is still at an early stage and you would like to discuss it first before writing a formal book proposal, contact us; one of our commissioning editors will get in touch with you.

We're not just looking for published authors; if you have strong technical skills but no writing experience, our experienced editors can help you develop a writing career, or simply get some additional reward for your expertise.

OGRE 3D 1.7 Beginner's Guide

ISBN: 978-1-849512-48-0   Paperback: 300 pages

Create real time 3D applications using OGRE 3D from scratch

1. Easy-to-follow introduction to OGRE 3D

2. Create exciting 3D applications using OGRE 3D

3. Create your own scenes and monsters, play with the lights and shadows, and learn to use plugins

Linux Shell Scripting Cookbook

ISBN: 978-1-849513-76-0   Paperback: 360 pages

Solve real-world shell scripting problems with over 110 simple but incredibly effective recipes

1. Master the art of crafting one-liner command sequence to perform tasks such as text processing, digging data from files, and lot more

2. Practical problem solving techniques adherent to the latest Linux platform

3. Packed with easy-to-follow examples to exercise all the features of the Linux shell scripting language

Please check **www.PacktPub.com** for information on our titles

Lightning Source UK Ltd.
Milton Keynes UK
UKOW040155140212

187199UK00001B/159/P